Understanding Design in Film Production

Great visual storytelling is possible on a minimal budget, but you have to spend a lot of energy thinking and planning. In *Understanding Design in Film Production*, author Barbara Freedman Doyle demonstrates how to use production design, cinematography, lighting, and locations to create an effective and compelling visual story, even on the tightest of budgets.

Featuring in-depth interviews with production designers, set decorators, construction coordinators, cinematographers, costumers, and location managers talking about the techniques of their craft, it provides you with a feel for what everyone on the visual team does, how they think and plan, and how best to utilize the knowledge and skills they offer.

This book guides you through how to find, secure, and manage the best locations, how to create and dress a set, and how to make old look new and new look old—all on a tight budget. With insights from experts at the top of their field, sharing how they plan for the real-world application of large-scale ideas, you'll be able to see ways to apply their techniques to your own smaller-scale productions.

Understanding Design in Film Production is a practical, hands-on guide for any aspiring filmmaker who wants to understand the basic principles of visual design in order to create exceptional looking films.

Barbara Freedman Doyle began her film career as the assistant to the Senior VP of Worldwide Production at Tri-Star Pictures. She continued to work her way up the freelance production ladder as a production coordinator and production supervisor on projects for CBS, NBC, Disney, TNT, Showtime, Hearst Entertainment, Hallmark, 20th Century Fox, Morgan Creek Productions, and Alcon Entertainment. She is the current Professor of Producing and heads the College to Career Program at Chapman University's Dodge College of Film and Media, and is a former Associate Dean of Production at the American Film Institute. She continues to consult on production for narrative and documentary film projects.

Understanding Design in Film Production

Using Art, Light, and Locations to Tell Your Story

Barbara Freedman Doyle

Routledge
Taylor & Francis Group

NEW YORK AND LONDON

First published 2019
by Routledge
52 Vanderbilt Avenue, New York, NY 10017

and by Routledge
2 Park Square, Milton Park, Abingdon, Oxon, OX14 4RN

Routledge is an imprint of the Taylor & Francis Group, an informa business

Library of Congress Cataloging-in-Publication Data
Names: Doyle, Barbara Freedman, author.
Title: Understanding design in film production : using art, light & locations
    to tell your story / Barbara Freedman Doyle.
Description: London ; New York, NY : Routledge, 2019.
Identifiers: LCCN 2018046087| ISBN 9781138058699 (hardback : alk.
    paper) | ISBN 9781138058705 (pbk. : alk. paper) | ISBN 9781315163642
    (e-book)
Subjects: LCSH: Motion pictures—Art direction—Vocational guidance. |
    Motion pictures—Setting and scenery—Vocational guidance.
Classification: LCC PN1995.9.A74 D69 2019 | DDC 791.4302/5—dc23
LC record available at https://lccn.loc.gov/2018046087

ISBN: 978-1-138-05869-9 (hbk)
ISBN: 978-1-138-05870-5 (pbk)
ISBN: 978-1-315-16364-2 (ebk)

Typeset in Sabon
by Swales & Willis Ltd, Exeter, Devon, UK

Contents

Acknowledgments

Thank you to all the colleagues and contributors who helped to make this happen, and to all the interviewees, who were incredibly generous with their time, insight, and experiences. In order of appearance:

Alec Hammond

Brendan O'Connor

Josue Fleurimond

Michael Villarino

Dave DeGaetano

Lee Ross

Shirley Starks

Brian Haynes

Timothy Hillman

Bill Dill

Johnny Jensen

Rachel Kunin

Vanessa Vogel

Steven Levine

Bill Kroyer

Jamie Burton-Oare

Jon Milano

Brenna Malloy

Rahma Farahat

Nick Ramsey

Sarah Wilson Thacker

Steven Snyder

Rachel Aguirre

Ryan Broomberg

Mian Adnan Ahmad

Amanda Renee Knox

Andrew Johnson

Chris Read

Jim Fredrick

and especially John Chichester and Priscilla Elliott, who were not only generous with their time but with their contacts, and Michael Keane at Dodge College of Film and Media Arts for helping with the photographs.

Photo Credits

Chapter 19: photos 19.22–19.25 courtesy of "Night Call"; director Amanda Renee Knox; footage shot by cinematographer Michael Phillips.

Chapter 19: photos 19.26, 19.27 courtesy of "Grandpa's River"; director Andrew Johnson; photos shot by Andrew Johnson.

Chapter 19: photos 19.28–19.31 courtesy of "The Lost Captain"; director Christopher Read; footage shot by Stephen J. Root.

Introduction

You are making your first movie . . .

Whether you're making a short, an internet series, a feature or a television pilot . . . you have a golden opportunity. You may only get this one chance to prove to the world that you can tell a story people will want to watch.

You probably don't have much money and you don't have a lot of experience . . .

You've got the script you like, and you have the right cast. A crucial element of the process that separates a beginning filmmaker from an experienced one is the level of preparation that becomes second nature to veteran filmmakers. Filmmaking is not just going out and shooting. Filmmaking requires massive amounts of tedious preparation. The more you prep, the closer you will move toward a professional level of production. So now it is time to prep for shooting.

When we think about the people involved in filmmaking, most of us think first of actors and directors, because they are usually the most publicly visible faces of the movie. They're the ones interviewed. Beyond mentioning the cast, people say they've seen "the Spielberg" film. Or "Ridley Scott's new one." The cast and director are, of course, key figures in the final piece of work you see in the theater or on TV, or online. We all know (if only from the title) what the screenwriter does. And when they announce the nominees for Best Picture on the Emmys and Academy Awards, it is noted that the names that are read are the names of the producers. But there is an army working behind the scenes on every film and TV series, and those troops are responsible for most of what goes into the way you see the show. As an aspiring filmmaker, you MUST understand not only what these people do, but how to communicate with them, how to recognize the choices and skills they offer you.

My hope is that you will use *Understanding Design in Film Production* to push yourself to a higher level of visual storytelling, and that you will earn the reputation of someone who prepares skillfully, with perfectly chosen locations and beautifully designed sets, so that it all holds together, and your project comes alive for the audience.

Though every filmmaking craft is important, in this book we're concerned mostly with visual design, production design, location choice, costume, and cinematography.

These components of filmmaking should work in lock step to tell your story as effectively as possible.

Film is a visual medium, so your first question should be: what is the world of your movie? What do you want your project to feel like and what do you want it to look like? Is your movie reality-based, or does the story take place in a fantasy future world? Will it be a light comedy filled with pastels and bright color like *Legally Blonde* or *Clueless*? Is it about a treacherous world? Treacherous how? Like *The Godfather*, *The Exorcist*, or like *Seven*? Is your imagined world the frightening domain of shadows and psychotic killers of the *Friday the 13th* or *Nightmare on Elm Street* variety? Or is it a completely different kind of place, filled with strange sets, vivid patterns, and quirky characters like *The Royal Tenenbaums*?

You may not have spent a lot of time thinking about this. You might be so concerned with the script and the cast that your physical design seems like something you can figure out as you go. This is not a good idea.

To make your project work, to pull your audience in so that they are feeling your film and not just watching it, you must employ every available tool. You must have a great script, find an inspired cast, and create a strong visual plan that supports your story and characters. An outstanding design plan serves as shorthand for your audience. Great design can replace talky, expository scenes, get a laugh, or cause goosebumps.

Watch the original *Blade Runner*, directed by Ridley Scott. Fabulous story, great actors, amazing work—but when you think of that film, the first thing that comes to mind is the damp, dark world of the movie. It's full of rain, pollution, and neon. That world was no accident. Scott worked with futurist Sid Meade and production designer Laurence Paull. With Michael Neale, their location manager, they scoured downtown Los Angeles to find and alter locations, to design and build an imagined world of an ugly future. Oscar nominated for Best Art Direction/Set Decoration, the film has been considered a triumph of design for over 30 years.

You may be thinking, "Those guys had an army of people on their crews and buckets of cash. How does that help me with my zero-budget short or micro-budget feature? I'm lucky if my roommate agrees to help with the art department."

What about *Whiplash*? A few locations: practice rooms, a restaurant, dorms, a few clubs, an auditorium, and an exterior road. Every location was chosen with the intent of presenting the stark, pressure-cooker world of the screenplay. You could afford that.

In *Locke*, there is only one real location. The interior of an automobile. Yet through the design, the use of lights and camera (and masterful writing and acting), the world is compelling and authentic.

Watch *Twelve Angry Men*, *Sleuth*, *Reservoir Dogs*, *Phone Booth*, *Panic Room*, *The Inside Man*, *Dog Day Afternoon*, and *The Breakfast Club*.

The filmmakers chose to use only a few sets and locations, but the ones they chose and/or built are extraordinarily effective.

Great design is possible on a zero or minimal budget, but you must spend a lot of energy thinking and planning. You must be determined not to settle for the first easy-to-access and cheap location you come across. You should be willing to scout 20 locations for the perfect hallway, or to put up a screen to hide a window, or track down the wall covering that tells the viewer the year is 1890. Beyond thinking about lighting and camera work, you must be prepared to analyze, discuss, and experiment with shape, color, the proportion of objects, the height of ceilings and textures of walls—all with the goal of crafting a setting that helps you tell your story.

Many young filmmakers want to hurry up and shoot—to get to what they think of as the fun part. But creating an effectively designed film is a painstaking process. You think you've found the perfect location, then you see a different house and it's more perfect. Or you'll have a picture in your mind, but you can't quite articulate what it is about that idea that encapsulates the mood or environment that you're hoping for. You must be willing to research, to find photos or drawings or films, and to express specifically what it is about them, so you know, "*this* is it."

An example? I had a directing student who kept saying that he wanted his project to look like *Billy Elliot*. That was a film made in the year 2000. He was speaking to his production designer, who went off and watched the film. *Billy Elliot* is about a working-class boy in England who wants to be a ballet dancer. But the designer saw the film, and was puzzled. The director kept talking about the foggy blue. After an hour of talking across each other, they discovered that the director was describing a mood—and was referring to the lighting, not the actual color palette. You need the correct vocabulary to connect what you want with what you'll get.

I am not a member of any of the design departments, but I've worked with brilliant designers, set decorators, cinematographers, costume designers, and location managers. As someone who has supervised and/or managed projects with budgets ranging from zero dollars to many million, and who has worked extensively with young filmmakers, I promise you that the size of your budget is not the determining factor when it comes to an exceptional-looking film. Money makes things easier, but imagination, resourcefulness, and a great eye do more.

This book is full of questions. That's because design for film is the practice of solving problems and creating visual strategies. Knowing the questions to ask yourself is the first step, and there is no single right answer, there are only solutions that work, solutions that work better, and those that don't work at all. "Working" in this case means helping to tell the story.

Beyond the trial and error of doing it all yourself, the best way to begin to understand the effective use of design for film and television is to listen to the thought processes of people who have themselves succeeded at making a story better because of their work.

There are books out there about stage craft, graphics, cinematography, costume, and the science of visual design. They are far more technical and academic than this book, and you should read them all. In *Understanding Design for Film Production*, you are getting a practical, hands-on perspective from people who have been there before. Whether you are looking toward a career as a writer, director, producer, hopefully you will be more aware of the silent contribution of design in visual storytelling—and you'll be able to communicate more effectively with your team.

There is nothing as valuable as hearing from the experts. You'll read in-depth interviews with production designers, set decorators, construction coordinators, cinematographers, costumers, and location managers. They'll talk about the techniques of their craft. You'll also hear from former film students who made projects for very little money but with great success. Their films have been shown at numerous festivals and have won major awards. We'll see how you can create Boston in Brooklyn, find the 1940s in 2018, and the Old South in Bulgaria. Key members of the filmmaking team will talk about how they work as collaborators, about building sets versus finding them, where a filmmaker should put their money when they don't have much, how to make old look new and new look old. Once you get a feeling for what everyone does and how they think and plan, you'll see some ways to apply their large-scale work to your smaller-scale productions.

You'll notice that the people who design for film and television don't merely create the visuals. The reality of the filmmaking process is that everybody has to deal with the politics of the set, the production budget, and schedule. Logistics and budget play a major role in every person's artistic life, whether the project is a multimillion-dollar extravaganza or an indie that is just one step removed from a college film school project.

Finally, you will learn how to take the elements of visual design and use them to make your movie look great.

Note

At the end of this book, you will see a suggested viewing list of titles. These are films that are either referred to within the chapter contents, or that illustrate the points made by the filmmakers interviewed. You may have seen some of them already—and loved or hated them. Some may have inspired you to become a filmmaker. Some may have convinced you that you just don't get it. At the very least, if you make a point of watching the films listed, you will have seen some outstanding work. As you are watching, keep in mind that all the films listed make use of the fundamental principles of design, and are prime examples of films that play on both your intellect and your emotion, usually without you noticing.

Clips of many of the scenes referenced throughout this book can be readily found on the internet.

Section 1

Understanding Design in Film

1   What Is Your Movie *About . . .?*

What is your movie about? Not the plot. What is the theme of your movie? What are you trying to say? If the answer is, I'm not trying to say anything, I'm just trying to entertain (get laughs/scare people/cause people to leave the Cineplex humming), you're off to a weak start.

Even the silliest comedies, goriest scare-fests, and musicals with the thinnest plots need a theme that holds everything together. Otherwise your comedy is just a series of punchlines and sight gags with no payoff. Your horror film will be repetitive and lack tension, and without tension and surprise you have no horror. Your audience may watch for a while, but without a strong narrative, a unifying concept, and interesting conflicts the audience is going to wonder why they're bothering. They'll get irritated, switch the channel, or exit out of your movie, because the action comes off as random or gratuitous.

Audiences have lots of choices these days and they're sophisticated. They tune out easily. There should be a motor, a force that moves toward the resolution of your central conflict. That means you must understand what your central conflict is.

There are countless lists of common themes in fiction, and critics, professors, and storytelling sages have their consistent lists of favorites. The variations are in how purely they are defined. That said, here's my top ten:

1 Man vs. the natural world—and by extension, Man vs. the supernatural world and, again by extension, do *not* mess with Mother Nature.
2 Man vs. Man—again, by extension, good vs. evil (and this often ends up including Man vs. himself and Man vs. society—or justice).
3 Loss of innocence (or loss of faith).
4 Revenge.
5 Redemption or the sins of the father (overcoming the past).
6 Acceptance (learning to live with . . . something).
7 Power of love
8 Follow your heart (and when pushed to the extreme, obsession).
9 Prodigal son (the ne'er do well, the addict, the spoiled brat, the screw up) comes home (which in a happy ending results in numbers 5 and 6).
10 The sacrifice of a few vs. the good of many.

Seem simplistic? It is and I'm sure there are more basic themes out there. But most movies concern themselves with one or more variations of these problems to be overcome. This doesn't mean your project has to be deep and meaningful. But there should be something that holds your story together, so it isn't just a series of events. *Deadpool* is a comic book movie but it uses good vs. evil and Man vs. Man to make fun of comic book movie tropes. *Get Out* isn't just a mash-up of a funny horror movie, it transcends its genre because the underpinning of the film is social satire, and Man vs. Man.

Alec Hammond is the production designer on features such as *Allegiant*, *Insurgent*, *Non-Stop*, *Man on a Ledge*, *RED*, *Flightplan*, *Donnie Darko*, and art director on *The Cat In the Hat*, *Men in Black 2*, *Austin Powers: The Spy Who Shagged Me*, among others.

Alec Hammond

What we do, almost completely, is tell human stories. Even when we tell stories that are about animals or robots really those are just stand-ins for humans. And those human stories almost always involve conflict and involve conflict between people.

You let the text and the director speak to you about the things that are important in the script. To steal a description from Jodie Foster, who mentioned this when we were doing *Flightplan*, "What's the big beautiful idea?" at the center of what you're doing. That was a wonderful way to say a similar thing a theater director I worked with said: "what is the spiritual envelope around those actions?"

Having started in theater, John Chichester went on to become an art director, set designer, and production designer, before becoming head of production design at Chapman University's Dodge College of Film and Media Arts. Chichester has credits ranging from huge feature projects like *Cowboys and Aliens*, *Get Him to The Greek*, *Tropic Thunder*, *Spider Man 2*, and *Alien Resurrection*, to episodic television and smaller, independent films.

John Chichester

Consider character. How can you develop this character in their environment? How can you show vulnerability in them? Designers should be thinking, how can we flesh this story out? How can we bring these characters out so that we can bring the audience closer to them and to their conflicts?

Point of View

Whose story is being told—and to whom? Who drives the action? In whose shoes are we standing? Point of view is an important factor in a screenplay and a key element in how a film is designed and shot. It boils down to who is telling the story and how they feel (how they see or how they *process* what's happening). This is significant because the goal of a filmmaker is always to bring the audience into the film. Their attention and their emotions should be *with* the film. That's how a viewer participates in the storytelling experience.

Picture sitting in the dark with 100 other people, watching a movie. There are lots of potential distractions. Candy bars being unwrapped. Popcorn. Whispers. How can you catch and keep an audience's attention? By involving them. And the way to involve your audience in a film or television show is to get their buy in. Make them part of it. A major factor in your ability to do that is point of view.

In the classic *To Kill a Mockingbird*, there is a scene where everything unravels, and it leads to everything being revealed. This is how the sequence is presented:

Scout Finch, an eight-year-old tomboy in a small southern town, is walking home from a Halloween celebration, accompanied by her slightly older brother Jem. They walk through a dark, wooded area. In the eyes of the two children, it's a little spooky. They're alone at night. Scout is dressed as a ham (it's 1930s Alabama). Her movements and vision is hampered by the costume. Jem hears something behind them. They stop walking. We can see (they can see) there's nothing there. Jem is nervous. Scout tells him that all she hears is the rustling of her costume. She starts to move again, then she hears the noise. The camera is close up on her face, and we can only see her eyes, but we are *with* her, emotionally. The two turn and we see what they see, an empty path in the woods. But we know what they feel, that there is something there. Jem keeps looking back. Because we are close on him, we are looking back also. We watch them speed up. Suddenly a dark shadow bursts out from the trees, attacking Jem, pushing Scout down. Scout, because of her costume, can't see anything and she can't escape the costume. Jem is thrown down, unconscious. We see the dark figure start to go after Scout. Out of nowhere comes another person, but like Scout, we can't tell who it is. It's a point-of-view shot of the hands of the attacker and the hands of the person trying to stop the attack. We see Scout's eyes. Again, we are with her. All she can see are hands—as one man struggles to hurt her, and another to protect her. Finally, we see only the feet of the man who saves her as he lifts the limp body of Jem and takes him away. Scout finally extricates herself from the ham costume and what she sees is the back of a man, in the dark, carrying her brother off in his arms. Why does this work? It's the *mise-en-scène*—the design of everything we see. It's the intentional decisions the filmmaker has made—where to place the camera, how close to come in to the children's faces, what takes up the space in the picture, what the woods look like, how dark is it, what the ham costume looks like (the costume choice is taken from the novel). *Mise-en-scène* also describes where in the frame (the single image that makes up a shot) the action occurs and how placement in the frame affects how we feel about that action. That scene could have been constructed many ways, but because of the choices the director, Robert Mulligan, made, the audience is living the action, feeling what the characters are feeling—and that's why a film made in 1962 still works today.

In Baz Luhrmann's 2013 version of *The Great Gatsby,* Nick Carraway is an observer to the glittering, splendid lifestyles of his cousin Daisy and his new friend Gatsby. Everything is over-sized, shiny, and luxurious, dripping with bright objects. Nick is the outsider, often caught by the camera as lost in the sea of guests who mob Gatsby's never-ending parties. He's not important. Although he is a bit cynical about it, he still wants to belong. Once things go sour, Gatsby's place is void of life. There is no sparkle. Nick walks through the great house and no longer sees a shimmering world. The basic set—Gatsby's mansion—doesn't change. But the way it's lit and decorated, the now silent rooms that once teamed with noise and celebrants, show us (and Nick) that everything's changed. By the end of the film, Nick has learned about love, betrayal, and emptiness.

Tone

Tone is a little more specific than point of view. Tone can tell you something about the way the filmmaker feels about the story and the characters. This is something you want to ask yourself. How do you feel about your film and how do you want your audience to feel? Is your film funny? Is it a black comedy? Whimsical? Is it a thriller? Are you aiming for reality or an ironic or detached comment on reality? *Edward Scissorhands* sets up a fairy-tale-like reality. For the movie to work, the audience must accept the premise of the gentle guy whose hands are dangerous blades. Director Tim Burton creates a highly stylized world, but his point of view about love and human nature and being different is authentic. The audience accepts the outrageous conceit because Burton presents it in a way that you have to take seriously. The first thing we see is a dark castle looming high on a hill. It's snowing. Cut to a woman staring out at the castle from the window of a house. She's a grandmother, tucking in her granddaughter. The granddaughter wants to hear a bedtime story, and so Grandma begins. But as she does, the filmmakers transport us to a different reality. The camera swoops from inside the cozy home, through the window, out over the neat town with its uniform houses, yards, and fences, and we travel to the castle. The camera move brings us from one world to the other. As the story begins, the grandmother as a young woman is selling door to door in the cookie-cutter pastel town. The camera move is the bridge. The visual design—the color, the light, Edward's wondrous topiary—creates the new world and we go with it.

What Does All This Have to Do with You?

As a filmmaker, your job is to use all means available to best tell your story without hammering your audience over the head. There are layers in storytelling. There is text and subtext (which often sends us back to the theme). There are only so many stories out there, and in their most basic sense they can be described as: somebody or something wants something. Somebody or something is standing in the way.

This holds true for all genres, whether romance, cautionary tale, murder-mystery, or sci-fi. When you consider your theme, your point of view, your tone, you are deciding how you want to tell your story, and it's how you tell your story that distinguishes your project from the thousands of other films out there.

The most talented people in the industry are those with expertise in bridging the gap between what you see and how you think and feel about what you see on screen. When they talk about what they do, their first statement was always about script and storytelling, and about the importance of recognizing that what they do is in aid of more effective storytelling.

John Chichester

Don't fall into the designer trap. Don't think you have to take off your storyteller hat and put on a designer hat. The thought process shouldn't be any different no matter what your position on the movie. As a designer you're visually developing character and situation to help tell the story. Don't *ever* let the storytelling be subservient.

2   Some Components of Visual Design

You're making a film. There's dialogue and performance, but ultimately everything is dependent on the visuals. If this isn't the case, your story might be perfect for a podcast. Everyone involved in storytelling on film should have at least a rudimentary understanding of the fundamentals of design. When you are looking at a film, you're seeing action happening in a specific kind of space—a flat one that has a top, a bottom, and sides. Your visual world exists within a frame, and as a filmmaker you control that frame.

For the purposes of this book, and your desire to make a film that really works visually, think about that flat space not only containing your actors, but being made up of colors, textures, and lines. Think about the relative volume of all the objects and bodies within the frame and how these design elements interact and generate a psychological and emotional response.

Color

It should come as no surprise that we have both a visceral and an intellectual reaction to color. Some of our response to color is cultural. In the West, we associate white with purity. Our brides usually wear white. In China, brides wear red because red symbolizes good fortune. Some of how we feel about color may seem to be more organically baked in. Green is the color of nature. We associate particular shades of green with youth, freshness and abundance. Certain colors and tones are thought to be calming—or not. You will rarely see schools and hospitals with brightly painted walls. Therapists don't have orange slip-covers or upholstery.

Our reaction to color varies with the shade and circumstance—and culture. Color is contextual. Yellow is the color of the sun. We tend to associate that with warmth and a pleasant sensation, but brownish-yellow speaks to us of aging and deterioration. What about purple? Is it the color of majesty or dread? Is black mourning or elegant chic? When we see a green reflection on someone's face, we assume they are ailing—or evil. Do you remember the close-ups of the wicked witch in *The Wizard of Oz*. In Martin Scorsese's *The Aviator*, a film that is in part about the tragic mental illness of multi-millionaire Howard Hughes, Hughes' entire home has a greenish tinge. The color of illness or money or both? A filmmaker can't ignore the role color plays in storytelling.

Some color terminology you may already know from art classes: magenta, cyan, and yellow are primary colors. Secondary colors (two primary colors mixed together) are green, orange, and purple. Complementary colors are opposite each other on the color wheel. Two complementary colors together can create visual energy. There are cool and warm colors. Warm colors are the reds, yellows, and oranges. Cool colors are blues, most greens, and purples. We tend to perceive warm colors as moving toward us and as taking up more space. Cool or drab colors feel as if they recede. Red pumps up our emotions and can make us restless. It can be claustrophobic. Blue can be reassuring, as in "true blue," or innocent—"baby blue." Blue can feel expansive, like the sky.

Color is tonal, meaning that it varies in intensity (or concentration). A primary color is intense and saturated. When someone (a painter or a production designer) says that something is "true red" or "true yellow," they are talking about that color that isn't *ish*. For example, aqua, greenish-blue, is not a true color. Reddish may be orange-y or scarlet. It's not true red.

If you add color to a primary color, you get a shade or a tone or a tint. Adding white to a pure color will lighten it. Adding gray to a pure color will tone it down, making it less saturated and intense. Adding black will darken it. When we talk about color in terms of a film, whether we are thinking about a wall, or wardrobe, or even a mood, it's important to be very clear, and use paint samples or photos. Descriptive words mean different things to different people. If you look up "crimson" in a thesaurus, the synonyms offered are, *pink, cherry, red*, and *cerise*, which are all quite different.

Color can affect our perception of size, particularly when something or someone is being photographed or filmed within a frame. To confirm this, find two identical and identically fitting long-sleeved T-shirts, one black, one white, and two pairs of pants; one black, one white. Put on the white T-shirt and pants. Stand in front of a full-length mirror. By standing so that your entire body, head to toe, is reflected, you are in essence, putting yourself in a frame. Notice how large or small you look in that frame. Now put on the black T-shirt and the black pants. Stand in the exact same position, same distance from the mirror—instant diet! You look smaller and thinner in that frame. You haven't changed, so what has? In the context of the frame, you appear to recede and take up a little less space. A bright yellow box will appear to advance, so will look bigger than the same-sized box that is dark blue or black. You will also feel differently about that yellow box or shirt. You may not like yellow, but your associations with the color might give you the idea that what is in the yellow box will be happier, nicer, more pleasant, than what's in the dark one.

When filmmakers talk about color palette, they are referring to the recurring use of colors and/or tones that enhance the theme of the movie. For instance, in *The Truman Show*, it's not just that the houses in Truman Burbank's neighborhood are light-colored, and so not in any way threatening. There's also something safe about the Crayola pastels. Contrast the use of color in that film to the use of color in *La La Land*, which is about dreams, particularly Hollywood dreams. In the opening musical number of the film, there's warm, bright color. The cars on the freeway are a rainbow of energetic color. A truck filled with musicians is bright blue. People wear yellow, orange, and pink. Color is youth and hope. As the film continues and dreams and romance falter and everything is not so lighthearted, the color is more subdued. In both films you might swear that your emotional reaction is to the actors and the plot, but would you feel the same way about Truman's town and Mia and Seb's lives if these movies were shot in black and white? Color helps tell the story.

Watch *Seven*. The film's unrelentingly murky green-brown tones are completely intentional, not incidental. In a film about decay and the bleakest side of humanity, the Production Designer and Cinematographer are not concerned with making pretty pictures. The film is masterful in its lighting and color design and it is ugly. Think about *Chinatown*, a period film about water—or the lack of it—in Los Angeles. Everything in that film is meant to emphasize the heat and dryness of the parched climate. But the front lawn of the of the rich, brutal water baron Noah Cross, is lush and green. He owns the water.

Neutral colors are whites, beige, gray. They're often employed to convey calm, but also up-tightness or dullness, or even the living space or wardrobe of someone obsessed with cleanliness. Another neutral—black—sometimes tells us we are in a place that's cool, or sophisticated. How many films have you seen where there is a party set in a hyper artsy or elegant place in New York and Los Angeles, and everyone is in black? High contrast "pops." As a filmmaker you can decide what you want your audience to notice, what looks hip, and what is a distraction. At your urban loft party or formal dinner, the awkward outsider might wear red (high contrast) and look out of place, pushy, and gauche. We know that person is either trying too hard or wants something. Maybe you don't want to be as obvious though. Maybe they'll be in black but positioned so that they are shrinking in the corner where the white walls meet. If it's a comedy maybe the frat boys will be in white dinner jackets and the outsider will be in powder blue. Colors, like all else that is visual, are only effective emotionally if they work *in context*.

If you're in the hot Mediterranean, the houses with their bright white stone walls seem to glow. If you're contrasting that to the blue, blue ocean you've made a statement about how your characters feel when they get out of bed in the morning and look out over that fresh horizon.

Schindler's List is about the Holocaust. It is almost entirely in black and white. There is no color (life) in this world of smokestacks and terror. Director Steven Spielberg uses color to ingenious effect. Oskar Schindler watches a little girl in a red coat wander through the streets amidst the murder and round-up of the Jews. He can't look away. We are seeing her through his eyes. Later, the red coat is seen on the dead little girl. Red is blood, life, and death. In *Schindler's List* the move from black and white or sepia to color at the end of the film gives life to the descendants of the victims.

In the final scenes in *The Road to Perdition*, there's the peace of sun-washed sand, the calm of sky blue. The killer (Tom Hanks) think he's has eluded the violence of his life, has taken his son to a better existence. Suddenly there is a gunshot and the intensity and horror of red (blood) that changes everything.

One of the best tools of a young filmmaker is color, because the thoughtful use of color can be extraordinarily effective—and color is free.

John Chichester

I designed a movie where the world of the bad guys didn't have any color in at all. And the world of the good guys had tons of color. They were gregarious, and color spoke to who they were.

An example of an expressive use of color is *The Last Emperor* (designed by Ferdinando Scarfiotti). It starts in golds and oranges, which is completely supported by the culture and by where they are, in Imperial China. Then the movie moves into cools as we get into the 20th century. By the end of the movie, when the deposed Emperor is in a prison camp, it's all gray. A brilliant use of color.

Alec Hammond on the Use of Color and Light

If you design a set or even pick a location without considering how light is an integral part of it, you're dead. Game over before you start. It can't be an after-thought. Cinematography and production design is a symbiotic relationship. It has to be together. Cinematographers light things, and if you don't light a set, or an environment, if you don't light a world, it doesn't look like anything. It's black. You have to be thinking about how the space is illuminated, presented,

(continued)

(continued)

angled, the direction, the intensity of the light at the same time as you're talking about color and structure and line.

If you look at the work Adam Stockhausen did on *Grand Budapest Hotel*—I would say that is a design of color and pattern in a brilliant way. A lot of Wes Anderson's things are like that. Almost all work on color, and blocks of color operating in a frame. There's a very cleanly defined border. In *Budapest*, looking at the color palette told the whole story for what that place was, for the time period. It became a show where the design and those elements of the design were a full character.

Texture

Film is usually exhibited on a flat screen. Texture is the feel of a surface. Since we don't literally feel a movie, how can texture be a factor in production design? Texture in film in some ways is about how your audience responds to the imagined feel. Texture is furry vs. silky, slippery vs. rough, shiny vs. dull, new vs. old. Texture is also about the depth of what you see. When you walk into a space that is flat and plain, it is without texture. When you add detail, it becomes a different place—a place that tells the audience something about the people. It's the filmmaker's job to make a conscious decision rather than a random choice when looking at the textures of locations, sets, cloth, building materials. Is someone starting a new life? Will everything in a recently renovated office be brand, spanking new? Or has the character saved a few things that were important to them? Depends on how they feel about the old life. Are there trophies on the bookshelves or are they stacked in a packing crate? Photos scattered or framed? This is a way you can say something about the character's story without on-the-nose dialog like, "I really miss playing football." You may think your audience won't notice these things—and they may not clock every single bit of texture. But subconsciously they will learn things in the best possible way—through your cinematic hints and clues, and those will add up.

Texture is often in the background. The camera may not focus on things but move past them. They may be lit subtly. Let's say you go to a friend's house for dinner. You're concentrating on the food and the conversation but, at some level, you are noticing everything around you. There are family portraits on the far wall, there are vacation souvenirs, toys on the playroom floor visible through the doorway in the hall. If you want to feel the effect of texture, try this: go into a house that's for sale and completely empty. Sparkling clean but not a stick of furniture. Then look at a house that has been "staged," meaning that the realtor has furnished or set up the rooms for display, with furniture, artwork, cushions on a couch. The theory is that a well-staged house—one with texture—delights the eye and helps the buyer (the audience) picture themselves owning the home. All other factors being equal, the fact is that an artfully staged house sells far more quickly and brings in a sales price that is thousands of dollars more than an equivalent empty house. A staged house targets our emotions.

Texture can be dust, which makes things look old and unused, or it can be a faint hint of dirt. It can mean using a touch of black powder so that it looks like you're in a sooty urban area, or constructing what is supposed to be an aged stone wall out of foam, painting it, rubbing it in so the paint settles, and making us feel that wall has been in your location for a hundred years. Texture gives three-dimensionality to flat surfaces so when lighted and filmed, they look real.

When you see a film where a surface is shiny, that's usually intentional, and again, contextual. What that reflection means is dependent upon context. Is the person slick? Vain? An egoist? Is there a repeated motif with mirrors, windows, reflective marble and tiled floors? On the one hand, things that reflect light look great on film, but on the other, a good filmmaker will make the choice of using reflections to tell you something, not just for an impressive shot.

When we watch a film, detail plays with our expectations and perceptions. At the simplest level, when you see an office full of polished surfaces, angular tables and couches, lots of glass and leather and chrome, what decisions do you make about the character inhabiting that environment? Is she/he cuddly? Old fashioned? Probably not.

When you see an apartment dressed with an over-stuffed sofa, woven throws casually draped on chairs, and lots of clutter, who lives there? In real life, people don't so obviously and closely resemble their environment. Perhaps it's not even really their environment—maybe they're sub-letting their place from their cousin. Maybe they moved into the glossy, sleek office of the former CEO and since the merger they've been too busy to redecorate. In movie life though, the audience has only a short time to get to know the characters. Detail is a short cut.

A simple example of texture—a chain-link fence is generally thought to be unattractive. It's a relatively inexpensive way to either keep people and things out or keep them in. The use of that type of fencing gives us the sense that the occupant of the fenced place is not friendly, or is off-limits. If you take the same structure of fencing (same height, same panel sizes, and inter-crossed design) but change the materials to something like woven cedar lattice—like a garden fence or a privacy fence—that place immediately becomes more welcoming. Is your character hemmed in, psychologically stunted? Your free-spirit probably doesn't live behind chain-links.

Texture is peeling paint and stained paper to depict age, jagged edges to impart instability and risk. It doesn't cost much. You can find a location with plain flat walls and give it texture. You might hang a tapestry, creating the impression of old money or Grandma's house. You can replace Venetian blinds, a staple of Film Noir, with lace curtains if your setting is an early Sixties blue-collar home in the mid-West or on the East Coast. These examples are not meant to tell you what to do. Some of these examples are too heavy-handed. They're intended to get you thinking about the connection between what you see, or as a film-maker, what you choose, and what information that visual choice has the potential to impart.

Plain, cream colored walls aren't very interesting—but they can be useful if your setting is meant to feel generic. You can transform that same, plain room into seeming to be older by adding crown molding— very inexpensive at your local building supply store. If you're building a set and want to suggest something about a family living in the house, think about windows. Do you want to use double hung windows? Broad, uninterrupted expanses of glass? Are we in the Thirties or Forties or Fifties? What about glass-block windows that let in light but no one can see anything through them?

Is your location a hipster café? What posters should be on the walls? What graphically reads hipster? Is the set a little girl's room? You can go the pink princess route but it could be more interesting to think about the character and decide what this specific character, not a generic little girl, would own. Which dolls are on the bed, or would there be dolls at all? Is she a Disney princess or Princess Leia? Does she pretend to be a girly-girl but hide a catcher's mitt under her pillow? And don't spend your hard-raised cash at the sporting goods store for a new glove. If she's a secret tomboy she would have found a battered old glove some-where and polished it up. It would have patina. Go to a thrift store. Give us clues about the inner life of your characters and they become three-dimensional. Texture adds up.

If you look at the bedroom of Seb's apartment in *La La Land*, you'll see there isn't much there. The walls are pretty bare. We know by the lack of texture in the room that this character is not settled. He's waiting for his life to begin.

In *The Godfather*, Don Corleone's home office is paneled with dark wood. The Don is a frightening guy but he respects tradition. He is a man who has killed and orders killings, but he prizes family. There are family pictures on the wall. He doesn't smoke but there's an ashtray on his desk. He's hospitable to those who come to pay their respects.

When the Tom Hagen character, the Don's consigliere (counsel) vis-its the home of Hollywood studio chief Jack Woltz, the two men are seated at opposite ends of a long dinner table. The use of the table as staging visually indicates the divide between the two men. Using texture and scale, the filmmaker emphasizes the tension. There will be no compromise.

Size

Size in this case means scale. How much space does something or someone occupy in the frame, and how much of a difference is there between that person or object and everything else? Back to the Hagen/Woltz scenes in *The Godfather*.

Woltz takes Hagen on a tour of his estate. His house is palatial. The grounds are vast. Woltz and Hagen dine beside a mammoth fireplace. The scale of the set signifies the reach and power of the studio chief, or at least Woltz's idea of how important he is.

In case we still don't understand Woltz's out-sized ego, we see him later in his bedroom, his private space. On the nightstand is an Academy Award Oscar statue. It isn't featured, just set to one side. He keeps it close, where he sleeps. There is no better way to show what that gold statuette means to him. Just as the Don is the ruler of his 'family', Woltz is king of his territory. (That is, until the private space is invaded, and Don Corleone makes his point with a bloody horse's head. Then the contest is over.)

If the way a set is dressed is the micro of scale, the way space is used in the frame is the macro. Alexander Payne's *Nebraska* is a modern film shot in black and white. The film is about family dynamics, dying communities, and in part about how insignificant these characters feel. Often the flat landscape fills almost all the frame. There is little space left for the actors.

In *Lawrence of Arabia*, there are times when the actors appear as specks dwarfed by the relentless heat and vast brutal emptiness of the desert. But when Lawrence celebrates a triumph, when he leads a band of men in successfully blowing up a train, he strides atop the destroyed train carcass, holding out his white robes to appear larger than he is. He's a leader. Though slight of build, for that moment he's a big man.

Scale often plays a part in our reaction to Point of View (POV) shots. Crane shots from on high are sometimes thought of as the God POV because they're usually about something more powerful than the small people, cars, or neighborhood in the shot.

When you look at size, you are often looking at emotion. How do you feel watching a person walk through a 20-foot high archway? How about one where there's an inch of head-room between their head and the curve? In a movie, when we see someone large squeezing into a tight space, depending upon the context, we either assume it is supposed to be funny or awkward, or that they're in danger.

Alec Hammond

Volume is the most important thing to get right as a designer. If the person who is supposed to go through a doorway comes up almost to the top of it or only to the doorknob you've told a completely different story. With one single door, you've put the person and the world that person is inhabiting in a completely different realm. It has a different emotional impact—a little teeny person walking through the door or a little teeny door with a giant person walking through it. The person doesn't change but you can tell a story just by having the door be a different size.

Because of that, in design we have to be very careful even when we're dealing with something as simple as an opening in a wall. We need to always look at what we do in terms of the characters in the world and what it says about them. Looking at the actual size of space, camera and crew requirements aside, it's important that you have considered the volume for the action that is happening in the space. I used to have a slogan above my drafting table that said, "Should it be ten times bigger? Should it be a tenth of the size?" It was just a way of breaking myself out of thinking, "it's a room. It's a bedroom. It's a living room" and to really think creatively about every aspect of the space.

A mentor of mine told me this anecdote: he was looking at these old Newport mansions for a set. I think it was supposed to be for the bedroom of the Queen of Spain as a little girl. There was one scene where they were looking for the bedroom of very, very young royalty who was clearly not of age to assume the responsibility of her position.

They were looking for—for lack of a better term—"girly" interiors. Lightly colored, overly detailed. Baroque, Rococo-style interiors. They kept finding them, but they weren't quite right. Then they walked into a room that was incredibly huge and dark, wood paneled and carved. He thought at first, this isn't good. But then he changed his mind. He said, "You know, this is really good. You have to think of it as more than the room. You think about putting a gigantic bed in the middle of it with a little girl in a pink dress jumping up and down on the bed—then you have the whole story of who she is. Of her being still a kid in the midst of her being manipulated and controlled by the men who were the power structure around her, yet she has the power." That is a function of volume. That's a strategy to get to the vital visual drama of that scene. That's allowing the visuals to tell the story of that scene in a different way.

Photo 2.1 An example of the use of both size and forced perspective. Due to
the way the photograph is shot, the airplane appears to be bearing
down on the car in a threatening way, although in reality it is very
far away from the car.

Source: David Cibley.

Forced Perspective

As a filmmaker thinking about size, you can employ forced perspective to
help tell your story. Forced perspective is essentially an optical illusion. By
manipulating the way something is viewed, you can make it look further
away or smaller, or closer and larger (see Photo 2.1). This way you can
afford to do things on a very low-budget project by using models (miniatures, for example) and building sets to a scale different than they are in real
life. This has to be done cleverly to work, but imagine the partially buried
and burned fuselage of a plane in the ground. You can get that shot using
a model plane in a sandbox filled with dirt and debris. Depending how you
light it, your choice of lenses and angles, and how you edit it, your audience
won't know you didn't spend a night in the desert. You can have a shot that
appears to be from the inside of a house to the outside prairie beyond. If you
build, set up, light, and shoot your miniatures and backdrops correctly, it
can appear that there is an entire frontier town in the distance.

Line and Repetition

When you think about line, you're thinking about movement and direction. Verticals move the eye upward. Horizontals direct the eye from

side to side. Diagonals give the impression of motion. Crossed lines can evoke conflict. We respond to line without knowing that we are doing it (see Photos 2.2, 2.3). Think about the POV crane shots you've seen

Photo 2.2 The lane lines on this road direct our eyes to follow the curve.
Source: David Cibley.

Photo 2.3 The perspective of this shot gives us a sense of the train's movement
that we would not get if the photo was shot straight on.
Source: David Cibley.

of packed freeways at night. You can't see the specifics of the vehicles, you see the lines of head and tail-lights intersecting. From that shot you instantly understand how complex, busy, and possibly indifferent life is in the big city.

When an army approaches, men and women marching in unison, we feel the strength and authority. The machine-like straight line, the repetition of the uniforms, and the force of the unstoppable progress of the marchers can give us a sense of relief if they're the good guys coming to save the day. If they're the bad guys, a shot of that line fills us with dread. Compare that visual to one of the same number of people dressed in a variety of costumes and colors, milling around. They aren't frightening. They aren't in control. Unless they're supposed to be an angry mob. Then you might completely fill the frame with them, getting uncomfortably close up so you see their rage. Faces and bodies crowding the frame does something else to us—our eyes go everywhere, from one to another—and that's disturbing.

Another Use of Line

Through movement, line affects our perception of size. Back to your T-shirt collection. Find one with wide horizontal stripes, maybe bright blue stripes on a white background. Your eye will move across the shirt—therefore, you will feel that that shirt is wider and more substantial than a version of that same shirt in a solid color. If you wear that shirt, you'll look broader. Same goes for an outfit with narrow verticals (pin-stripes)—you'll appear slightly taller and thinner. As a filmmaker, you can prod your audience to look in a specific direction by the use of line. For instance, your scene is about a fifth-grader caught cheating on an exam. He walks slowly down the aisle, between long rows of low, kid-proportioned schoolhouse desks. By placing the camera specifically, or by using a lens that makes the walk seem more a walk of shame, the walk toward the much bigger, taller scary teacher's desk can seem to take an eternity. You can rouse your audience to sympathy, apprehension, or just anticipation. You can nudge the audience by directing us along the line of his path—the gauntlet.

In *La La Land*, Mia leaves an audition and she sees a row of women who are waiting to read for the same role. They look a bit like her and are dressed like her. As we follow her down the hallway it is evident that she feels ordinary. We are pretty sure she won't get the job. We're moving down the assembly line of actresses with her and as we move with her and take on her point of view, we identify with her. If the shots were designed differently—for instance, if she left the room, saw her rivals but they all looked and were dressed differently, then she walked down the hallway alone, we would still get the point. But because we are heading down the same path as she does, it feels more immediate and uncomfortable. The visual echo of the aspiring actors, the length of the hallway, and the camera move work in concert to bring us emotionally closer to Mia.

The set is not a major, expensive piece constructed on a stage, it's a hallway with some chairs. By carrying us along on her journey, the scene works our emotions.

Alec Hammond

Design allows for the actual filmmaking experience and the events that take place within it but it also operates as something you move through. The camera moves through things, the characters move through things. The dynamic quality of the environments and the worlds that you're creating is equally as important as what it actually looks like.

Another example of the use of line you've seen before: filmmakers often use high-rise buildings to communicate that a person inside is important. The offices have banks of windows and overlook a cityscape or a body of water. The interiors of the offices have high ceilings and bookcases that draw your eyes up. A formidable executive is introduced as part of a sequence of a) establishing shot of the high-rise where his or her office is located, b) a cut to his or her office where our eyes are directed by lighting, furniture arrangement, and color, to the command center, c) the CEO at the desk.

Now, transpose the gist of that scene—our first sight of the person of influence—to a period film. You've seen it before. The impressive palace, a long dolly through high-ceilinged chambers with enormous pieces of furniture and murals or huge framed portraits on the walls, then massive doors opening to a very long walk forward where our eyes are directed to the Royal on his or her throne. In both the case of the high-rise and the palace, line (and scale) tells the story. No need for the intrusion of lines of dialogue letting us know who these people are. No exposition. We know we're visiting the halls of power.

Fences are essentially lines, and can make you react in a variety of ways. If they're low—a short wooden or stone fence is clearly just a border that marks territory but does it in an approachable way—you might want to visit that house. When fences are high, made of tall and elaborately twisted wrought iron, they can be used to intimidate, or to convey a period or location feel. Bright white picket fences are often a statement—these fences can be a throwback to a simpler time, or stand for all that's wrong about contemporary suburbia or small-town America.

Weight

How much weight does something in the frame have in comparison to everything else? Weight in the frame is a function of: foreground or background, sharp or soft focus, lit or indistinct, a color or texture that draws attention (see Photo 2.4). As the filmmaker, you decide when you want to make use of visual devices that pull us in a specific direction.

As you're imagining your sets, choosing locations, deciding on wardrobe, think about how and where you want everything to appear in the frame. This will be a discussion with your art department (or maybe you *are* your art department), your cinematographer, and your costume designer, and everyone should be aware of what you're going for. You may wonder if your favorite filmmakers really say, "I want this to fill the lower eighth of the frame"? Or, "We're using fuchsia and puce because . . ." Some do. They look at pictures. They use reference materials. You should too. You also have the freedom to experiment. See what you notice out of the corners of your eyes. Remember, you don't want to be obvious. You want to be subtle and discerning. Your goal is to get your audience on board for the ride.

Photo 2.4 In this image, the scale (relative size and light on the left section of the fence) draws our eyes from left to right.

Source: David Cibley.

3 The Vision—and Collaboration

There are directors who are design-savvy and know exactly how they want the film to look. They want someone to give life to the pictures in their heads. Some are hoping for a creative partner who will create a style that enables the story to be told in the most effective way. But some directors don't really want to be involved. They want remarkable sets and locations and costumes to just happen. They assume they'll know what is right for the movie when they see it but don't know what they're hoping to see. They like their department heads to bring them lots of choices and assume that something they see will ring their bell. Some directors are micro-managers. Some assume that once they've hired a good team, they've done their part. A director who has a background in the theater might have a different way of relating to a set than a director more experienced in commercials and music videos. One director may feel more inspired by a set that is practical (meaning a real location), thinking that a scene will come across as more honest if it is shot in a setting that really exists. Another may want the control that comes from building sets and having the freedom to remove walls and hang lights from an overhead grid.

Note that on a television series, unlike on a feature film, it is usually the showrunner (head writer/producer) who is the conceptual person. The showrunner and the staff writers are the constant participants and they hold the power on a series. The directors may change with every episode.

Production designer Brendon O'Connor received his BFA in Interior Design at Harrington College of Design and his MFA in Production Design from Chapman University's Dodge College of Film and Media Arts. He has worked as an art department, assistant art director, an art director or a production designer on television series, including *Shameless*, *Mr. Box Office*, *The First Family*, *A to Z, Studio City*, *White Famous*, *Mr. Student Body President*, *One Mississippi*, *Love*, and features including *Happy Birthday*, *Hacked*, *The Barber*, *Beyond the Lights*, *Bounty Killer*, and *Feeding Mr. Baldwin*.

Brendan O'Connor

In order to get the best creative out, you have to be willing to offer up as many ideas as possible. You're going to be researching, finding photos, finding images of what the set could be, video references, you've got to do a lot of digging. If the director doesn't have a design concept, it's your job to create it. You've got to be able to adjust—and adjust quickly when they're not happy with what you came up with. You cannot take it personally. You have to be able to be flexible. If they didn't like one idea you should have two more waiting in the wings, and be ready to say, "how 'bout we do this instead?" That's the communication that's important. I've seen a lot of designers get caught up when their creative idea gets rejected and they can't pivot to something more positive. And I've seen that with cinematographers as well. Cinematographers who walk in and start with a "no." "No we can't do that." The director wants it this way and they say, "we can't do that because of this and that and whatever" and the director is ready to pick up the camera and shoot it himself because he knows that it can be done. You have to be able to roll with it. Each production is different. You can't get married to something and think it's not going to change—because it's going to change.

Alec Hammond

At the end of the day the production designer has very much a go-between job. It is not a fine art form. It's a collaborative form between ourselves, the director, and the script. It's a particular vision of a particular set of words on a page. Primarily it's the director's vision but you always come back to the words, you always come back to the page. You're volleying between your own personal view of those things and the director's, and how she's going to shoot it, You create that visual envelope that wraps around that dialogue between you and the director. That dialogue is vibrant. The hardest thing about learning to be a production designer is that there is so much practical and technical that you need to know—but in some ways the hardest thing to do is to have that collaborative dialogue.

John Chichester

Have a conversation with just the director. The fewer people in the room, the more relaxed people can be. Often people feel uncomfortable saying, "you know, I don't know. Let me think about that," if they're in front of a large group of people because they think that can make them look like they're indecisive, or that they're incompetent or something. Try to meet one-on-one when you can, so you're talking about nothing but story. It (getting to the design concept) is like planting a tree. You've got to water it. You've got to see it grow before you get into the practicality.

Until you feel you're on the right track, until you've laid the groundwork try to pose as much as you can in a question so that you can gain common ground. Once you've gained common ground (about the story) then you can start brainstorming. You can start really moving.

John Lloyd Miller has directed, produced, and written feature films, documentaries, commercials, and television. He has directed music videos, for top recording artists, including Garth Brooks, The Smithereens, Eazy A and NWA, The Goo Goo Dolls, Joe Cocker, Billy Ray Cyrus, Reba McEntire, George Strait, Patty Loveless, and Vince Gill. His commercials and short films have been nominated for and won numerous international awards. Miller is a graduate of USC Film School and currently lives in Nashville, Tennessee.

John Lloyd Miller

For me, no matter what field I'm playing in, whether it's music videos or commercials or film, the goal is to make some sort of emotional connection. Visual storytelling is all about emotion. I try to deconstruct the story into its most basic elements. In terms of emotion, I break down the script and every page can have a different emotional outcome, and a different emotional intention. From there, I begin to build what becomes the visual design of the project. The budget is never a consideration because on a real base level, if I'm trying to create an emotional response, there's always a way. It's easier if you have lots of money. But even then, sometimes people get caught up in how much they can do instead of how much they should do. When we're making decisions about what color the wardrobe should be or what something should look like it always comes down to, what are we trying to convey emotionally? What is the story about? That's everything. Every lens we pick, every light we decide, every angle we shoot from, how we're treating the material digitally, all those decisions are based on emotion and emotional intention.

There is not a one-to-one relationship between what the character is feeling and what the audience is feeling. Sometimes starting filmmakers think that if they cause an emotional reaction in a character that the audience will have some kind of one-to-one relationship with whatever that character's going through, but I point out that the Three Stooges could take a two by four and whack a guy on the head and you'll laugh. But the guy who got hit with the two by four is not laughing.

On Design Choices

Everything is about context. It's always anchored by: will this tell the story? I made a period piece that jumped around in time a lot. Early on, we made the choice, we're going to do it in black and white. Our reasoning was, it's going to make it easier and less expensive to recreate the early Sixties in black and white. And in fact it was, but there is a section of the film that is a flashback within a flashback that's in color. Very pastel. And it's the only calm time in this character's life. It really jumps out at people. If it was a normal color film, it would have been meaningless. Just that decision helped sell the time period. It made the setting feel older.

An Example of a Film That Demonstrates a Great Use of Color and Design

There are so many. But *The Verdict* is one. It's a film that in every way is so remarkable in terms of the design choices. There's not one frame of that film that is not completely controlled and intentional. The camera movement is non-existent until the point in the trial where a key piece of evidence is revealed—and then the whole film turns. And there's this slight move in. Because the camera has been so rock-steady the whole time until then, until that little movement, you feel like you're going to crash into the wall.

(continued)

(continued)

The film is meticulous in every aspect of design, including color. Or lack of color. It's a film where color is almost the enemy of the main character. We meet the Paul Newman character in this colorless dark place. His relationships are colorless and dark. And in the end—it's not a happy Hollywood ending, but there's a sense of moving on. It's not *The Wizard of Oz* where it moves from black and white to color. But the color moves ever so slightly, and you move with it. It takes you as an audience.

Design in film is the result of the collaboration of dozens of people. If you look at the credits of most motion pictures or television programs, you'll see a seemingly unending list of departments. It may seem like a no-brainer that the production designer and art director are the key folk in the design chain, because it is their responsibility to create the look of the world we see. But they don't operate in a vacuum. There is the cinematographer, the costume designer, the set decorator, the props person, the location manager. The length of the list of contributors to the visual design of a project can be quite short on a micro-budget or student film where a single person fills lots of slots. Alternatively, the credits list could be on the screen for several minutes because it might take hundreds of people to support the design of a Hollywood sci-fi/comic book spectacle.

Depending upon the script and genre, the art, construction, set dressing, and greens departments on a big budget film may look like this:

Production Designer

Supervising Art Director

Additional Art Directors

Assistant Art Directors

Concept Artists

Storyboard Artists

Illustrators

Set Designers

Set Decorator

Set Dressers

On-set Dresser

Leadperson

Set Decoration Buyer

Art Department Coordinator

Art Department PA (Production Assistant)

Graphic Designers

Construction Coordinator

Construction Crew

Scenic

Propmakers

Greensman

Add to that the construction department, the cinematographer, the costume designer, the property master, the location manager, the special and visual effects designers—it's a lot of people and they must all work toward the same goal: everyone dealing with visual design must understand the director's vision. At the same time, their plans must be feasible given the production schedule and budget. It should be obvious that good communication is immensely important. At any stage of production, whether in prep or on set, things can get confused. Or it can be found that items cost too much or activities take longer than expected. It's even possible that someone with more clout may change their mind about the look—suddenly, in their mind, it won't work. Then the carefully thought out plans must be scrapped. If this happens, and it occasionally happens very late in the process, there's no time for recriminations or anger. One of the traits of a great department head is to know when to voice objections, and when to bite the bullet. And a great department leader has learned that part of the job is to develop the ability to turn on a dime.

How does this communication work? How can so many people who are often not even working in close proximity to each other communicate effectively, understand how their departmental needs interface with all the other departments, and most important of all, how do they enhance the mood, how can they help bring the story over the finish line? Every bit of visual design is meant to carry the audience into the world of the film, to move the story ahead—and to do it seamlessly, without you even noticing.

Section 2
The Collaborators

4   Designing, Building, Painting

As we've seen, it really can take the proverbial village to create the visual world of a film. Your own team will likely be much smaller than the average feature film crew. Fewer people will take on more and different combinations of responsibilities. It still helps to have a checklist of who all those people listed are and what they do in the professional world, so you can be sure your two-person crew has all the bases covered as completely as possible.

The Production Designer

First, there is the production designer, the head of the art department. The production designer's name appears in the main titles—the credits at the front of the movie. The production designer is what is called a "key creative." This means the designer is expected to have a great deal of input in the artistic aspects of the process. Usually, the designer has a crew of people he or she has worked with in the past. Once the designer is hired, the rest of the art department team falls into place. Please note that it is definitely a team. Once you've been involved in a few projects, no matter how small, you develop a group of people whose work and work ethic you respect. On a professional film, department heads fight to bring on their regular people. There are so many things that can go wrong on a project. It's reassuring not to have to reinvent the wheel and start from scratch every time you start a film. You want to surround yourself with those who have come through for you in the past, whether creatively, budgetarily, or with 25 hours of commitment during a 24-hour day.

The production designer is responsible for the overall look of the film. In consultation with the director, he or she strives to generate a physical representation of the literal, psychological, and emotional setting of the movie. The production designer oversees the look of anything designed, constructed, painted, and/or decorated. Whether it's the Shire of the *Lord of The Rings* trilogy or 1860s *Five Corners*, Manhattan in *Gangs of New York*, Gotham in *Batman*, the hotel in *The Shining*, or the New York school and jazz clubs of *Whiplash*, mostly shot in Los Angeles, the

production designer is responsible for taking the settings described on the script page and interpreting what is written so what you see supports and enhances the characters, the tone, and the dramatic action.

Film production has a hierarchal reporting structure. Everyone in the art department either reports directly to the production designer or to someone at a lower level, who then reports to the production designer. Depending on the intricacies and physical requirements of the project, the production designer might start work anywhere from several weeks to a year before shooting begins. He or she is one of the first people hired when a film is given a green light. (A green light is the signal that a film has moved from script stage to the point when a project is going to be made and money can be spent.)

Prior to being hired, a production designer is sent the screenplay. He or she reads it, then begins to formulate ideas as to what the movie will look like, thinking about the possibilities. Is it a comedy or a thriller? Period or contemporary? Will it be moody, or light-hearted? Will there be a thematic color choice? Should there be anything unusual about the overall scale and scope of the sets? Is the world of the project realistic, stylized, exaggerated, or bizarre?

A designer must understand the story and the subtext of the screenplay so they are able to translate vague descriptions on a page into a visual statement. INT. UPSCALE DRESS SHOP can suggest a variety of images. It's their job to come up with the best images for this story, this setting, these characters? SPACE—THE YEAR 2050 can mean anything. What can it/should it/could it look like? The production designer's point of view has to mesh with the written material and with the concepts of the prime storyteller, the director. The designer's ability to develop and communicate an original take on the visual world of the screenplay is vital. If it's in accord with the director's vision, then they are hired. If not, no matter how brilliant they may be, probably the director will look for someone whose thinking is more aligned with their own.

The production designer must be able to articulate ideas to the producer, the rest of the art department, the set decorator, the costume designer, the location manager, and sometimes the special effects or visual effects team. This is important because at some point, art, dressing, costume, and location come together. Design has to be cohesive. For an example of this, look again at *The Truman Show*. Truman's world is consistent. Scores of creative people worked on the film, but the world is precise and not at all ambiguous. The choice of the location (the film was shot in part in Seaside, Florida) underscores the premise of a place too good to be true, where everything is ship-shape and standardized. Truman's environment is pretty, and feel-good in its conformity, like an old-fashioned illustration in a child's book. This location was a design choice. Without a line of spoken dialog or explanation, it tells us what we need to know about Truman's idealized reality-show life. For another classic example, look at the original *Blade Runner*, set in a future Los Angeles filled with smoke pollution, darkness, and neon. The look is one of deterioration. The choice of color is the lack of color. This is a world of people drained of joy. It's difficult to tell the humans from the replicants. In both films, directors Ridley Scott and Peter Weir knew precisely the stories they wanted to tell, and how to use light, color, and design to do it.

When you write a novel, you can devote whole chapters to description. In a film, using production design and lighting you can communicate it with a 10-second shot. *The Truman Show* and *Blade Runner* tap into both our consciousness and subconscious. For most of *Blade Runner* it's raining, and the ground is wet. Everything is degraded. Life in the Los Angeles of the future is inhospitable and cold. In *The Truman Show* all is spotless, orderly. Nothing lurks in the shadows. Truman world is airy and neat as a pin, devoid of conflict. There's no fear in Truman's artificial stage-set world. The night sky is bright and beautiful. Only when there is an intrusion from outside, is there actual darkness. Are we supposed to notice that? Not in an obvious way. But we are meant to pick up on the emotion conveyed through the design choices on both films. Anxiety and foreboding is part of *Blade Runner*, where in *Truman* world, everything is like a sunny smile, welcoming Truman home.

The Business Side

As the head of a major department, the production designer also over-sees the department budget. The production manager, who supervises the overall project budget, often does a preliminary estimate of the cost of labor, materials, and personnel for each department. This sometimes happens before the department heads are even hired. That can mean that the people with the true expertise in the area haven't weighed in. As experienced as production managers are, it's impossible to decide what the art department will need without there being a plan. For the plan, you need the designer. What this amounts to is that once there IS a designer hired, there is often a tug of war between what is needed and what has been allotted. Frequently the production manager says, "You have only X amount," and the production designer says, "Unless you give me Y amount, it can't be done." Then everyone goes back to the drawing board to figure out a compromise. Why isn't this done in a more logical order? Why doesn't the production manager wait to do a budget until all the information is in? Because a budget is usually a factor in the decision-making process of the studio, the production company, or the investor as to whether to make the project at all. Without a budget, there is no funding. Without funding, you can't hire a production designer. So, the production manager makes an educated guess and once the production designer is hired, the negotiations begin.

Great sets are impressive but not if the cost of building them is out of proportion to the rest of the production cost. The designer must also have a sense of logistics. How long does it take to do what is planned? How many people are needed? Should a set be found or built? The designer works in consultation with art director, the construction coordinator, the set designer, and the location manager. Sometimes the art director manages the budget on a day-to-day basis, but the designer is ultimately responsible for making sure the art department comes in (spends) at the amount budgeted, once the project has wrapped.

In an ideal world, by the time building, painting, and dressing begins, there are no surprises, but since the production schedule and budget of a film might be locked before all decisions are made, the production designer adapts, and after a while, acquires a sense of which battles are worth fighting. The way unforeseen costs work on a film is, IF unanticipated costs arise, there is a scramble. The producer and production manager, who are responsible for making sure the film is made for the money available, are charged with managing the funds. Studios, production companies, and investors don't want to spend more than the amount they've originally committed to, so where does the money for unforeseen expenditures come from? The money is pulled from somewhere else in the department's budget. Need more cash to finish that spaceship interior? Then the scene taking place on the alien planet may have to go. Miscalculate what it would take to build that high-school locker room and the argument between the jocks, written and planned to take place as a fight/stunt sequence ending up under the showers, might be moved to the football field.

Reworking of things at the last minutes occurs more often than you'd expect and sometimes you may never know the real reason why something that had been OK'd has now been tossed aside. Sometimes it is budget, sometimes it is poor communication, sometimes it's just politics. I worked on a film where everything had been shown to the director in advance, it had been approved weeks before. As the crew was pulling in to the location (a storefront playing a restaurant) early, ready to shoot, the director stated that he didn't like the way the table settings or the napkins or the tablecloth looked. The set dresser and the property master had to find an open store, find and choose new props and dressing within an hour, then be back to set up in time to shoot the scene. They took care of it. They probably were not smiling as they did it, but it happened. Recovery is a major part of the job.

Another example of change at the very last minute: a director arrived on set of a major studio film for the very first day of shooting. He had praised the primary location of the film when he'd walked through it just days before. The crew was ready to start lighting. The all-star cast was in make-up. The director pulled his producer aside and said, "It's all wrong." Luckily there was an alternative location ready to shoot. The original set was re-done—but to be honest, it wasn't extremely different.

Why does this happen? In both these cases, the directors were very experienced and, in the second case, the director was what the industry refers to as "A List." It could have simply been a case of the jitters on their part. They're not comfortable with the scene or the actors or something is keeping them up at night, and they're displacing that anxiety. Maybe the director was looking for an excuse to fire the designer. (In the second case, the designer was replaced a few days into production.) Or maybe he had had a fight with his wife. It doesn't matter. Pros just deal with it.

When a designer has a first meeting with the director, he or she is not only thinking about the creative possibilities of the project, but about what they know about the director. Collaborative? Decisive? Difficult? When a director has an existing and strong relationship with a production designer that's who gets the job, sometimes with just a phone call. But if that person isn't available, or the director wasn't happy with the most recent experience, the director will want to meet new designers. At those meetings, after a few pleasantries, invariably the first question asked is, "What do you think of the script?" This doesn't mean the director is expecting story notes. The director is listening for concepts regarding the physical design of the spaces in which the story takes place.

In addition to an artist and a manager, the production designer must be something of a psychologist. Each project is different, and directors have different ways of working. There are months of discussion, meetings where drawings and photos are viewed and approved, plans made for the manpower and materials needed, location scouts with all the pertinent people on the scouting van, and many "show and tell" sessions, and this is all to facilitate a shared vision of the film.

John Chichester about His Process

You've got your script. As I'm reading the script, I make up a set list. Every set, interior or exterior. I'll also make practical notes: the building blows up. The house burns down. Those little things. You get an overall sense of who the characters are, of what the story is. You go to the meeting where they see whether to hire you or not. Probably bring some visual imagery to the meeting. Then I help define where they want to go with this. You can gauge from your director what the tone is that they want, if it's going to be bold and visually extreme or subtle.

The designer, as quiet of a job as it is, can really determine a lot. Tone. The movement of the actors in the space. Ultimately the work of the cinematographer and the director and how everyone moves in the space is defined by what the space is.

(continued)

(continued)

Research is vital. Do conceptual research, and do research into whatever the subject is of the movie. Look at artists, photographers at work that you think this movie could look like. Then print the images so you can lay them all out on a table and your team can look at them all at the same time. Anything that looks wrong—discard it. That way you can immediately start editing and narrowing it down to the images that your director and your teammates react to the strongest. Then give them to everybody so everybody's got them up on their wall and can look at them and think about it.

The Art Director

The art director is the second in command in the art department hierarchy. The art director's responsibility is to oversee all the departments that are part of art, so that the designer's vision of what the world of the movie should be can be realized. Like the production designer, they deal with the construction and graphics departments, the set designers who draft plans for building, the visual effects people to coordinate the use of set extensions. A set extension is the created background or painting of an environment that is meant to ultimately be coupled with a real image as a composite. This process can be used to combine the image of a jungle behind a model King Kong, to add buildings, or to erase pine trees and street signs. It can be used to create a city where there isn't one, and to shoot a scene in an empty warehouse that is dressed as a cave, then filled in with stalactites and stalagmites.

In addition to being creative, the art director must be skilled in logistics. The art director is a sort of project manager for the art department. She coordinates disparate departmental (and sub-departmental) schedules so that everything is ready to shoot when needed and tracks the day-to-day expenses of all these activities. On large projects, he may supervise a team of art directors. On smaller projects, the art director and the production designer may be the same person.

Art director Priscilla Elliott has come up the ranks of the art department, from researcher on *The Cat in the Hat, Charlie and the Chocolate Factory, The Corpse Bride, Flight-plan, The Fantastic Mr. Fox, Charlie Wilson's War, Star Wars: The Last Jedi,* to assistant art director on *Southland Tales,* to art director on *The SpongeBob Movie, The Hunger Games 2,* to the Los Angeles portion of *King Kong: Skull Island,* to supervising art director on the new TV series *Too Old to Die Young,* the films *Tag* and *In Time, The Invention of Lying,* and *The Back-up Plan* plus several episodes of *Castle.*

Priscilla Elliott

You read the script and you come up with your idea of how you understand the visual world of the script. The first thing you do is literally write down everything as you read it. We're inside a hotel. We're on a freeway. We're in a car. We're in a subway. Your first breakdown is a rough set list. From there you go into your interpretation of the mood of the story. You might go through your art archives and come up with 20 pictures that relate to these 50 sets. You start having a conversation with the director. You start talking about what kind of details that mood is going to take on and you start working from there.

Go to people's homes. I did a movie on soldiers with PTSD so I went and photographed a guy's home. What books did he have on his shelf? The way he set up the shelves was so poignant. Because these bookshelves had all these self-help books. How to get rich mixed in with war books. And he had this go-bag with an AK-47 right by the door and the refrigerator was stocked with bottles of vodka. He was ready for trouble. When anyone lets you get inside, it's amazing. Because that's where you get ideas and you say, "Oh my God, this feels right."

I thought *Beasts of the Southern Wild* was amazing. Their decision was that they wanted everything to be real. They raised these baby pigs. They slept with baby pigs. Someone on the crew raised these baby pigs so they would be tame. And he started dressing them up in costumes so they could wear the tusks because the director didn't want a CG [Computer Generated] pig. That's how they solved this problem of "where do these beasts come from? What do they look like?" You could have made them cartoon beasts. They could have been animatronic beasts. They could have been CG. But because they knew what they were doing in terms of the visual flavour . . . it was the right thing emotionally.

The design in *Fight Club* is a high. It's such a potentially ordinary situation. You have these guys living in a shitty squat. This guy works in a boring office. And he lives in a boring apartment. But the visuals are crazy and it's because they did all these amazing things. One small example, they didn't use an ordinary stack of books. The place is a mess, but they didn't just use a stack of books, they had a carved stack of books or magazines that was leaning too far over for gravity. They carved the thing so it looks messy. The design strategy was doing just that little extra "too much" all the time. There was a huge effort in fabricating the "too muchness" that gave it a heightened unreality, set in a potentially mundane environment.

As an art director, Elliott has had to be a problem-solver, from finding a creative solution for something in the script, to dealing with a massive but leaking water tank (working all night long with a crew to drain it, fix it, and get it re-filled just in time to greet the crew arriving to shoot early the next morning), to helping to find and choose a distinctive-looking parking garage for the TV crime series *Too Old to Die Young*. (The challenge was to find a unique location in a city where it seems that every single nook and cranny has already been filmed.) Elliott began as an art department researcher and she still relies heavily on research.

Priscilla Elliott

Amazing set design is thinking it through all the layers. That doesn't cost money. In something like *The Hunger Games*, because it's a sci-fi concept based on the reality of the story, each zone (in the movie) has a different job. One zone makes coal. One does something else. The people who live in each zone, their life arrangement would be based on what they make. If you're in the coal environment, you're going to be using coal. You have coal fires. Everything you do is going to be based on the material you have available and the technology you have available, based on the artifice of the story. You want to think about, what kind of plates would they use? The more you can think about what the story suggests about that reality, whether it's a story about a soldier with PTSD or it's a sci-fi story where there are no cellphones and no cars—what does that mean? You try to find a specific psychological reality.

Walk the streets. Study them. Don't be lazy and make it up. Look at pictures. Libraries are great. Search. It's free. You want something to look like downtown LA in the future. You drive around downtown LA. Take a photograph of every sign. I did a movie called *RV*. The director sent me out for ten days with a car and a camera to shoot trailer parks across the US. We got stuff that's not going to show up on the internet.

The Set Designer

The art director also works closely with the set designer. The set designer's job is to draft plans for whatever is being built. Set design is the physical blueprint for building or altering existing sets and locations for production. Some production designers do this themselves but, depending on the number of built sets there are or what their individual expertise may be, some have a set designer on their team handling this area. Under the leadership of and in consultation with the production designer, the set designer generates technical architectural drawings. The production designer, art director, and set designer on a big project will work with the construction coordinator and construction crew (carpenters, welders, painters, plasterers) to ensure that the two-dimensional renderings are accurately brought to three-dimensional life. This may mean the design of walls that are 'wild' (can be removed to achieve more shooting flexibility in an existing space), staircases that lead to non-existent second floors, grand canals that can be filled with water and built on a soundstage, etc., or the design can include erecting a false facade so that a building in Long Beach in Southern California can 'play' a brownstone in Brooklyn, New York. Depending on how extensive the building plans are, the set designer might work alone or they might have a crew of draftsmen working under their supervision.

Art Department Coordinator

There is often an art department coordinator who helps manage and track information and receipts. On most projects there is a lot of buying and renting going on. There can be changes in the script and in the schedule and everyone and their multi-person crews needs to be made aware of any revision to the plan that might factor into the art part of the pipeline. Art department coordinators also sometimes deal with legal clearances for the use of logos, posters, etc.

Concept Illustrator

Josue Fleurimond is a fine arts painter, who works independently, either commissioned by clients or on his own, to creative artistic works. He works across a variety of mediums—paper, metal, clay, photographic film, and wood. His work hangs in museums and art galleries—and he works in film as a conceptual illustrator. His credits include *X Men: Dark Phoenix*, *Mary Poppins Returns*, *The Predator*, *Captive State*, *Assassin's Creed*, *Batman vs. Superman*, *The Revenant*, *Deadpool*—and that's just in the last two years.

Josue Fleurimond

I consult primarily with the director and production designer, to illustrate and express the look, atmosphere, and emotion that move a story. This is in order to communicate this vision of the script to the entire production crew, and collaborate consistently with the second unit, stunts, special effects, visual effects, and numerous other departments.

The concept illustrator, in other words, is a visual bridge-builder. They are hired to paint or draw someone else's idea but rather than just taking a description and drafting or sketching the literal description, they must also be able to illustrate mood and create atmosphere. The concept illustrator should understand perspective, focal length—all the elements of what the camera can do, so they can take the idea of a shot design or a superhero and translate it to paper. That way the design doesn't live in the director's head but can be shared with the art department, camera, costume, and effects.

Storyboard Artist

The storyboard artist creates frame-by-frame drawings of a shot sequence. Directors may work with storyboard artists in different ways. Some use them extensively, some for stunt and effects sequences, some not at all. Storyboards are used to plan action. They can look like stick figures, or the detailed frames of a comic strip or they can look like diagrams. Ultimately the intention of a storyboard is to work out and communicate how something will be visually presented and shot.

Researcher

It should be clear by now that pretty much everybody does intensive research as part of their job, but there is sometimes a separate person whose responsibility is only to research. The researcher finds pieces of art, maps, and objects that may be applicable to the design of the movie. If the story is set in San Francisco in 1890, the researcher will create files and collect photos that show exactly what the city looked like then. They won't stop until they've covered every relevant neighborhood in depth. The material they hand in to the designer or art director will cover not only the prevalent architectural styles of the time, but the idiosyncrasies of one street vs. another, whether the roads were made of cement, cobblestone, or gravel, where did people who are of the same type of social and ethnic or economic class as the characters in the screenplay live, eat, and play. They'll unearth pictures of vehicles that were driven, signage, they'll find sketches of shops in the "nice" neighborhoods and in the neighborhoods that were less nice. By the time they've done, they'll be able to tell you what kind of toys little children in 1890s San Francisco had for the scene of the kids playing in front of a building and whether a child would be permitted to be outside playing at all. The researcher pulls images and finds all those tidbits that help inform the design team.

Construction

The construction coordinator oversees the actual construction of sets or the altering of existing locations. There are films with very little construction, and a crew might be hired for a week to build one structure—let's say, a closet with removable sides is needed for shooting (from all angles) someone trapped in the closet.

On huge productions a crew of 50 might start building six months before shooting begins and continue building as production progresses. Then they might spend a month striking (disassembling) once they have been shot out (once the scenes have been shot and the set is no longer necessary). On productions of that size, the construction department will have its own accountant to track costs and, due to the potential for accidents and injuries (power tools, heights, electricity), construction has its own medic.

The Construction Coordinator

Michael Villarino began his career in the art department as a Propmaker in the late 1970s, fabricating props for films such as *One From the Heart*, the *Beastmaster*, *The Natural*, *Star Trek 3*, became a construction foreman in the 1980s and 1990s on *Lethal Weapon 2*, *Days of Thunder*, *The Two Jakes*, *Edward Scissorhands*, *Toys*, *Jurassic Park*, *Jerry Maguire*, *Castaway*, *AI*, and *Minority Report*—and that's just a few. As a construction coordinator, Villarino's credits include *World Trade Center*, *Get Him to the Greek*, *We Bought a Zoo*, *Straight Outta Compton*, *Nocturnal Animals*, and additional photography on *The Greatest Showman*, *Justice League*, *Doctor Strange*, *Avengers: Age of Ultron*, *Fast and Furious 6*, *Unstoppable*, and *Anchorman: The Legend of Ron Burgundy*. He has worked with many of the most revered production designers and directors in the film industry, and at the time of this interview, he'd just started on the pilot for the TV series *L.A. Confidential* (based on the 1997 feature film).

Michael Villarino: Flexibility Is Key

Through the whole film you're bouncing up and down. Things get added and things are eliminated. Things grow bigger and things get cut. You have to roll with it. It's a never-ending process of additions, eliminations, changing schedules, and locations. That's the craziness of our business.

Probably the most challenging thing I think I've worked on was *World Trade Center*. We had to build Ground Zero. Oliver Stone [the director] was adamant about the realism. The Ground Zero

(continued)

(continued)

set covered almost three acres. It was outside of Playa Vista (Los Angeles). We would try to figure out how to make a set that big look real and to be able to get everybody in and out of it without getting hurt, because it's all debris and a lot of it is steel and sheet metal, and a lot of it was elevated. We had to come up with ways to make all these parts that looked like the building, that were huge. We had pieces that were 20 feet by 50 feet long that looked like parts of the outside of the building. We ended up using 200 sea containers [the kind of containers companies use to travel goods on cargo ships] lots of foam, and some real steel to support things. We put the containers in as an underground maze of tunnels. We cut the ends out, and opened them up and connected them so you could walk to wherever you needed to pop up, and there were ladders or stairways that went up to where you needed to be, so people could be safe, and no one needed to walk through the debris you see on camera except for short distances.

Most of the sets we build are meant to be struck [taken down, and stored or trashed] when we're done. Sometimes we fold and hold [pack and store] them and put them in a warehouse until the movie is released, then they throw them away. Sometimes things have to be built even stronger than they would be in real life. On *We Bought a Zoo*, we built a house. But they wanted each room to be able to hold 50 people and a camera. That house was built to be sturdier than it would be if it was built to code [normal construction building code].

The prints [blueprints] for a film are not like prints for the real world. We get prints that are aesthetic. This is what it looks like. We have to figure out how to make it safe, how to make it come apart or do whatever they want it to do. Once in a while we do things like the Tim Burton films, where you're building things that don't exist in the real world, which is the most fun. Building 15-foot high mushrooms!

Of the films I worked on, my favorite was *The Color Purple*, even though it was a difficult shoot. We were in North Carolina. It was 90 degrees and 90 percent humidity every day and it would rain a lot and just get hotter and wetter. We were shooting interiors with atmospheric smoke and no air conditioning. Long days. We bonded to be the tightest group I've ever worked with. We were all friends. We were in the middle of nowhere. We spent all our weekends hanging out together. Everybody was the same whether you were Whoopi Goldberg or a laborer. There were not a lot of egos on that show, it was just everybody walking up the hill together.

Dave DeGaetano, construction coordinator, started in episodic television. Among the series he worked on were *Hill Street Blues, Thirtysomething,* and *Star Trek: Deep Space Nine,* then he moved to such feature films as *Primal Fear, L.A. Confidential, Pleasantville, The Sum of All Fears, Catch Me If You Can, The Last Samurai, Smokin' Aces, Fast and Furious, Little Fockers,* and *Bridesmaids.*

Dave DeGaetano

I started construction coordinating in '78. In '92 I went over to Paramount and started working on features. Started on *Indecent Proposal* with Mel Bourne. After that I just kept doing features. I worked with a lot of good people. I got connected with Jeanine Oppewall, Lily Kilvert [all are legendary production designers].

Generally, I would get the call about the project, read the script. Set up a meeting. We (the production designer and I) usually have a little time to do some talking before we get into pre-production. I'll go over the script and talk about what the builds look like, what their preliminary budget is, is it going to be building as opposed to location work. What size, how many people will be involved, how many crew. I've had a crew with me for the last 40 years and they've stayed pretty busy, but the size of that crew would go up and down depending on the scope of the movie. That's the first thing: how much of a build it is as opposed to how much on location.

Most of the production designers I've worked with ask me to do a preliminary budget, a ballpark to let them know, so they can proceed with production and have some idea of what kind of money I think we're talking about. Do we need to scale something back or even possibly change the script if the budget doesn't allow for that much expense.

Generally, on a feature level, they've done their research, they probably have some sketches, sometimes they've even got a storyboard artist on (payroll) to present to the director. Often I'll be doing that (sketching), even on a cocktail napkin. Doing a layout. When we did on *Last Samurai,* we had model-makers who were just getting on board. We knew that we had a Tokyo street circa 1874 to build. You had some pictures, you had the scale, and I would work with that kind of information, after having read the script, knowing what scenes they were planning to do there and what scenery we would have to work on. Of course, there were

(continued)

(continued)

scouts we went on and we hired crew in New Zealand, a splinter unit went to Japan, and the rest, the bulk of it, was here (in Los Angeles). That's the job, coordinating the different elements and the crew. It was a pretty good size show. I think we had at one point a 230-person crew on in LA and another 40 in New Zealand.

I did a lot of period shows. It's much more difficult now to work in LA and find anything practical. On *L.A. Confidential* (the film) that motel with the shoot-out was the biggest location build. We did a lot of work to individual locations, but it was mostly house-keeping, making everything electrical look period correct. But we did build the (Victory) motel in the oil fields in Baldwin Hills [a neighborhood in Los Angeles].

That was a pretty big build from the ground up and had a lot of effects work—bulleted walls. Eric Rylander was the special effects coordinator on that. We read the script and worked with Eric and Jeannine (Oppewall) and the art director with the storyboards because those are very helpful to make sure we're going to give the director what he wants. It's got to be choreographed. We'd sit down with the storyboards and lay out where the (bullet) hits are going to be, where the principal actors are going to be. We had to protect them yet design these walls, in this case to be built out of plaster drywall and lathe and plaster and a lot of those have to be plugs for multiple takes. [Plugs are pre-assembled pieces that can be "plugged in" to replace other pieces—possibly movable walls that are moved out for a quicker changeover.] We designed these walls for that motel to be able to be removed and replaced based on what the shooting schedule was, hopefully with a little time between. They'd go shoot something else while we're scrambling to get the wall replaced.

Stunts

On *Last Samurai* we had a pretty big fight scene where Tom Cruise takes on assassins on a street. It was a very complicated, choreo-graphed sequence with sword fighting. He's attacked and defends himself. He did most all of that himself (not with a stunt person standing in for him). We needed to make the space safe for him to work in. They had the choreography work done. He'd been train-ing with stunt people for weeks at a facility in Burbank. The moves were down, they knew where they needed to be, but they had to find an area on that street where that could happen, where it would be incorporated in the set. We were asked to help design this area. We poured rubber street dirt and built some of these elements he was interacting with out of foam. We could cast these elements, some wood, some stone, some dirt skins [skins are coverings used to change the look of something—for instance, decals that would be added onto a picture car to make it appear to be a realistic police patrol car]. We poured the rubber, painted, and put dirt on it. That way they could do their falls and their stunts.

I did *Fast and Furious 4*. There was a lot of car activity on that show. A lot of wrecks, a lot of ramps, and a lot of effects work on the cars themselves. We were creating the space where that all happened. We built tunnels where they did the racing. We built the tunnels out of sea containers, big 40-foot shipping containers. We stacked those into rows and covered them with a gray material that's like a green screen [green screen is a process by which two visual components, separately filmed, can be digitally combined to appear to be a single image]. Then they (Visual Effects) could add the elements of a cave inside them while the cars were racing through. We shot in San Pedro at a big fruit shipping warehouse. I think we had 200 containers where we created this raceway green screen cave. There were a lot of elements that were in the cave when the actors were out of their cars interacting, and (our job) was creating the spaces.

Building on a Practical Location, Rather Than a Stage

Whenever we go to a practical location there's almost always work to do there. I haven't been on a lot of projects where you (just) walk in and shoot. On *Catch Me If You Can*, we went to a Downey, California facility and created FBI headquarters. Coming in, there were columns that were kind of puny looking, it didn't look like a federal facility. We changed windows out, we built around the columns with cement-looking things. We changed out all the lighting fixtures and created cubicles inside the space. They had to have that space for the size they needed to shoot, but we had to create the whole office because they weren't able to find anything that was the size they wanted that we could take over. It would've had to have been a huge corporate office building that was available.

The Process

We all read the script because it means there are that many eyes on the project. Hopefully we come up with some things that a director might like. In the art department we always have (concept) meetings, discuss options. A lot of times the production designer might be asking for suggestions. You get people who have done different things, put them all together, we all can contribute what we know might work.

Greens

A Greensperson is responsible for finding, placing, and maintaining plants, flowers, and trees for the art department. For scenes that are interior, the Greensperson takes care of all decorative greenery and foliage, real or artificial. For exteriors, the Greensperson also works on the layout, including hardscape (pathways, rock designs). The Greensperson works in consultation with the rest of the art department, and with the set decorator.

Lead Scenic

The scenic artist is a painter who is expert at creating texture where there is none, or altering existing texture, by painting. The lead scenic creates faux surface finishes, such as using painting techniques to simulate aging. The lead scenic alters and uses materials so that they create the illusion of being some other surface when photographed by the camera. For instance, a lead scenic may paint foam so that it appears to be stone. Why would you need this kind of treatment? An actor may need to throw something that would normally be too heavy to throw (maybe the tablets of the Ten Commandments). Or a set may have to be easily movable. Or you may not be able to afford the marble flooring, but the look can be achieved by painting a different material so that through the camera, it appears to be marble.

Lee Ross has painted sets on over 77 projects, including feature films and episodic series. His feature credits (as either lead scenic, camera scenic, on-set painter, or lead scenic on additional scenes or reshoots) include: *Kong: Skull Island*, *The Purge: Anarchy*, *Frost/Nixon*, *Party Crasher*, *Gangster Squad*, *Zero Dark Thirty*, *The Master*, *Water for Elephants*, *Hot Tub Time Machine*, *Zombieland*, *A Single Man*, *The Fighter*, *You Don't Mess with Zohan*, *Rush Hour 2*, *Smokin' Aces*, *Bad News Bears*, *Miss Congeniality*, *I Heart Huckabees*, *Dodgeball: A True Underdog Story*, *Laurel Canyon*, *Three Kings*, and many others. His television credits include 52 episodes of *Grace and Frankie*, 14 episodes of *Mad Men*, and again, many others.

Lee Ross: Learning on the Job

I absolutely did. Never had an art class in my life. I figured it out. One of my strengths is problem solving. If I have five minutes to figure it out, I'll figure it out. I come at my job with an art director perspective. I deal with everything in the set, and interface with all the departments. I try to understand what the director and production designer and art director are imagining. It's layered. It's not just painting walls. Part of our job is to take artwork and turn it into reality that's shoot-able. We take these renderings (sketches), and these blueprints, these pictures and manifest these ideas into an actual set piece that can be utilized.

On *Kong*, for example, we had the Kong Wall. They give you a digital rendering made in Sketch Up where they create a 3D mock-up. It was like a line drawing, not much detail. Then we look at photos, we research. We decide on the amount of bark, the amount of green. There are these big thick tree stumps, some real, some molded (a resin), some molded bark skins (another resin) wrapping big tubes. We had thick vines that flowed in and out of the cracks between the trees, trying to create this opening that was kind of stealth and secret.

In the script the wall was built by natives to keep out the monster. I was out there with a headlamp taking fake moss, literally impacting the moss into the little crevices and gluing it on to these vines. The moss drastically improved it. That moss was the last touch. We only finished one side of the wall because they were convinced they wouldn't even need to see the other side. But sure enough, on the day (of the shoot), 20 people were scrambling to change what we'd done to make it look different, so they could shoot what was supposed to be the other side.

On Color and Texture

Some of my favorite big iconic movies, the Tim Burton stuff, *Honey I Shrunk the Kids*, *What Dreams May Come*, really use texture and color to help tell the story. That's what design is about. An example of a great use of wall coverings: in *The King's Speech* there's a wall with great detail. It's supposed to look like wallpaper that's been torn off.

I'm working on *Grace and Frankie*. In the series, Lily Tomlin's character is an artist. One of the sets everybody loves is her art studio. There is an artist who is responsible for creating the character's art, but it's hundreds of paintings. What they do is make prints. Then I will take them and embellish them with a gel medium. When light hits things you can see the texture. When the light hits the (gelled) prints you see the build-up of the material. That takes a print and makes it look like an oil painting.

(continued)

(continued)

There is a plot point, (on *Grace and Frankie*). This character, Martin, does musicals. I'm doing all these over-the-top wood grained bleachers, creating the illusion, sometimes more theatrically, sometimes more realistically, taking flats and turning them into something else. [Flats are constructed, movable walls.] We take a flat with some holes cut out to look like windows and we'll do an interesting forced perspective on it, but if you look at it from the side it's just a wafer. That's what we do.

Ross's View of the Scenic Department's Relationship with the Director and the Production Designer

They have the dreams, we make the dreams.

5   The Decorator

The set decorator is in charge of "dressing" the sets. The decorator researches, finds, or is responsible for the manufacture of all aspects of all décor. This includes furniture, lighting fixtures, curtains, wall and floor coverings, artwork, photographs and posters, and decorative touches such as pottery, the books on the shelves, the knick-knacks for both interior and exterior sets and locations. If it's on the wall, on the floor, on the ceiling, or it's something embellishing the décor, it's set dressing.

One example of great set dressing that subtly communicates story, character, and theme is the film *Almost Famous*. Set in the late 1960s and early 1970s, we see the lead character's house. William Miller, teenager, aspiring rock journalist, lives with his professor mother in a San Diego bungalow, a prototypical middle-class home, complete with shag carpet, lots of fuzzy textures, lots of family photographs. This is a warm, nurturing environment. William (Patrick Fugit) is well-loved. His idol, cynical rock critic Lester Bangs, lives alone in complete disarray. Bangs (played by the late Philip Seymour Hoffman) is a shambling, outspoken bear of a man. His typewriter, racks of record albums, papers, and dishes are all within easy reach. This is his lion's den. When William goes on the road with Stillwater, a rock band, we see hotel rooms littered with empty bottles, ashtrays, and clothing strewn everywhere. There's no reason to clean up. The band's life is transitory. The groupies who trail along beside the musicians hope to land a permanent place in their lives. They make their presence felt by throwing brightly printed scarves over harsh hotel room lamps in an attempt to filter the light. This is their chance to help the hotel feel like a home. When Russell (Billy Crudup), a rock star temporarily disillusioned with his bandmates and unreal lifestyle, visits a party-house full of adoring teenagers in Topeka, he strides through the living room and spies a lampshade. In nostalgia and stoned excitement, he exclaims, "I grew up with that lampshade!" The details of the dressing help us understand what these people want, what they need, and what they ultimately get.

As a filmmaker, you can be thinking beyond the pages of the screenplay. What are your character's histories? Were they part of a happy family and now they're not? Were they miserable failures and now they've made it? Are they conflicted about their lives? Would there be great inconsistency, an obviously pricey item on the shelf next to one from a discount store? What kind of artwork is on the wall, on the shelves? In *Ordinary People*, a classic film about a family coming to grips with the accidental death of a child, we see a house that is beautifully and tastefully decorated but looks so perfect it's as if no one really lives there. Eventually we learn that this is a family concerned with display—about how things look, rather than about how they are or might be.

Is your character hiding their pain, looking for control? Or are they unraveling and are things half-done, half-perfect; at first glance it all looks great but there are old milk cartons and half-eaten sandwiches lying around?

Shirley Starks has been a set decorator for over 20 years. She's worked on films, network and cable series, and television movies, with budgets large and small. Her credits range from the classic feature *Mi vida loca* to 20 episodes of *Monsters*, 23 episodes of *Crossing Jordan*, 26 episodes of *Summerland*, and 27 episodes of *Jericho*.

Shirley Starks

A set decorator works very closely with the production designer to create the environment that tells the story. With the production designer and director, we set about putting things in the room that help create the character. The art director and construction give us the walls and the floors, and anything from the walls in, floors up and ceiling down, pretty much is set decorating.

We create the doctor's office or the library or the nursery for the baby or grandma's house, and grandma's collection of ducks or birds. If we're in the library, what kind of books does that person read and how do those small pieces put everyone in the right environment for this story—the actor most importantly.

What is most important to me and to most set decorators I know is that we work as a unit with everybody because everyone on that set is working together to make this story. We do that by acknowledging and agreeing to keep our commitments—we've broken down the script, we know the props and if it's day or night, we know where we are, who is in there, how it's written.

The Crew

The set decoration crew consists of a lead, an on-set dresser, the swing gang (or additional set dressers), and sometimes a buyer. The leadman (who could be male or female) coordinates the dressing activity. The art department schedule is an organizational puzzle, with purchased and rented items coming and going from vendor or store or manufacturer, to storage, to set, then back to storage or finally back to the rental vendor. Or sometimes things end up at a warehouse space. Once it has been determined that an item is "wrapped" and doesn't have to be held for additional photography, it is either returned or sold off. Selling purchased items helps offset the inevitable costs of loss and damage that occurs when furnishing and pieces of dressing are packed, unpacked, and constantly on the move. The leadman supervises the swing gang, which can consist of anywhere between two and ten workers. The swing gang move set dressing from wherever it originates to wherever it is stored to set and back. They dress the set per the direction of the decorator. Not every project has a designated buyer, but when they do, the buyer deals with money and the delivery logistics of hundreds of pieces of dressing.

The on-set dresser's job is primarily one of continuity. Picture this: you're shooting a scene set in a dining room at lunch. A mom, dad, and three kids sit around the table and you want a master (an all-encompassing shot) and then you want singles (shots of each one of the lunch-eaters), and maybe a few two-shots for reactions to whatever is going on. To get the necessary coverage (camera angles), the camera moves, the lighting changes, the flowers on the table are moved out of the way for one angle, the place settings are moved for another. But when the camera moves for a view from another side and the scene is edited, it can't look as if things suddenly disappeared or got closer. The on-set dresser is there to a) re-set the dressing so that everything looks the way it was decided it should look and b) to freshen the flowers, refold the napkins, make sure that it looks as if the lunch is taking an hour rather than the 12 hours it is taking to shoot. During production, the production designer and set decorator start the day at each new set or location for a final approval viewing with the director, then move on to ready the next day's location. There's usually nothing for them to do once shooting begins. The on-set dresser is the link between the art department (who work ahead of the production team so things will be arranged for the next day) and the production team itself.

Starks on Collaboration

Sometimes we use boards—we have a feel board, or a color board—an idea board to set the tone, so that everybody knows from the very beginning—not necessarily that this couch is the couch, but

(continued)

(continued)

this is the flavor of what we're all doing together. The director of photography will be asking, what practical lights are you going to give me? That's wonderful because if I give them practical lights they're going to shoot more of my set. They'll use them to light the actor. We are very much working together.

The creative process of translating the character in the script to fabric and color and style: I read the script first just to see where I'm at. I read the script a second time and do the breakdown to see who the characters are. What clothing is scripted—often you get notes on who the character is by what they're wearing. What are the props, where are we in the locations? After that I go back through scene by scene, page by page and write all that down for myself.

After that process I look at the overall picture and who these people are. For instance, in (the TV series) *Jericho*, the actor Gerald McRainey, who played Mr. Green. It was decided early on in several meetings with the creators and the director and unit production manager and the producers and the writers. Everybody met together to talk about who he was. Mr. Green is a manly man. He's the mayor of our town. He would have taxidermy in his office. He would have deer heads and fish. He's that guy. He's a hunter-gatherer, he provides for his family, he provides for his town. It was a wonderful experience because when Gerald McRainey came onto the set for the first time, he looked around, he moved a couple of things, he opened a couple of drawers and he said "Oh, perfect." He was at home. Then he said, "I have something I want to bring." He brought in a boar's head that he had shot in Africa, it was on my set for the 20 some-odd episodes that we shot. It sat right behind him on his credenza the whole time. That told me I was right on the money. There were a couple of awards I'd given him, and he said, "Oh, I don't want them there, I want them in my drawer. That way if I open my drawer we see them." He felt his character was a modest military man.

We were doing *Summerland*. We had the beach house. We built Leo Carrillo Beach on stage at Raleigh Studios because we had children, and the tides don't work well with assistant directors (who are in charge of safety on set and who set the shooting schedule) and children working at night with bonfires. We built the beach house on the stage, with sand dunes and water. Bernard Hides was the production designer. We had a collaboration that was precious. I could drag in a piece of iron that I saw on the side of the road, not knowing what it was for, just that I loved the shape. Next morning, I come in and he's cut a hole in the wall of the restaurant set and that iron is now in the wall so then you had a see through with a camera port! There are magic moments when you work together.

When we created the house—we created the entire house on stage—we had a berm which you walked up over on stage and there was a little awning and then the stairs went down. On the actual Leo Carrillo Beach, we had the awning and the stairs going down. It was a seamless tie-in. It worked beautifully. And the house, when we got done, everyone said, "Oh my god, it's beautiful. I want to live there," but it was just a set on a stage at Raleigh Studios.

Part of the decorator's job is to do your research. If the show is based on an Indian reservation—what is on a Paiute Indian reservation? There are different tribes and what is the reality of the Paiute? Let's create that. I don't want Indians from a 1950s western. On a feature that I did, I went to a reservation and I said, I would like to do this properly. I asked the questions. They gave me amulets and eagle feathers and a Chief came and blessed the set. Maybe you think you know but if you go to the experts and ask questions—not once in my years of experience has someone not helped me. Given me advice, shown me tools.

Often, it's left to me to bring in my thoughts as to who these characters are. There are times when they'll say, "No, maybe not." But there will be times when they say, "Yes! Of course she plays the violin!" If you don't do your research, then you're limited to your own personal focus—and that's not your job. It's not about what I like, it's what tells the story. That's my commitment to each project. I'm here to help forward this story.

I have the characters in my head, I've discussed them with the production designer who has the overview of the entire project. With any luck we've had tone meetings with the producer, director, costume designer, and the assistant director. If you know who the people are, and you know what they're doing, and that this young girl is very athletic and she's into sports, she skateboards and she's also on the track team and excels in stuff like that, you know she's probably not going to have ruffles. I'm not going to put Priscilla curtains in her bedroom. [Priscilla curtains have ruffled trim running from the top down the sides of the panels.] If it's a young, bright teenager I'm not going to go with cabbage roses.

On the other hand, if it's an eight-year-old girl who is dressed in frills and bows then she might have Priscilla curtains and a canopy bed and the whole princess look. That would depend on the mother and the house they live in, because often the choices are also dictated by their wealth. Is the mom a schoolteacher? Then the choices are

(continued)

(continued)

made on what a teacher could afford, if it's a single mom. If they're living on one of those huge estates out in Chatsworth [a suburb of Los Angeles in the San Fernando Valley] and the father is a billionaire . . . then you would go for the high end of everything because that's who your characters are. We have to be careful with budget, so you can't go out and rent a $12,000 sofa, but a lot of what we do is have things fabricated, we change it a little so it's still in the designer world, but it doesn't cost that much.

Working on a TV sit-com is not like that. On a sit-com what you're thinking is, what can you find to re-cover that exists (and is affordable) or what can you buy on-line. Now with things being at everybody's fingertips (on-line) there is the thought that everybody's a decorator. That's true if it's your home but not everybody can decorate to tell a story. That's two very different things.

The Devil Is in the Details

I was on a panel at a school and they were designing a 1940s office. Somebody had put a chair in one of the offices and I said, "where did that chair come from?" And the student said, "I just like it." I said, "show me where that chair was in 1940. Show me your research." And she said, I just liked it. That day I realized that some of those students thought that research was obnoxious. It was extra. They didn't want to do it. But you have an opportunity to step into another environment. That's your commit-ment. If you're putting a 1980s chair in a 1940s office, that's wrong. You think they're going to hire you again? They're not going to let you get through the day.

They really hadn't thought about it that way, that research was a way to step into the shoes of another human being and see their world. A chair can be just a chair because somebody needs a place to sit. But maybe it's not the right chair. Maybe it's a chair made of material that didn't even exist in 1940.

Color

Colors set the mood. Your story is about an old man who lives by himself and he's lived there since his wife died. And you can barely open the door because the newspapers aren't even undone, they're just piled to the side. And it's dingy. He's not going to have a bright red anything, everything will have that aged look. Because the story you want to tell is the sadness. Maybe it changes when the little kid next door comes and brings flowers, whatever the story may be.

Or maybe it's the color. An avocado (colored) refrigerator—where does that put you? You're in the Sixties. Avocado and that wondrous awful yellow in your kitchen. Put those two elements in and you're there. Nine times out of ten you'll work with the production designer on colors. Often the costumer is involved in that as well. You don't want a blue shirt on a blue couch against a blue wall. You don't want to put anybody on green sheets unless they're supposed to be really sick.

Working with a Changing Storyline on a Television Series

If you have a grocery store, which I did on *Jericho*, you've got a working grocery store on every week that's got to be replenished every week. [The series was about the aftermath of a nuclear bomb and the residents of a surviving Kansas town.] In the series when the Chinese did a big supply drop, everything in the market that had been almost empty, was now (going to be) Chinese. We made all kinds of Chinese labels—and now my mom and pop supermarket was the center for anything and everything.

(In the series) nothing worked after the 1970s once the bomb dropped. So that was an opportunity. We've got a hospital, we have people who are wounded, we have no electricity. We had to figure out, what do we do to sanitize and clean the sheets? We got big vats and put them on barbecue grills and boiled the sheets out back. We made a whole chain of how the sheets were hung out to dry because you couldn't just throw them in the washer. What would you do?

Dressing Exteriors as Well as Interior Sets

Exteriors—you have to make sure the plants are all right. Obviously if you're shooting in Los Angeles and you're supposed to be in Baltimore, you make sure you don't see any palm trees. You work with the greens department, which is under the art director.

The front of a house needs to invite you into the environment. Is there a child (in the story)? Are there toys in the front yard? Is there a broken-down swing in the front yard with newspapers piled on the front porch? Is the swing a bright happy red and yellow with everything perfect because the kids just got it? Is there a sign outside of a store? Am I hanging plants? Am I doing a display out front?

(continued)

(continued)

Are there tables and chairs for people to sit? Is it welcoming? Does it look like maybe you don't want to go in there and get a coffee?

If you're at a house you have to make sure that the window treatments that you do inside tell the right story outside, because often drapery is white on the back and sometimes that's problematic (to shoot).

More on Working with a Team

There are people who say, "That's not my job," but we also need to work together. If the rest of the crew cares about you and they understand that you're looking to make it all work for them, you're showing them where the wild walls butt up, and how this works with that, and how you set it up so it's easy for the juicers (electricians) to unplug it and move it—that's a camaraderie that helps us work and function together. If we make it easy for them, they make it easy for us. When you sign on to a show you are signing on to be part of a family. The purpose of the family is to tell this story, to make this movie. You do it all together. Everybody loves it when it works—but you have to remember that you're dealing with type-A personalities—a whole lot of them—in one room, or on a stage or back to exteriors—at that house. Where are they going to put their cables? Oh, they need me to bring in hedges. OK. Or they need me to give them flowerpots to put their lights behind!

Shooting on Location

We are intruding on people's homes and I find that goodwill goes a long way. If a little old lady or man lives there, I'll have the guys repair the light fixture, we'll tighten the doorknobs. We'll plant flowers out front. I'm there three days before everybody else (to prep) and I'm there two days after (to strike and restore). I take it upon myself to include in my budget something that can be left behind, that leaves a good taste rather than a bad taste. I've been in that situation, coming after those people (who don't treat people well). It's a nightmare. I never want it to be a nightmare.

You make a lot of friends. Hopefully you don't make too many enemies. It's a very small town.

6   Locations

John Lloyd Miller

I think any successful film you think of, you can look at the choice of locations and it's critical. All of John Sayles' movies were very much of the place where he shot them. He found places that spoke to the story. Woody Allen—*Broadway Danny Rose*, *Stardust Memories*. *Apocalypse Now* wouldn't have worked shot in Topanga Canyon.

People settle. It makes it easier. But it's extraordinarily important to not only find the right locations but to actually be inspired by the locations. You want to know, what is it you need emotionally from this location? What is the purpose of this? If the scene is by a lake—it's not about a postcard or a vacation video. So just finding the lake isn't enough. Maybe it's a scary scene, a suspenseful scene? What is it and what kind of location by a lake would be appropriate? Somebody said that casting is 90 percent of your job as a director. That's true. And locations are 9 percent of the other 10 percent. It's so important, it's just like casting. You wouldn't just settle on someone, you wouldn't say, well I need a guy who's 40 and here's a guy whose 40 so let's cast him. You're going to keep going until you find the right person for that part. Locations are the same thing. They are a character in your film.

The job of a location manager is tough and thankless. When things on location go right, it is almost always seen as someone else's victory. When things don't, all heads turn to the location manager. They must be multi-talented and multi-functional. A good location manager must first have a great temperament. Location managers are "people persons." They often serve as the face of the production. It's the location manager and his or her staff who knock on doors and ask to be invited in to a stranger's house to see if it passes muster. It's the location manager who negotiates for the fee to shoot there. They deal with the handholding and care and feeding of the owners, so that they don't grow impatient with the inconvenience and change their minds. Their job is to convince people to do something very odd—to let a group of strangers into the privacy of their homes or to allow them to shut down streets and businesses, all in the service of someone's future entertainment.

The location manager has to cope with homeowners who say, yes, you can use their house for the negotiated fee, but no, they won't move into a hotel, they want to stay and watch. Then they offer their suggestions to the production. Why would you want to put their wall art in storage, they are positive the director will adore the clowns and dogs playing poker on black velvet. It's the location manager who speaks at town meetings to obtain permission to block off Main Street for a chase scene, and knocks on every door in a 1,000-foot radius for residents to sign off on the company's ability to shoot until midnight. It's the same person who talks a street of homeowners into shutting off their interior and exterior lights for three hours to satisfy the production designer and director's vision of what a black-out should look like.

The location person must be personable, unfailingly pleasant, reassuring, and above all, tactful. They are asking to disrupt people's routines and use their stuff. That takes patience, salesmanship, and a lot of charm. When a home or store owner is approached by someone, they are suspicious. Is it a scam? Is it porn? Once the property owners are positive the people involved are reputable, they think about mitigating their inconvenience in ways that don't work for production. They are happy to have filming there but for just four hours at a time. They're flattered that you want to shoot in their café, but can you work around their customers? Usually not.

The location manager must be an educator. This is what is going to happen, this is how many people will be milling around your house, this is where they'll park and eat and go to the bathroom. Your dog is adorable and doesn't make much noise, but it would not work for the film, or for the dog, for him to be there even if he is in his crate. There is insurance and you will be covered. We will repair your wall/floor/staircase/front lawn. And by the way, could we paint the living room wall and mount a light on your garage roof?

You may say, I'm a great talker. How hard could talking people into letting you shoot be? Well—here's an example: the 1985 classic, *Witness*, a crime thriller set in Amish Country, in Pennsylvania. The Amish are a religious sect who are not supposed to see movies or be photographed. However respectful the filmmakers might have been, one can only imagine the challenge that location manager faced.

How do you move into a community and avoid offending or enraging the neighbors? The location manager must be a diplomat and an authority at the same time. Although the homeowners, landlords, and cities are being paid, they are still the production's hosts—and that makes the filmmakers guests. It is the location manager's job to make sure that the production is not destructive or overbearing and that at the end of the experience, the location will be happy to have them return.

The location manager must also have a visual sense. It takes an "eye" to see that a building that looks great when you're standing in the lobby may look like nothing when filmed. The location manager gets the first look at places and must be able to make a preliminary prediction as to whether the lobby or the exterior will work, not just logistically, and budgetarily, but creatively. When something is photographed, it flattens out and is transformed from three to two dimensions. Production design and lighting defines the space, but it is so much better if the location is interesting even before it's transformed. The production designer makes the call, but the location manager is the first filter.

The location manager must intuit the production designer's creative concept, however ambiguous, and be capable of interpreting abstracts. A location manager friend of mine was once given the direction, "The house has to suggest the future, without being futuristic." (He found a 1930s Deco house, and everyone loved it.)

Finally, the location manager must be able to understand and work with the production manager and assistant director in terms of budget and schedule; must have a sense of how contracts work; must work with the production designer, set decorator, and construction department so everyone knows which floors can be distressed and which flowers can be dug up; with camera, grip, and electric so the locations are accessible; and with transportation and catering so whichever way the camera wants to point, the shot won't be ruined by the sight of a fleet of trucks and people preparing lunch.

The location department usually consists of a location manager and at least one and sometimes as many as ten assistants. On a big-budget film with lots of locations or where the locations are spread among several cities, states, or countries, there is often a key location manager who supervises subordinate location managers and their assistants. When films are shot on distant location, there is usually a key, a local key who is native to whichever area the film is shooting, and assistants and PAs.

The location manager is one of the first people hired on a production. Often a production designer wants to work with the location manager he or she has worked with before because, once again, there is a short-hand between them. They start work months in advance of shooting and go through the same process as everyone else, reading the script a couple of times and creating a breakdown. They have to consider whether the project will be shot locally or on distant location or if it will end up being a combination of both. A mix of artistic, logistic, and financial factors go into that decision, which may be finalized early or left so late that everyone has to have a plan A, B, and C.

Wherever shooting is located, how many of the locations will be found and how many will be built? Does the location as written actually exist? If the script calls for The Alamo, it exists but it's a major tourist attraction and you probably won't be shooting there. And strangely enough, though a historic landmark, it probably doesn't look the way you'd want, and it couldn't be made to look the way you'd want. You couldn't break apart the walls so you wouldn't have much room to shoot. The Alamo, though a real place, will be a build, either on stage or on a back lot. On the other hand, if the script calls for Yankee Stadium and your film is not X-rated, you have a lot of cash, and can work with the season's schedule, you just possibly could make that happen.

When does the story take place? *LA Confidential*, a film set in 1950s Los Angeles, might seem a natural for a "build" show, but as we've learned from the construction coordinator, almost all the locations were practical (real). The location manager and production designer found buildings that worked for 1950s Los Angeles. One of the only constructed locations was the motel used for a climactic scene between the corrupt cops and the clean cops, in part because the gun battle is so violent that the building is virtually splinters by the time it ends.

The film *L.A. Confidential* was shot in 1996. In 2018, *L.A. Confidential* became a television series, and Mike Villarino, the construction coordinator on the series, has found that he is basically building almost everything, in part due to the expense, in part owing to the difficulty of finding, and shooting in the right locations in a city where location rentals average $5,000–$10,000 per day and the tendency is to tear down or remodel any building more than 20 years old.

Downtown Abbey was largely shot in two locations. A real castle was found to play the Crawley family's country place and soundstages were used for the work rooms and servants' rooms. *Mad Men*, a TV series set in 1960s Manhattan, was shot mostly in Los Angeles, on stage, and in restaurants and bars around town. Both *NCIS*, set in Washington DC, and *CSI Miami* were shot mostly in Los Angeles.

If the decision is made to find a practical space, the location manager starts to scout. Experienced location managers keep extensive files of photos and information on the off chance they may someday need that diamond-shaped café with the life-sized bucking bronc sculpture out front. They know their own territory well and, if they are out of town on location, they learn the new environment with lightning speed. They know how to research. They make hundreds of calls to find just a couple of places worth checking out. They drive (or, as you will see, sometimes fly) around. When they find possibilities, they photograph or video those places from all angles. They weigh the pros and cons of what they've found. Convenient to a freeway? Accessibility is good. Too near the freeway? Is there too much noise? Some noise can be handled but what if the building is perfect but next to an urban police station where on any given day, the production will be interrupted by the sound of sirens? No matter how much money you have to spend, you're probably not going to convince a police department not to sound the sirens when needed. Is the perfect space on the first floor? Great! On the tenth? How easily can the grips get the equipment up there? The scene is written to take place at night. If shooting can be on the ground floor, windows can easily be blacked in with fabric and you can, to make the schedule work, shoot during the day. If they're on the second floor, the grips can use scaffolding and lifts. Higher than that, and the perfect location starts to feel like less of a find.

The location manager will think about cost, availability, and the willingness of the owner to rent the location and allow the kind of activity planned. He or she will find out what, if any, restrictions exist per the city or town where the potential site is located. If there are strict rules regarding the use of firearms (even prop guns, or real guns with blank ammunition, with stunt people and a licensed armorer) the production might have to jump through special hoops or not shoot in that town at all. Is filming not permitted after 10pm because the location is too near a condo complex? The location manager finds out that there were problems with a commercial shoot the year before in the same city. The lighting people on the commercial bathed the parking lot in high-intensity lighting until three in the morning. The Mayor's Office is not anxious to repeat the experience, and get all those complaint calls, money or no money.

The location manager will get the photographs to the production designer, but not until they've confirmed that the possible choices are available. No one wants a situation where their boss sets their heart on something then can't have it. People get emotional. They see something they like, the wheels start turning and it's radar lock. No one wants to recalibrate. It may seem ridiculous. How can anyone be passionate about an office reception room, a garage, or a tide pool? But that happens all the time. When it clicks it's hard to unclick. Everything else looks not as perfect. So, it's important politically that the location manager knows everything about what they present before it becomes the unattainable answer to everyone's prayers. Once availability is confirmed and the initial meetings have taken place, the location manager scouts the possibilities, taking video or photographs to bring back to the production designer. There are the creative requirements—does the location work for what the director and designer want? There are the logistics of the location. Is it accessible, affordable, does its availability fit with the production schedule? Might it work with the other locations so that if there are only a few hours of work to be done there, there's another nearby location that works to fill in the remainder of the day? There are times when a fabulous location doesn't mesh with the schedule. Then, as expectations have been raised, the location manager must find another, even more fabulous location that does. Sometimes the location works with the schedule and the deal is made—then the schedule changes.

And the location manager has to return to the property owner and the city to renegotiate.

When discussing their potentials with the designer, the location manager will need to know what's good, what's bad, what's close. If nothing is what the designer had in mind it's back on the road. If close but no cigar, it's back on the road. If it's OK but not great, it goes in the OK pile but it's back on the road. Until there are very strong choices, scouting continues.

Hopefully the designer is an effective communicator. Good feedback helps the location manager's scouting yield progressively better results. Once there is an array of acceptable possibilities, the designer will weed out his or her top picks, then bring those to the director. This prequalification by the designer happens for several reasons. First, the acknowledged expert in design is the production designer. Therefore, there can be logistically and financially viable locations but the designer might not like the look of them and might assume that the director won't either. Pre-production is a busy several weeks or months. It's not constructive to waste the director's time or to have it appear that they don't understand what the director wants. Or, the designer might suspect that the director might like the weaker alternatives, so they might not want to even open that door. This may seem disrespectful and under-handed. Isn't it after all, the director's preference that counts? It is, but it's also the designer's job to help the director get to the strongest visual choice. The director is not necessarily as adept or practiced at picturing how a location can be worked on and made fabulous versus another location that will only ever be OK.

On occasion, there are still even more layers of approval. If the financing production company had issues with a particular location on a past project, there may be an unanticipated battle of wills when they exert their authority. What kind of issues could there be? One example: there is a spectacular-looking house outside of Los Angeles that has been featured in films, television shows, music videos, and commercials. This is a unique structure in an equally unique setting. Due to the way the place is built, almost every project that has shot there has incurred charges of several thousands of dollars for damages to the location. In fact, the property owners will not agree to use a standard studio or production company location agreement (contract) for the house. They have their own. In the property owner's contract, there is a detailed description of damages that might occur, the specific manner the damages must be repaired, and the cost of the repairs, per damage. It may or may not be true that the property owner has been able to collect enough money from damage repairs to buy an entire additional house—but that isn't relevant. No one is forcing anyone to shoot there. But production designers and directors see this place and fall in love. Then the tug of war begins. Because the production company has been through this before they know that the cost of using the location won't be what the contract says. It will be several thousand dollars more, because there have always been—there will always be—damages. Who wins? Depends who digs in harder, the creative or the business people. If it's the creative team, the poor location manager spends the entire time the crew is shooting there policing the place, trying to be sure there is no damage. But there always is.

The negotiation for a location can be simple—x amount of money for x amount of days. It can also be surprisingly difficult. The location manager has to learn to survive the natural inclination of people to hear "movie shoot," and recall all they've read in the tabloids about inflated star salaries and decide that it's their turn to get theirs. When people think movies, they see green. The "business" of the film business in many ways, is quite public. It is much written about and discussed. There have been so many reports about film budgets of hundreds of millions of dollars. It isn't the job of anyone who is outside of the business to understand that there are *X-Men* and *Beast of the Southern Wild* budgets. For many people, if it's in the theater or on TV, it's all the same. So why wouldn't a home or business owner see dollar signs when approached?

Brendan O'Connor on Collaboration with Locations and Camera

Regarding the aesthetics, I think you have your low, middle, high. The location manager might find three possible locations for one set. One of them you love. One of them is a middle—you have to do a little bit of work, change out some sconces or light fixtures or stuff on the wall or something like that. One of them is a low so you're OK to see it go when the director doesn't like it. That has to be your balance. You hope that the majority of the time, the high that you love is going to get it but sometimes the director is going to see something else, maybe a camera blocking that you didn't see—how he's going to move the characters through the space and how he's going to shoot something—and that might put you in the mid-level.

In design in general, it's a lot about taste and your taste level and style. But in design for film, you have to understand the difference between a low-end crack house, and a high-end mansion and you have to think about how to make things as authentic as possible.

You've also got to think practically about how that location is going to be best suited to the production—is it easy access? You don't want production to be pushing carts up a hill just to get there. You've got to think about which way the light is coming in, what direction the windows are facing, what's outside the windows. You're trying to sell

(continued)

(continued)

that you're in small town Illinois but you've got palm trees outside. If you don't have money to use greens [bring in bushes or plants] to cover that, that becomes an important battle. Do you need to spend the money to place the greens outside or do you limit the direction that the camera is facing? How do you make that decision with the cinematographer, and do they feel comfortable working with that? Do you feel that the location is important enough to limit the frame?

That's really important, to learn the camera angles, what the camera can do, where it can be placed, if there's a Steadicam, is there enough space for it? In film you have to think about [the fact that] there's a person on a digital monitor who is pulling focus and where they can be in relationship to the camera so they aren't visible. Where is video village? [Slang for the area where a group of people—the director and specific key crew members—huddle around the on-set monitor screen to see exactly what the camera is seeing.]

Brian Haynes' first job in the film industry was as assistant to the Vice President of Europe and the Middle East for 20th Century Fox International. He spent four years in Paris, London, and Madrid. When he returned to his native Los Angeles, he worked as a production assistant on *Blade Runner*, then moved into location management on *Fast Times at Ridgemont High*, and the James Bond movie *Never Say Never Again*. Since then, his credits include *Dave*, *Bye Bye Love*, *Down Periscope*, *Never Been Kissed*, *The Gilmore Girls*, *Deadwood*, *Private Practice*, and *How To Get Away With Murder*.

Haynes has traveled the world in search of "the perfect location" for a movie. Charged with finding a gorgeous coastline for the James Bond film, *Never Say Never Again*, he flew to Corsica, rented an airplane (he has a pilot's license), and scouted the island by air, flying the length of the coast of Spain, from Barcelona to Gibraltar. Then he went on to the French Riviera. Nice work. But many of his most challenging location situations were closer to home in Los Angeles, and almost always the biggest issues involve dealing with people.

Brian Haynes

I break down the script. Sometimes I make suggestions on my breakdown as to what I think should be a set vs. a practical location. I would make my suggestions to the production designer and the designer would make their suggestions to the director. My break-down would reflect the name of the location as stated in the script, a small description of the action, if there is anything special—gunfire, explosions, because it will have an effect on the final decision. If it is a final script (meaning the final revision or shooting script) I would write the scene number and the number of pages so we would know approximately how many days we would be at each of the locations. For films, a location might last ten days but in television usually no more than two.

When I'm looking at a location, I'm looking for something that will photograph well, and look interesting. I look for something that's never been filmed before, which is a rarity in the Los Angeles area. For the last 20 years, there have been 84 companies a day filming. It's pretty unusual to find something that hasn't ever been filmed.

I look at the budget. If it's a big feature, then it doesn't usu-ally matter how much you spend. If it's a TV show, I know those amounts based on my experience. Depending on the house it can be $2,500 to $30,000 a day.

I consider logistics. How easy or hard it is to film in those places. For example, in one city you can film between 7am–7pm in a resi-dential neighborhood, 7am–10pm if you get signatures from the people who live within a certain distance of the location. Some places aren't friendly when it comes to extended hours.

I think of the logistics of getting a filming company there. There are a lot of trucks, you need parking (there can be 70 crew members, all driving their vehicles to work), you need to have a basecamp (where the star trailers, the dressing room trailers, and the cater-ers set up). Some things to think about. You couldn't shoot where I live, even if it looks great, because I live up a very long, narrow, winding canyon road. They just couldn't get everything up here. It also depends on the neighbors. Maybe they just say no. Sometimes they are happy for you to come but they do nefarious things to get more money, like having a gardener come in with a leaf blower on a day when they usually aren't there. At one point I had an issue with a neighbor who was a sound man in the industry. The day before we were due to come in the guy called me and said, "Oh by the way, we're going to have a backhoe coming into our property." Looking for money.

We show the designer 20 pictures of houses and he or she wants to see four of them. We go out to look at them. Of those four he might pick two that he or she wants to show the director. When we go out with the designer we talk about the logistics. What will

(continued)

(continued)

we see in the reverse [shot]. If you're filming on the street in front of a house you want to see everything that works—and everything that doesn't. You check out the geography of the house. I go out to see the places before we go out with the production designer and director. I'll go to a house or a market, a potential location, and I'll approach the owner, say we'd like to use the place and go over things, is there gunfire, are there explosions, car crashes, rain effects—so they aren't blind-sided when we get there.

I'm always friendly, always honest. I believe that's part of the deal. If people don't want filming, other than money, what can per-suade them? More money. But I can usually convince people to accept filming because I have a good reputation. I offer references, explain how the process and the clean-up process works, and give them a security deposit to seal the deal.

There's a saying in the film business that I've always objected to—it's "Do we own the location now?" Which means, have we gotten the agreements signed, do we have the permits, have we paid the money? But we never own the location. We're visitors. It's their home or office. A lot of location managers treat locations as if they own them and once the shooting company moves in to work, it's like, tough, we're here. We'll take over. But you never want the location team to think "this is my neighbourhood," just because we made a deal.

I found out that you can ask for ridiculous things and they'll sometimes say yes. On *Harley Davidson and the Marlboro Man* we wanted to stage a motorcycle chase through Century City. [Century City is a busy, high-end and high-profile business and residential area between West Los Angeles and Beverly Hills.] We had two motorcycles, one a Harley and one a futuristic-looking one. They came up a ramp, did a motorcycle jump and went racing through Century City. I was astonished that the city let us do it.

Other surprising requests: on a film a long time ago, we needed an airplane, a 707. What was supposed to happen was the airplane was supposed to go sailing down the runway then explode. Setting up the scene, I had to deal extensively with Ontario Airport, Ontario Security, the Fire Department, the Control Tower, and the FAA.

We had it set for a particular day, we had a 707, we went out to Ontario Airport. The plane was a jet that had been painted in a very specific manner. It didn't look like any other plane. But the fellow I rented it from had neglected to tell us that there was a lien on it and the bank had repossessed it. So, we were waiting at the airport and the plane never showed up. That was bad. I had to find another

707 quick. I looked around, looked around, and finally found one. A beautiful privately owned 707. All of the interior was custom, the fixtures were gold. But we had to paint it so it would match the one that we didn't use because we'd already filmed a miniature version of the other plane. We had to match it. I rented the jet, we painted it with water-based paint, so it would come off and we flew it to Ontario. Unfortunately, it was raining. The plane got to Ontario with most of the paint either running or off. The next morning, the art department rented a paint gun and we sprayed the paint on the plane before the company arrived.

What we did for the explosion—obviously nothing really exploded. Since it was night, the plane ran down the runway, ran out of sight, out of the lights and basically disappeared. Then at the Universal backlot, the FX guys took lots of gasoline, put it in buckets and blew it all up. It was impressive. They married that footage to the footage at the end of the airport scene. I was probably 100 yards away from it and you still got the blast of heat.

Second Unit

Second Unit is a unit or a period of shooting where there is no cast present. The First Unit would be what we usually think of—the director, the actors, the crew. Second Unit is often supplemental action, with stunts or special effects, and may be directed by either the film's director or a stunt coordinator. There may be a completely different crew. If there is talent on camera, they are stunt people or stunt doubles. If the director is not present, there is no acting and no dialogue is recorded. The intention is that the Second Unit footage will be smoothly edited into the Main Unit's footage and the audience will see the star leap from the plane or crash the Mercedes.

Brian Haynes

I was on for the Second Unit of *Terminal Velocity*. My two locations were in the Saline Valley, where we were dropping two Cadillacs out of a cargo plane. Also the final scene is somebody parachuting into a wind turbine, like the electricity generating wind turbines they have in Palm Springs. We had to drop them down on a line to

(continued)

(continued)

make it look like they were parachuting into the windmill and there was a lot of editing to make it look real.

For dropping the cars out of the plane, we had to clear a huge stretch of desert road. There were highway patrol men out on the road. We were filming close to a wilderness area. Wilderness is a special thing, environmentally protected. You're not allowed to have motor vehicles, you can't fly within 2,000 feet of the ground. We were just outside of that area, dropping the cars. That said, unfortunately one of the cars landed in there. We got in there, we cleaned it up, we paid a mitigation fee. The Bureau of Land Management was with me the whole time and it ended up fine.

The scene we were shooting involved people fighting in the plane, the car being pushed out the back of the plane, people fighting in the air, pulling somebody out of the trunk, holding them, and the person who was getting them out of the car had to take her out of the back of the car, hold her, then parachute to the ground. Each car had a rocket parachute on it, so they would come out of the plane and at a specific altitude, it would trigger the rocket and it would fall to earth.

There was a little town there, kind of a ghost town, with one person who lived in the town. I had to make sure the guy didn't come out of his house while we were dropping the cars. I sat with him watching the cars fall.

My favorite show that I worked on was *Deadwood*. What was interesting about *Deadwood* is that you'd leave 2005, drive to 1876, be immersed in horse shit and oxen and cowboys all day and go home, take a shower and be back in 2005.

Timothy Hillman has been a location manager on a staggering 43 film and television projects, including features *Most Wanted*, *Scream 2*, *Wag the Dog*, *Lansky*, *Magnolia*, *What Lies Beneath*, *Castaway*, *Road to Perdition*, *50 First Dates*, *National Treasure*, and series *CSI NY*, *CSI Cyber*, *Shameless*, and *Lethal Weapon*.

Timothy Hillman

I get the script and try to read it two or three times. The next step for me is to sit with the designer, the director, and the producer to figure out what's going to be built on stage, what's going to be on location.

If we're building the interiors on stage will we be shooting any exteriors? Because the exteriors have to be found first so we can match the inside and outside.

Sometimes they ask for something that doesn't exist. They ask for a laundromat near another location and there isn't one. But I know of this really cool bakery that's around the corner from where we have to shoot that day. If the story isn't about the laundromat, it's about what's going on in this guy's life, we might move it to the bakery. I try to get inside the director and the designer's heads. Try to see what they see. The hardest part is nailing down the designer, when they say, "I'll know what it is when I see it." If you can't tell me what you want, I can't find it for you.

The cost of a house location in Los Angeles can vary between $3,000 and $25,000 depending upon the house. Average these days, $5,000 to $10,000 a day. Let's say we need a house in the suburbs. The questions I have to ask: what's the socio-economic level of the people living in the house? What do they do for a living? What are their hobbies? How big is the family? Is it a single mom, is it a mom and dad? Are they about to get divorced? Where are they in their lives? Is this the house they grew up in that they took over when their mom and dad died? Would it have some of those elements to it?

The toughest location I had to find—the crossroads in *Castaway*. Took me six weeks and seven states. I would get on a plane and fly into a town, then I'd get on to a smaller plane, then get into a car with a map book and a GPS, and I'd find the crossroads. It had to be very specific. Zemeckis [Robert Zemeckis, the director] wanted a four-way cross with nothing around it. Preferably paved. The problem is when you have a crossroads in the middle of nowhere, when you get to the part where the crossroads intersect, there is usually something there because everybody gathers there. There's a 7-Eleven, a grain elevator, a gas station. I was in the Panhandle of Texas, I had been in Amarillo for two weeks, and I'd put 1,700 miles on my rental car, looking. Someone said, you should try Canadian. That was a town 93 miles northeast of Amarillo right on the Oklahoma border. I went, and I found the Chamber of Commerce office. I said, "I'm looking for this and this. And I also need a house like that." There was a photograph, it was a Sears kit house, an 1890s house. The woman there said, "Oh that's the Arrington Ranch. I can get you out there in about 20 minutes. And about three miles from that, there's a crossroads." As quick as that, after all that searching.

(continued)

(continued)

What is the personality you need to be a location manager? You need to be calm. You've got to be able to think on your feet. "You can't do that." Alright, I have to come up with some way to do it and I've only got an hour. And it has to work. And it's very rare that we can't come up with something that works.

Places "Playing" Other Places

John Miller

I wrote a script that took place mostly in LA because I was in LA. But there's a section that takes place in New York. And I managed to find an area downtown in Los Angeles. It was supposed to be Brooklyn. I found a street with triple-deckers that looked like New York. I could only shoot it from one angle because if I shot it from any other angle it didn't look at all like New York. It was one of the first times I realized that cheating was available as an option. When you start making films you start off being so literal—but what we do as filmmakers is, we cheat everything. We make 500 people look like a crowd of 5,000 people. Everything we are doing is an illusion. No one questions it.

I had a professor when I was in film school. We were on a tiny sound stage. He said, "A lot of you will be shooting scenes that take place in a home. Now, what do I need to show to convince the audience that I'm in a kitchen?" A lot of students had opinions. "You should see a table and a refrigerator and a stove . . ." and he took this one piece of a table that had the right kind of counter-top on it, and he lit it in such a way that you just saw one corner of that and you saw the character behind it. We're all looking at the video tap, seeing what the camera is seeing. And it's definitely a kitchen. We don't have to build things out, we just have to show enough so they believe it, so we can get that emotional impact we're going for. I shot a movie where I used a corner of a room as Sun Studios in Memphis. [Sun Studios is a legendary recording studio where Johnny Cash, Jerry Lee Lewis, and Elvis Presley made records.] People who'd been to Sun Studios did not question whether it was Sun Studios in Memphis. They just assumed that's where we shot.

It is possible that your screenplay will be set in a specific place but for reasons that are either financial, or logistic (weather, no local crew, height of tourist season), you just aren't able to shoot there. Assuming the location of the setting is important to the story and shouldn't be changed, what can you do?

Analyze the visual aspects of the setting.

Break it down to its basic components. What's the geography of the setting? What does the scripted location look like? It can be rolling hills or flat, mountainous or not any of these. There may be a seashore or a lake. If there's a beach, what kind of beach? Hyannis is different from Malibu and neither of them look like the Outer Banks or Mendocino. Do you need dunes or rocks and cliffs? If the film is set in the desert, it can look like White Sands, New Mexico, or Saudi Arabia. Be specific. Is the action in the heartland, or on the plains, or in the woods? Tropical growth or scrub pines?

If you shot or purchased stock shots establishing the Eiffel Tower and the Seine, could you find cafés and apartment buildings that could be dressed as Paris? It's been done.

Do the characters have a lot of money and live in expansive minimum acreage-communities or in cookie-cutter housing tracts where most of the houses were built at the same time?

Are the streets in the real location narrow or broad boulevards, winding, gravel, dirt, asphalt?

If the screenplay takes place in contemporary times, your research is easy. Even if it's a period picture, you can get online, go to the library, and find photographs.

Ever see the movie *Anaconda*? The tropical gardens at the Huntington Library in the lovely suburb of San Marino, California, "played" the Amazon jungle. Indian Dunes in Valencia, a suburb of Los Angeles, is now closed to filming but in the not-too-distant past it's played the Mexican jungle, Vietnam, Brazil, Africa, and Afghanistan. The terrain was overgrown, and its configuration was such that you could shoot at night without seeing the city lights, although it's a stone's throw from the Six Flags Magic Mountain amusement park. For decades, the now-razed Ambassador Hotel in the middle of Los Angeles starred in hundreds of period films including *Bobby*, *That Thing You Do*, and *Catch Me If You Can*. The Ambassador was huge and once it became a full-time film location for rent, there was so much shooting there that there was a permanent film production office, staffed by veteran location managers who operated as liaisons to the industry. The Ambassador was home to the famous Coconut Grove nightclub. It's a pretty sure bet that if you've seen a movie made before 2005 and there was a vintage nightclub set, an elegant old-fashioned restaurant, bar, coffee-shop, or a drive-up entrance under a broad portico, you were looking at the Ambassador. It didn't matter where the film was

set—you could've been in Baltimore, DC, or Chicago. The filmmakers decided what you saw, and you never saw anything beyond the boundaries of the camera's frame. Though these places are now not available for filming, there are other similar locations. You may not have to travel to find your script setting if you develop the ability to focus on specific elements rather than an entire landscape.

Another example—a film was going to shoot on Cape Cod. The screenplay was written as a Massachusetts beach area and the Cape was a perfect fit. But when the team went to scout the area, the production problems with shooting there quickly became evident. The location would be too busy, too populated, too expensive, and there wouldn't be enough housing for the crew because it had to be shot in spring, and the production schedule would carry into summer. Spring and summer were the run up to, and the height of, the tourist season. The team re-evaluated. They looked at the necessary production elements. 1. Seaside town. 2. Terrain that could play New England. 3. Lots of local Nantucket-like character. That film ended up being shot in Nova Scotia, about an hour outside of Halifax. In addition to getting the desired look, the production company was able to take advantage of the discrepancy between the Canadian and US dollar. That enabled the production to put more of the money where it counted—on the screen.

Issues of non-native vegetation can be solved by bringing in greens or blocking existing trees that aren't right, or by using digital techniques to make them vanish. You can buy flowers and plant them temporarily. They may not live long in the wrong climate but they'll help sell the look of where you want your audience to think they are.

What type of buildings exist in the actual setting and what are the materials they are made of? Are they high-rises, brownstones, brick, wood? Are the buildings old or new? What are the styles? Colonial, Federal, Spanish, are there columns, pillars? Pastel stucco? Even if you can't find areas with those elements, you'll know to avoid certain areas because they'll be too new, made of materials that weren't used, or are just too identifiable as the wrong place. You need a house in Connecticut. Easy if you're based in New York, Chicago, or Los Angeles. You can find a "Connecticut house" outside of Vancouver and Montreal. Not easy if you're in Florida. You'll look at your research. You'll have to find a wooden or brick house, either a Colonial, Salt Box, or cottage style. You'll avoid seeing pink stucco or Florida foliage. Maybe you'll bring in plants from out of state. You'll limit your exterior shots, and it won't be ideal, but it can be done.

If you can't shoot in the location the script is written for, what can you do? You can get the answers to the questions listed above, then you can scout locations to find some of those elements that will "sell" the place you are shooting so that it will appear to be the location in the script. Then you can dress and disguise the exterior elements that don't work.

Before tax credits, incentives, and a state and city government that sought to encourage production, it used to be very expensive to shoot in New York City and in Boston. Even studio movies with substantial budgets didn't want to pay the kind of price it required to shoot (back then) in either of those cities. Filmmakers began with shooting establishing shots of iconic Manhattan landmarks, or shooting a big exterior scene or two with the leading actors to set the location in the audience's mind. Then they shot the rest of the movie in Toronto, where they could find areas that were close-enough looking to parts of New York City, including brownstones, high-rises, a river, and wide boulevards. The transportation departments found yellow cabs and property masters used skins (peel-off stickers) on them. Being able to find New York in Canada at the time meant: paying for traveling and housing the stars and a few key creatives (producer, director, sometimes the cinematographer and production and costume designer), hiring highly experienced local crew, finding actors in Toronto who could do an "American" accent (they all can), and saving millions of dollars, due to incentives, a favorable currency exchange rate, and less expensive union rates.

If the script was written for old Boston or Philadelphia, it was pretty much the same situation, but maybe the production would shoot in Montreal, where the age of the buildings and the narrow streets, some of them cobblestone, could be made to match both of those cities and some European cities.

You can find Miami in Los Angeles, and New York City's older areas in downtown LA. You can shoot the Pacific Northwest in Vancouver. A major scene in *Black Rain*, a film about the Yakuza in Japan, was shot in Northern California. As previously mentioned, *Mad Men*, set in 1960s New York and its suburbs, was mostly shot in Los Angeles, both on a sound stage and at locations around the city. The TV series *Dawson's Creek* was set in Massachusetts but shot in Wilmington, North Carolina. *Gladiator* was shot in Morocco, all over Europe, and in the US. The Clint Eastwood "spaghetti westerns" were shot in Spain. *Unforgiven*, set in the Old West, was shot in Alberta, Canada and Sonora, California. *Pretty In Pink*, set in suburban Chicago, was shot in Los Angeles, as was *Grosse Point Blank*, set in Grosse Point, Michigan. There is a farm in Gilroy, California, that played an old homestead in Nebraska. You can pull it off. It's all about supporting the story. Famously, the 2003 film *Cold Mountain*, about the American Civil War and set in North Carolina, was shot in Romania, in addition to Virginia and North and South Carolina. (It can occasionally go the other way—the TV mini-series *The Starter Wife* was set in Hollywood but shot in Queensland, Australia.)

Dave DeGaetano

What are things you can tell people in terms of selling the design of a location if you don't have that kind of money? I would tell them there's not necessarily any reason to go to New Zealand (for example). I would suggest they look at some local locations, hilly, beautiful fields. There are locations in the Los Angeles area that would surprise you. We shot very little on location for *The Last Samurai*.

Scale down the scope of your shot. Instead of having a street in Tokyo that's split five ways just run an L and build some plugs. That will change the look. On *Samurai* we'd have some shots on one part of a street front, maybe you'd do a 90-degree turn, then we'd change over and have some plugs that would go in front of that, so it would become a restaurant row.

Nowadays you could easily make use of green screen, change some foreground elements that change the look, and put something in, in post, shoot some plates. That's still money but it's going to be cheaper than housing, the crews, the transportation, the shipping, that adds up really fast. People fall in love with the location and think that looks great, and it does, but there are a lot of ways to skin the cat.

7   Lighting and Picture

What about the cinematographer (otherwise called the DP, DOP in Canada and England, or director of photography)? Isn't the look of the film his or her job, too? Cinematography is an art, a craft, and relies heavily on technology. The director of photography is responsible for lighting and photographing the world that the production designer creates. Through the choice of lighting design, lens selection, and digital presentation and processing, the cinematographer has an enormous impact on how a film, television, or digital project looks. You can say that cinematography is the art of capturing an image, but it's much more than that. A cinematographer is an artist with light and the cinematography uses, manipulates, and controls the way information (the image) is documented, and then how it's altered before we see the result. Cinematographers work with the director to use light the way the art department uses color, texture, etc. The cinematographer collaborates with all of the visual design departments, particularly art, set decoration, and costume.

An example: a party scene. One person is sharply in focus, in the foreground. Other party-goers are chatting a couple of yards away, in the background. As the scene continues, an action or piece of dialogue moves the background group more clearly into the forefront, joining the original person's range of conversation. This may be the director's vision and design for the scene, but this seemingly simple action involves planning by several departments. What is the location and does it offer the correct size and configuration? (That will be the production designer and location manager.) The cinematographer will look at the lighting, lens, and camera-movement necessary to make it work, and that may become an equipment discussion with the gaffer and key grip. How close in are the shots? What will show in these spaces? (Set decorator.) If the "fuzzy" party-goers are not meant to draw attention to themselves until the second part of the scene, the costume designer is going to have to know that because the party outfits should not be colors that pull the eye away and distract from the main focus. Sounds like a lot of fuss about a few seconds of viewing time—but it all must work together because when it doesn't, the audience notices. Seamlessness takes time and care.

In post-production, the cinematographer is involved with the color-grading process. Color grading is the digital altering of the color of the footage to correct problems (you'll want to achieve a uniformity to the look of a project that has possibly been shot over several days, weeks, or months under very different conditions, so that it looks as if all pieces are part of the same movie) and to alter or enhance the footage for an emotional or story effect. Color correction and color grading usually takes place at the final stages of "picture" post-production, once a final edited version of the project is complete.

The cinematographer is the head of the camera department. The camera team usually consists of the director of photography, sometimes a camera operator (sometimes the cinematographer acts as his or her own operator), and a first and second assistant. The operator physically operates the camera, frames the shot, and executes camera moves (pans, tilts, etc). The operator may take the camera from the dolly or tripod. Then the shot or sequence is considered hand-held. Doing this requires the ability to maintain rock solid steadiness while moving or following action, and it's not easy as even a millisecond of shaking can distract the viewer.

The first assistant cameraperson (AC) has the nerve-wracking job of maintaining focus. The sharpness of the image depends upon a combination of the lighting, the lens, and the movement being photographed. First ACs are meticulous and exacting. When a shot is soft—just a fraction out of focus—the first AC is in the hot seat. Directors aren't happy if an actor hits the perfect performance note but the scene must be reshot because it's a little fuzzy. Actors aren't thrilled either. The logistics involved in reshooting when the problem is viewed a day later, once the set has been wrapped and the shooting crew has moved to the next location impacts both the budget and schedule. It's no wonder that the first AC on your project may be a bit tense.

The second AC is the person in charge of the slate (the electronic blackboard that tells the editor which scene and take he or she is saying once they receive the footage). The slate also generates a signal so that sound and picture can be synched. The second AC also takes care of the paperwork (camera reports that document what scenes and takes were shot on a specific day).

Although the grip and electric department are not actually in the camera department they work in tandem with the cinematographer and are there to serve his or her needs. The grip department deals with camera and electrical support in terms of rigging. The grips build and set the equipment (dollies, scaffolding, stands) that hold the lights and camera. The grip department is headed by the key grip, whose second in command is the best boy grip. The electrical crew controls the lights. The chief lighting technician is the gaffer. The second in command to the gaffer is the best boy electric. There are additional grips and electricians who take their cues from their department heads, and carry out the lighting and lighting support functions.

The director of photography, working with the director, designs the lighting and execution of each shot so that each image contributes to the mood and intention of the screenplay. How does the director of photography look at a screenplay? Like the other department heads, they read it to digest the story, the tone, the point of view. This sounds as if it should be obvious, but occasionally aspiring and student cinematographers immediately go to their comfort zone—lights and camera gear and cranes, etc.—and don't look at the basics of story, characters, who wants what, and what's in the way. That's understandable. Every department eventually reads a screenplay with their own area of expertise in mind. But great cinematographers examine the text and subtext of the drama or humor or action of the project as a whole. Then they think about lighting design and incorporating it into the telling of the story. They meet with the director and share ideas. Sometimes the DP has worked with the director in the past and they have a kind of short-hand. They understand the director's style. Even then, the discussion must be had. This may be a project where the director decides that everything will be different.

The cinematographers is often hired after the production designer and the location manager, so although they have input regarding the locations, the bottom line is that their job is to figure out the best way to photograph the actors, and the location.

Bill Dill is a veteran cinematographer—his credits include feature films, television series, and documentaries, among them *Soul Food*, *Dancing in September*, *BAPS*, *American Playhouse*, *The Five Heartbeats*, *Sidewalk Stories*. More than that, Dill is recognized by literally scores of cinematographers as a master educator. A highly revered professor at top film schools—the American Film Institute, the University of Southern California, and Chapman University, Dill is a long-time member of the American Society of Cinematographers, an invitation-only organization that recognizes notable cinematographers.

Bill Dill: How the Cinematographer Works with the Director and Designer

It's important to have a really deep understanding of the story, first and foremost. Second, what is this director's particular approach to the story? You've got to have both of those together. Which is one of the things I'm surprised that people don't understand—that cinematography is storytelling.

(continued)

(continued)

Most people think cinematography is just this technical manipulation of cameras and lights and lenses as if somehow that comes out of a vacuum, when the thing that defines all of that is the specific nature of the story you're going to tell. It's the technical in aid of the storytelling. And your technical ability has the veto power over your aesthetic choices. If you don't have the chops to pull off the idea technically it doesn't make its way to the screen.

The reality is, most cinematographers if you ask them, they'll tell you they've got a great DIT. [A Digital Imaging Technician is the camera crew member whose responsibility is to be sure that all the digital data on set is captured in its most accurate technical state. DITs in many ways bridge the technical gap between what is shot in the camera and the post-production process.] And they've got a great camera assistant. Most cinematographers spend more time thinking about the visual storytelling effect of color, of light and dark, or near vs. far, the impact that the lens has on that, the impact of what we're doing with the camera, what the production designer does, plus the costume designer, plus any effects people— what they're doing and the impact we have on that and what we want to achieve with that, than they do on what specific switch gets flipped to do what, which codec [digital encryption] are we using, what's the most effective workflow. We do have to have a sense of that but that stuff isn't all that useful unless it's in the service of something else.

The cinematographer has to be aware of where we fit in the context of all that. It's all at the service of what do we want to say about that particular character? One of the things that I find to be the most problematic for young directors is thinking you've said something you actually haven't said. And saying something you don't know you're saying. You want to direct the eye. Where do you want the audience to look? What's important in that frame, and how do we communicate the importance of that thing to the audience in such a way that it isn't on the nose and obvious and presentational and, on the other hand, it isn't in your mind but not on the screen.

Ways of Seeing

The built-in conflict between the cinematographer and other creative partners in making creative decisions is in part because they tend to look at something and make their decisions on how it looks in the environment right now. We have to look at it through this lens, through this camera, through this filter, through this codec, through this color space, and that's a different thing. The way I try to describe it (to my students) is, you shoot an image with your eye and you just use the camera to show it to other people.

The Perception of the Audience

When you photograph two characters you're photographing the relationship between those characters. One of the most fundamental parts of our visual pattern recognition system is the notion of proximity. How close am I to you? How close do I appear to be to you? How close is the audience to the characters? How close does the audience feel they are to the characters?

Invariably the audience is creeped out by this [describing a very close frame], a little more comfortable by this [a mid-distance], and distanced by this [a long view]. We are hypersensitive to this idea of violating someone else's space. If you want to watch a character here [close], it's different than here [mid-distance], and it's different here [distant]. Focal length isn't just coverage. It isn't just, how much are you seeing. A lot of it is hooking into the audience's unconscious sense of things and how it works at this moment in the story. Are we OK being close to that person right now, or are we uncomfortable being close to this person right now?

Using Expectations to Tell the Story

That's fundamental to how cinema works. Cinematographers photograph either change or the absence of it. More often than not, we establish patterns just for the sake of breaking them. This idea of matching size and distance for both sides of a conversations? Shooting back and forth from one character to another who are roughly the same size in the frame? My students say, but that's a rule. Yes, and I'm totally cool with showing you how to break every single rule. Every single one. There's a reason for the rule. Almost always the reason is that you want to establish the pattern. And now we want the audience to pay attention because we're going to break that pattern.

I show my students Hieronymus Bosch. *A Garden of Earthly Delights*. This altarpiece, which is actually a triptych, a three-part painting, [portrays] the beginning of knowledge, the Garden of

(continued)

(continued)

Eden, the Corruption of Mankind, then the end result of that corruption. This is the painting that gets to what cinema does. One of the under-lying principles that filmmakers have to understand [is] the sequence of events has as much power as the single image itself. In other words, no single image lives on its own. All images have their impact because of the images that precede it. That's a basic part of the design idea. That's another reason the director and the cinematographer work so closely together in designing the look of the movie. It's about the progression of the images as opposed to looking at the set. It has to do with getting past how the thing in and of itself looks, or how it feels to us in the absence of the context of the story. Because context is everything.

Johnny Jensen has been a cinematographer on over 30 feature films and episodes of television. From Denmark, educated as a mechanical engineer, he immigrated to the US when he was 20, intent on a career building race cars. A much-abbreviated list of his credits includes *The Ladies Man*, *Rosewood*, *Three Wishes*, *Grumpy Old Men*, *Rambling Rose*, *Benefit of the Doubt*, *Angie*, among many others. He has shot over a dozen television movies; he was an additional director of photography, camera operator or assistant camera on *Because I said So*, *Bringing Down the House* (second unit and DP on the helicopter unit), *Exit to Eden*, the U2 documentary *Rattle and Hum*, and has been cinematographer and director on over 20 hours of television, including the series *Heartland* and *Dragnet*. He has been nominated for two Emmy Awards and is a member of the American Society of Cinematographers.

Johnny Jensen's Process and Bridging the Gap between Story, Camera, and Lighting

I feel the characters to begin with. As I read, I really write the visual language in my own head. As a cinematographer, nobody may ever hear about what I see, but my initial visual response is in my head. From the words and from the story. What I feel the first time I read the script, that is what drives me.

The first time I read a script is before I get the job. Then I need to meet with the producer and director. They are interviewing me and I'm interviewing them at the same time to find out what do we have, what are the resources, who else is involved as artists and collaborators.

"What do you think of the script?" is usually the first question that is asked and I have (what is) perhaps an unorthodox response. My response usually will be—I'll feel the room first—but without being short, I'll say, before I go into this "I'd love to hear what you have to say about the story. You have already spent months on this. I've had a day to read it and I've got a concept but in order to facilitate you and your process, why don't you start telling me how you see the story."

Now, of course I do have an idea but it's my idea and I'm not willing yet to share it. I could have a totally wrong idea. When someone feeds me something else that original idea could fly away, and I get a completely new idea. I don't like to put myself in a position where I'm glued to something.

Working with Actors

To me, both as a cinematographer and a director, it's a performing art. It's not just a craft. Nothing really comes together until the actors are there. [Director] John Huston said, "My job as a director is over when I'm cast. I sit back and watch." That's an idea I totally embrace. You bring the actors in because they inhabit the characters. Everything that we do in filmmaking is to coax the actors into feeling that they can embrace the characters truthfully and unencumbered. That is what our physical job is. Once you set that up, stand back and watch and interpret and see what it is that you actually have to do. The visual language is now there. You have to find it.

The actors bring an opportunity. A total opportunity. I worked as a focus puller on a film. The director cast brilliant actors . . . their performances were immaculate. But the principal actor struggled with the director because when we needed the actors on the set, he'd say, 'bring in the puppets." That's what he thought of the actors. He would ride the shot and look through the camera and he would be more worried about a foot being in a correct place than about whether the dialog was flowing out. This taught me a lot of things: to give the actors more room. I wanted to never be putting a burden on the actor, never to be a stickler with marks, lighting for marks, making an actor aware of them. [Marks are the pieces of tape put down on the floor of the set. An audience can't see the marks in the shot, but they guide the actor as to where to stand for blocking and focus purposes]. A good actor is aware of marks organically. I try to embrace the actors . . . my experience is that the first thing, when the director says "cut," the person that leading actor is looking at is the cinematographer. I present myself as a life-preserver. If they are going to stumble into the net, I've got the net.

(continued)

(continued)

I work hard on giving the feeling that when I'm in charge they don't have to worry about anything but what they have to do. That helps them and helps the storytelling.

One thing I always do . . . you call it a make-up test, the first time you're working with the actors. But you're testing everything. You're testing costumes, you get some flats in from the art department where you can see the clothing against what the walls are going to be painted like, so there's far more than make-up happening in that make-up test. One of the essential things that I find can be done in the make-up test, besides looking at these pieces of craft to stoke the artistic endeavor, is to show the actors that you care for them. You are showing that you care about how you're going to light them, that you're thinking about what their character should look like, and all of those things. That first impression as a cinematographer—this really happens on the make-up test. You're doing all these mechanics at the same time but to me the most important thing that happens is to make that impression. Here they have a floor to dance on and they're OK, no matter what.

The Art Department

Getting back to story and collaboration. A good production designer will take each character in the story and put a background to them so they have a basis as to where they are coming from. It is not in the script, this character's mother is never mentioned, but where does that character come from, who was the mother? How did that character grow up? So that in set decoration and the kind of choices the designer makes about the character's living space it is evident that it's coming from some place. Too often a director does not have time to do that, so a production designer will do all that.

As a cinematographer, when I get hired on a job I'm very interested in who the production designer is. It's the first person outside of the director that I collaborate with. I get friendly with the art department. I look at all the stuff they have accumulated, the reading material, as to where they're going. They've been on [the movie] for a long while before me. I soak that stuff up. I definitely lay out the friendship, so collaboration is at its utmost with the art department. They lay the groundwork for the visual language. They define the space. Of course, it is there in the story. The director is aware of all of that and feeling all of that, but not always either capable of or interested in illuminating each and every detail.

When somebody illuminates it for them it is an enhancement that they are happy about.

The story is basically there to begin with. You can take ten different people reading the same script and they could have ten different ways of looking at that script. Now the step is to get that together, to mesh. I do think a good team is the team where your desire is usually higher than what you can afford but that desire will usually drive you to do all that you can afford. You want to be where everybody understands each other within a filmmaking team. You need to know as much as possible about what everybody does because you're in that circle where the story is being cemented.

Color and Lighting

Color triggers emotions. We can use that, we can highlight it and we can dampen it. That's something that plays a part both in production design and cinematography. You can evoke an emotion. When you are desaturating a film, for instance, and using monochromatic images, you are already putting the audience in a mood that is on the downward side. You usually don't want to do that in a comedy.

What is it that you want to do? What are the characteristics of the piece? That determines how you think of color and how you want to feel the color, because color can be done in different ways. I think the subtleties of that is something you need to think about. You can use color on the lights [gels] and get a perception of emotion from the lights, or you can use lights to illuminate the colors already on the set. You want to put the audience in the place and time [when the story is set], whether it's in the past or in the future. You can do that with color.

Lighting and Location

When I look at a location it's about how to channel what it is that fits that story. What is the volume of the space, the place, the person in that space. What is the emotion? Does the set have a real relationship to what is happening? Or is it just a space? Within a space there are so many things you can do—you can make it feel as if it is trapping, you can make it spacious, you can make it so that the person in the space feels alone.

An example: when you're shooting a close-up with a wide lens, you're shooting up close but because of the angle of the view, you're seeing a lot of background. If you're shooting a close-up and you

(continued)

(continued)

want to see all that, that's one thing. But that might be too much, it might distract. If you're shooting with a long lens you can do a close-up and see nothing, no background at all. Now you have a better sense of how the person feels. There's no dialogue. That person is just thinking.

The human eye goes toward light. If you have a hot [too bright] window and someone in the shadow who is about to cry, that window should not be bright, you should have a backlight on the person even if they're in the dark so when you see that frame, you're on that person. You have to always be thinking about the audience and the characters. The actors are presenting what the character feels through their eyes and you are presenting that back to the audience. What do you want audience to feel? I always say that as a cinematographer, you're a puppet master. Where is the audience looking? Lights, lenses, shadows, locations. When that visual design is done right, you've got the audience feeling a certain way by making them look at a certain thing in a certain way.

It's about emotion. I hate when someone is talking about "the shot." It's the emotion. If they are talking about "the shot," there's a problem.

Director John Lloyd Miller on Lighting Design

There is no one way to light. Starting filmmakers tend to be afraid of the dark. They believe that moonlight is blue. Whenever there's a moon, they put so much blue gel on the light that it's like a neon sign blowing into their room. They make sure the whole room is lit up. The great filmmakers, the great cinematographers, only light what needs to be lit. There are exceptions: Lucas made *THX* and it's basically all flat and brightly lit, it's lit like the inside of a refrigerator. But that was a great way—and an inexpensive way (because it was a student film)—of creating that inhospitable environment. But most great filmmakers, filmmakers like Buñuel and Coppola, almost every great filmmaker for the last 30 years, understands that we don't need everything lit up like a Christmas tree. It doesn't help. Lighting is an element you control, so once again, what is the intention? What am I trying to get people to feel? And am I moving from the darkness into the light? Am I moving from the light into the darkness?

There's a difference in intention there. What is the emotional arc of this film, what is the story arc of this film? To me, the default is, it's dark until there's a reason and then you light only what needs to be lit. Your job as a director is to tell people where to look and one of the ways to do that is with light. In *Casino*, Scorsese and Robert Richardson have got these bright HMIs [a type of light that can give a very sunny daytime exterior look] shining down the middle of a table. Light that's coming from nowhere. No motivation. But it's where everybody's hands are, and it forces you to look at everybody's hands.

8 Costumes and Props

Volumes can and have been written about these craftspeople and artists. They are major contributors to the filmmaking process and their work touches every department.

Costumes

The costume designer is tasked with finding or creating the most effective costumes for the project. This could mean anything from drawing and overseeing the manufacturing of space suits, to going on a shopping trip to the mall or a thrift store, or visiting a costume house and renting historically accurate formal wear for an 1800s grand ball. On a micro-budget project, the costume designer might meet an actor at their home to rummage through their closet. If costumes are manufactured it's a long process. First there is the actual design, then a pattern is made, fabric chosen, tailors employed, fittings are made on the actor, and a final version of that piece of wardrobe is born. If the film is contemporary, the designer might still have a costume created or the costume designer takes the actors on a shopping trip, or visits the actor at home and together they rustle through the closets. It depends upon the film genre (rom-com, noir, drama, etc.), the period (future, current, Reformation), on the designer, and on the ever-present limitations of the budget.

Like the production designer, the costume designer is both the creative head of the department and the administrative chief. The costume designer finds or alters or creates the costumes that fit the mood, the style, and suit the cast, while supporting the director's storytelling vision. A costume designer usually has his or her own crew, a group of folks who work with them on everything they do for years—or until someone filling a subordinate role has a chance to move up to a higher tier of command. (Then they, in turn, begin to assemble their own team.)

The costume department on a micro-budget contemporary project might consist of only one person. On a lower budget film like *Get Out*, according to IMDb, there was a costume designer, a supervisor, a key costumer, an assistant costume designer, two costume assistants, and a seamstress. On the series *Downton Abbey* there was a designer, a supervisor, costumers, and assistants (who might also act as researchers). Much of the wardrobe on *Downton* was rented from a costume house, but it had to be historically correct—down to the undergarments worn beneath the wardrobe. *Wonder Woman* and projects of that size and type will have more costumers, buyers, costume propmakers, and modelers. *Dunkirk*, in addition to the usual crew, had a concept artist, a textile artist, and an ager/dyer. Whether the costume crew is tiny or an entire troop, the job of the costume department doesn't change. The actors must be dressed in the appropriate clothing, and the choice of materials, style, and color must enhance the story.

Once again, an interesting example is *Almost Famous*. The costume designer is dealing with a style that is period but still fresh in our collective memory. It could have been very easy to get wrong or ridiculous, but the costume designer, Betsy Heiman, gets the population of rock bands, groupies, fans, hip journalists, and regular people just right. They aren't caricatures, and their truthfulness helps us slide right into the world.

In *The Devil Wears Prada*, a film that is set in the fast-paced and frenetic world of fashion publishing, the lead character, Andy Sachs, is a friendly, earnest, intelligent assistant. She's an aspiring journalist who begins her journey as just-graduated-from-a-good-school nice girl. Style, particularly the hyper-stylized style of *Runway*, where she works, is not only not important to Andy, it's something she finds faintly comical. She is introduced to us as a girl dressed like a college student. Cable-knit sweater, wool skirt, sturdy shoes. The filmmakers (and the novel upon which the film is based) stayed close to realism. Andy's outfits, though on the frumpy side, say a lot about who she is. Attractive but not outstanding, a little awkward but not anyone who'd be out of place in "civilian" (non-high fashion) suburban life. But this is the big time in the biggest media city. Over the course of the film, Andy is transformed, and as she becomes more determined to succeed, she changes her clothing, her hair, her make-up, and even her walk becomes more glamorous and more confident. The transformation sequence is striking in its speed and its efficiency. We understand that Andy has crossed a line.

In 2015's *Five Hundred Days of Summer*, the object of Joseph Gordon Levitt's affection is the pixyish Summer. Levitt's character Tom is pretty much always dressed for work. He's serious. Summer wears flowery, flowy dresses that are pretty, lacy, and even a little "little-girlish." She wears ribbons in her hair. Even in the musical scene, when he's overcome with delight about his new love, Levitt's tie is only loosened a little. In the dance scene, everyone other than Levitt is dressed in shades of blue. Levitt, in his white shirt and dark vest, stands out. He feels different—he is different. But not different enough. Summer is a free spirit. The relationship is not going to work. When Tom meets Autumn (we presume she's his real soul mate) she wears a dark blouse, she looks like an adult—and she is dressed for business.

More recently, we have *Get Out*, where Chris, a black man, goes off with Rose, his white girlfriend, to her wealthy parents' country house. Chris is educated, a successful photographer. He dresses the role of an urban twenty-something visual artist. Work shirts, hoodies, subdued colors. Rose wears the uniform of the preppy Northeasterner. Their style is casual, comfortable, and somewhat similar in tone and type, lots of blue and gray. We immediately believe that they're a couple—that these two people look right together.

We know that *Ladybird* is a bit of an outsider who seems not to care about how she looks—but of course she does. She looks like she shops at thrift shops, not the mall. Her clothes are boyish. She's not quite comfortable with herself as a young woman but she does know she doesn't want to be exactly like the girls she's growing up with in Sacramento.

Rachel Kunin, costume designer on TV's *Jane The Virgin*, *Longmire*, the re-boot of *Dallas*, *The Good Guys*, *Three Rivers*, *The Ex List*, and many other series, started as an intern in the costume department for legendary producer Roger Corman and fell in love with the costume department. She says, "the minute I started, I knew I'd found my people."

Rachel Kunin

The Process

I do a read through and I'm coming up with ideas, I want to see what their arc is, how the characters change over the course of the script. In really good writing, the clues are subtle. If it's bad writing, they aren't there at all.

On a TV series, you're looking at the tone to the entire show. In television the character analysis is always there and present but it's broad strokes. It's different on a feature, where there's a beginning, middle, and end and you're pitching the character's style or taste. On a feature I have the full arc of the character and I can really dive in. You can get a little more detailed in your character analysis. If *Jane The Virgin* was a movie, she'd go from being a virgin to not being a virgin to getting married to her husband dying and then to being with someone else. You'd have all that information in a single shooting period. She would go from a little innocent and you'd know what you're heading toward, so you'd design heading toward something. For television she's done all of that, but she's had three years to do it. It's a more gradual character evolution. Since you don't know where your character is heading, that's the challenge, to make it seamless and consistent.

The Team

On my team for the series, there's a costume supervisor who manages the department. She breaks down the script, we do the budget together. I have a key costumer who runs the wardrobe trailer. She is the person who gives the costume to the actor. There's also a set costumer who is there to make sure that the person who is on set is wearing the right thing the right way. And If we shoot it again three months from then it will still be the right way, so the collar is inside the lapel, three buttons are open vs. it's all buttoned up. There's also a cutter/fitter, who does alterations. They are responsible for cutting the fabric and fitting, so it looks the way the designer wants it to look. They do all of the alternations or make pieces to order. And there's a shopper, for when I can't do all of the shopping.

On the show, it's contemporary but we also have a character who is in a tele-novella, and we also have magical realism. The character of Jane has so many changes—in one episode typically ten but it's gone up to 25 for maybe one or two episodes—and of course, there are the other characters. I consider myself to be a "method" costume designer, meaning I really try to shop where the character would shop.

I think of what I do as being a tool for the actor as well as being part of the painting of the picture. There's the painting and the clothes are just part of that person who is in the painting. That person has to wear them, has to act in them. It's their performance.

In my experience, for the visual design—I start with the director (on a feature) or the showrunner (the head writing producer on a series). Visuals can be distracting in a bad way but when they enhance a character, the costumes can add so much and be so good. So, I have that conversation. I can guide but it's really their vision.

One of the important things to keep in mind is that you can't deal with people's personal taste. It has to always be about this character, in this movie.

Vanessa Vogel has been a costume designer, an assistant costume designer, costume supervisor, and wardrobe supervisor on feature films, working with directors as distinguished as Gus Van Sant (*Good Will Hunting*, *My Own Private Idaho*, *Psycho*), Curtis Hanson (*Wonder Boys*), Nick Cassavetes (*John Q*), and Nicole Holofcener (*Lovely and Amazing*).

Vanessa Vogel: Character First

You read the script as if you were reading any piece of literature. Then you picture the character—who is it, what's going to work for them? A lot of times, there's a type, there's the young ingénue. And there's the hero. You read a lot of scripts that are the same thing over and over and you think, how am I going to make this different? You have to visualize the story. Sometimes you get great characters and you have the chance to really hone your stuff.

If you look back at a television series like *Friends*, because of the cast, the costuming is really important. There are a lot of characters and you have to differentiate them. They were sort of the icons of the Nineties. You get their personalities from the dialogue—this one's the ditsy one, this is the brainy one. Before you know who the actors are, you have to cast it in your head. You're making your own movie, that's the fun part of it. For that show (which is a good example because everybody's seen it), think of Phoebe. How would you convey the ditsy-ness? She wore a lot of odd prints, put odd things together. She was the character who would experiment with her clothes, in contrast with the other two. There's always the one weird character who has the most fun with their costumes.

Then there's the research. When you're doing research, that's when you start to struggle. Maybe you're looking for photos of drug addicts on the street in Seattle.

You have to find those images to help set the tone and hope the director will look at those and use them as a reference and move in that direction because you want that authenticity.

You might have your own concepts and you hope everyone agrees. But you have to be a collaborator. There are so many people you have to collaborate with—the director, the actors, the production designer, sometimes the cinematographer. You have to be a person who thrives on that. You can't be beholden to one thing, to your own idea. You have to be able to just move on to the next idea.

When you're starting on a project, you have an overall design concept but then the big concept shrinks to the minutiae of finding every piece, then to every piece as it is fitted on the actor. You're finding pieces. You may have to have 50 choices of each piece to find the perfect piece. You go through three or four racks of clothing to get those few perfect pieces. Then you might choose fabrics to remake them. In *My Own Private Idaho*, everything was from a thrift shop. Everything had a story. In *Wonder Boys*, we needed the perfect pink bathrobe. We had dozens of choices of pink bathrobes. Finding that one perfect piece, no matter how you're going to alter it— you know it when you see it. Maybe you know that little Seventies shoulder does the job, maybe it makes the character look evil. And then you go back to your research at the end of the movie, and you realize these choices really do go back to the research, they're not random, whether you realized it when you found the piece or not. Research is the foundation.

On *Lovely and Amazing*, when I read the script, the characters were ordinary, neurotic LA people, and it was going to have to be a very subtle thing. There's nothing in that movie that is particularly styled, it's very realistic. My research was, I went to the West Side [of LA] where the characters lived and took pictures of people. But when you work with a director like Nicole [Holofcener], the characters grow really easily over the course of the fittings. She was very specific. I went to the actor's houses. I brought the majority of the costumes, but they also used some of their own clothes.

You want to build up the actor's trust. You discuss the concepts with the actors because that trust is the most important thing. You want to give them options. You want them to be comfortable. The most important thing is to get the actors to look believable in their part, where you don't notice the costume. Ultimately the movie is based on what the actor is doing, and you're supporting it.

The One Most Important Thing People Should Know about Being a Costume Designer?

It's a strange combination of skills. You have to be a great observer of reality. You have to be a great people watcher. Everybody is so self-involved, it's hard to look at the world as an observer but that's what you have to do. Go to a café. Take pictures. Who do you think is interesting and looks like they have an interesting story?

But maybe the most important thing is, you have to realize that costume design has nothing at all to do with fashion. It only has to do with storytelling.

Props

Property is anything and everything an actor holds or physically uses. The property master (or propmaster) is a department head, and not part of the art department. The property master usually has one or several assistants, depending upon the scale of the project. If there are police or soldiers in a scene, the property master is responsible for the gun belts and holsters and works with an armorer who obtains and supervises the use of weapons, and a special effects person and stunt coordinator, so that everything is safe, consistent, and can be photographed effectively.

Props reveal character and push the narrative forward. A character is nervous, unsettled. What do they play with while they're speaking to the detective? A character, a CEO, is a kid at heart. The set decorator and property master (this is worked out between them, depending on what the scripted action is) may decide that on the desktop of the icy glass-and-steel office is a collection of wind-up toys. The actor may, on his or her own, reach for the toy when things go wrong.

What book is the character reading? When they open their wallet to pick up the tab, do we see identifiable prestige credit cards? Are there photos of their dog or cat or an old boyfriend? Does the teenager hug her ragged stuffed rabbit when she's sad, or is it a doll?

Props range from cell phones to magic wands. A script can call for a few flashlights the property master buys at Target, or 50 specially manufactured lightsabers. The props person obsesses about details. If there's a 1950s Marilyn Monroe-type starlet in a scene, she can't brush her hair with a plastic brush from 2018, and when she makes a call, it had better be with a rotary phone that sits on a table. A big trial lawyer's watch shouldn't be a Timex, unless there is a plot point the director wants to communicate about how careful she is with her money. The pro third baseman must have the right glove, which may mean one of a couple of specific brands. A prop person knows how to underscore the traits of a character with things, without being obvious. The right prop can be iconic, and can sell a time and place the same way a location might. There's the sled in *Citizen Kane*, Wonder Woman's "god-killer" sword. You know you're in the Sixties if there are glass Coke bottles and Hula Hoops. Satellite phones tell us the hero's in a remote area, and flip phones say it's the 1990s. A tea pot in a knitted tea cozy feels old-timey, tortoiseshell instead of chrome implies tradition rather than flash. Red Solo cups mean a party.

Like everyone else dealing with the visuals, the props person breaks down the script, researches, shops, rents, and gathers examples of possibilities. There is a "show and tell" with the director (or the producer, depending upon whether it's film or television). The director or producer approves all/some/none (hopefully not none). This goes on until everyone is happy with the choices. It can take months. The selection of one prop might be quick and easy, but another might be so important that the discussion and tweaking of a design can last weeks. Think of *Lord of the Rings* where the entire plot is driven by the ring and its power. In *Edward Scissorhands*, the little pastel blue case the Diane Wiest character carries. In *Almost Famous*, the musical instruments have to be accurate. And think of *Castaway*, where the star had to bond with his only companion, a volleyball.

If there's a wedding or banquet or restaurant scene and waiters are serving, the property master either takes care of the food or works with a food stylist. The props person on a low-budget project may handle the food styling themselves. The stylist's or property master's job in food scenes is to keep the food attractive and safe (if the actors are actually eating the food) or to construct faux food that looks real and delicious, while the lights are hot, the days are long, and things must continue to look (and possibly be) appetizing. In many cases, both the props team and the food stylist will work in concert with set decorating, so the food an actor eats will be real, the roast ducks and turkeys in the middle of the table may be plastic, and the ice cream pie may be colored Styrofoam.

Steven M. Levine has been a property master on over 40 major Hollywood films and series, among them *Cocoon*, *Pee Wee's Big Adventure*, *Tales from the Crypt*, *When a Man Loves a Woman*, *Apollo 13*, *The Cable Guy*, *I Still Know What You Did Last Summer*, and *True Blood*.

Steven M. Levine

What a property master does, the easiest way to describe it is, we provide everything that is handled by the actor. Anything that is being handled with, dealt with, referred to, is a prop. Pieces of ID— for instance if the character is working for NASA and has special ID; license plates; eyeglasses; wedding rings. If the scene is in an operating room, all the surgical instruments. If there's a bank robbery, all the cash, the ink packs. Everything.

When I did *Apollo 13*, I knew nothing at all about the space program. Everything involved, from the flight plans, the stuff at Mission Control, flight books, all the way to the things the astronauts carry from inside to outside the space capsule, it's a tremendous amount of stuff and I had to learn all about it. Sometimes something has to be specifically designed, then you work with a design team, and supervise the manufacturing.

You research in a lot of different ways, it depends on the film. If I had a Wall Street stock broker in a script, the first thing I would do is find a real Wall Street broker to talk to. I would ask, what are the basic tools that you work with every day. What do you carry in your pockets? What's on your computer terminal? If you're researching a cop, the script is not going to tell you everything, you have to put yourself in that situation. Maybe he's from Ohio. You have to research the color of everything the cop in that city or town in Ohio would have, the type of materials everything is made of. What do they use in certain situations? What kind of flashlight?

(continued)

(continued)

Then you have to show that flashlight to the DP to make sure it's bright enough (so it will read—be visible—on camera).

Think about a guy coming into a lawyer's office. What would he have as the client? What would the lawyer have? That's a lot—and it is different every time. I'm not in the least bit minimizing the talent of all the other departments, but there is a difference. Their equipment is basically the same from one movie to the next. But our stuff is subjective. And if you have three producers, two may love what you have, but one might say, "I'd like a cross between this and this"—then you have to find that.

The best time I've had as a prop master on a feature film—my favorite was *Apollo 13*. That was because of the director, Ron Howard. I loved working with him. As a prop master you want a director who knows what he or she wants. Ron Howard knows what he wants. He sees it, he approves it, and he's happy. When a director says, "I'm not sure. I don't know. We'll decide on the day," then you know there will be a problem.

9   Visual Effects and Animation

Effects

Everybody knows what special effects are, right? Maybe. Special effects are practical, meaning that physically something real happens in front of the camera. Special effects happen in a real space, in the context of a scene, and the effects person works in conjunction with the production design, the set decoration, and the location departments—and very often with the stunt unit.

An effects person can be a pyrotechnician using explosives, a generator of snow and rain, and/or a manufacturer and operator of a harness that allows the wearer to fly or hang in the air. An effect can be as minor as a pellet spitting blood when an actor bites down, or the slash on an arm when a sword comes down. When a director talks about effects he or she could also be contemplating stunt air cannons and ramps used for freeway bits where cars crash into each other, hurtle through the air, then burst into flames, courtesy of an effects supervisor. When this kind of thing comes up, the talk often shifts from practical 'on set' effects to digital, computerized visual effects.

Visual Effects and Animation

In these days of mile-long end credits on films listing an abundance of names in the categories of modelers, puppeteers, creature designers, compositors, fabricators, etc. it's easy to assume visual effects (VFX) and special effects (SFX) are different names for the same thing. But VFX are digital and created via computer, sometimes as the actual production is being shot, sometimes during post-production. These days SFX and VFX are often combined so that the basic scene is shot during production and then augmented by VFX during post. When a shot is practical, then combined with one that is CG or done by some other kind of movie magic (rear screen projection, for instance), the shot is called a process shot.

Bill Kroyer is an Oscar-nominated director of animation and computer graphics commercials, short films, movie titles, and theatrical films. Trained in classic hand-drawn animation at the Disney Studio, Bill was one of the first animators to make the leap to computer animation as computer image choreographer on Disney's ground-breaking *TRON*. He pioneered the technique of combining hand-drawn animation with computer animation on projects such as his theatrical animated feature films *FernGully* and *The Last Rainforest*. As senior animation director at Rhythm & Hues Studios he directed animation on scores of commercials and many feature films, including *Cats and Dogs*, *Garfield*, and *Scooby Doo*. Bill is a governor of the Academy of Motion Pictures Arts & Sciences Short Films and Feature Animation Branch.

Bill Kroyer: It All Starts with the Story

The first step in most visualization happens with the storyboard. It's been that way for 80 or 90 years and all the best directors still use storyboards, even if they're going to go out and shoot live or if it's John Favreau going out and doing a high-tech *Lion King*, they start with the storyboard artists.

What do the storyboard artists do? They are the people who start with the words or verbal description or the interrogation of the director, and they are tasked with being the first ones to put the description down on paper as a picture.

The power of the storyboard artist is, with a pencil, you can draw anything. The famous "Roman army coming over the hill?" You can draw the Roman army coming over the hill. If you have to draw a spectacular futuristic city, you can do it. If you have to design a girl's bedroom that gives a clue that she was kidnapped by a serial killer, you literally sit down and draw the little details on the desk that give those clues. The great thing about the storyboard artist is that the pencil offers absolutely no limitations. It is the ideal first step in visualizing.

The first thing the storyboard artist wants to do is understand the story that they're telling. In that respect they are like every person who works on a film. You shouldn't start production design, or visual effects, you shouldn't start any of that until you really understand the visuals you're being asked to create. The only way you can understand the visuals is by knowing, "What is the story I'm trying to tell?" You try to understand what the tone of the movie is. Is this a movie that's going to have relatively traditional cutting and editing and staging, a Wes Anderson, Kubrick kind of thing? Or is this going to be the frenetic Paul Greengrass look? You try to start to put those things together. What's the content and what are some of the fundamental ways I think the director is going to want to think about the visualization?

To me, content of story is the absolute key to this entire process. The irony is that a good writer will never actually write the content. If your dialogue is saying what the movie's about, its guaranteed to be a mediocre movie. What's the story underneath? Great writing describes a combination of the intent and the actions. The actions are not nearly enough to give the audience the complete message. There's the story and the plot. The plot is what's happening, but the story is what it's about. There is a difference between visualizing just what the script says is happening and conveying what it's really about. That's the trick. It's understanding the feeling and the mood and the subtlety and the subtext of what's underneath. That's the most important thing you need to know. Whenever I talk to anyone about a scene I always grill them.

The interesting thing about the live action business is that almost every person who works in live action approaches the film with an abstract idea of what the film is. Everybody has a different idea. In animation, the animator is used to making the entire film, and accounting for everything on paper. They do the production design, they do the characters, they do the posing, the gestures, they do the acting, they can think about the lighting. They're the people who are skilled at instantly taking the verbal or story abstract or concept and coming up with a way to represent that.

That's the advantage that animators have with their films. They board everything. An example—those walk and talk scenes at the end of *Coco*. He sings to Coco and the little visual things in almost every scene are so natural . . . If you watch the movie a few times and you pay attention you discover so much. The movie is 1,300 shots and every one of them is loaded, but it's natural, it doesn't feel contrived in any way. That's the thing about animation. Because we're used to boarding everything we have a chance to sit and really think about it.

"What is your character thinking and feeling right now in the scene?" They say, "well they're saying . . ." But it's not about what they're saying. What they're saying might have nothing to do with what they are thinking and feeling. It may be the exact opposite.

Again this is where the storyboard artist comes in. The way people look, the expressions on their face, what they're doing with their hands, how they're handling the mundane task that's being mentioned in the script, those things are meant to convey a very specific message to the audience. The first thing you have to understand is, exactly what is the scene about? What is the audience supposed to know at the end of the scene? Is it supposed to have

(continued)

(continued)

tension, is it supposed to be humorous? What's the mood of the scene and how's it fitting in to what came before and what came after and how is the information portrayed in the scene balanced with similar information that we're going to convey later? That's really important. Because a lot of times you want to feed it out. It's what we call progressive revelation. Progressive revelation of the visuals is what makes entertainment. You never want to give it away. No storyboard artist is ever going to show the wide shot and give away the point of the scene. They're going to start on the close-up and reveal the reaction to something that's happened, so the audience is going to say, "what did that?" And at some point, they will then reveal the kicker. That's entertainment.

More and more you find that live action people are doing the same thing. If you've ever seen Stephen Spielberg's storyboards, they're very crude, but they are totally clear. You can get what's going on. He absolutely understands where he's going. Although most people probably shy away from a beginning storyboard class because they have no drawing ability, I think it's a great thing to do because it forces you to actually do that process of visualization and take it from words or ideas into pictures.

Working with the Director

Every director is an artist with a different level of vision. In animation, we used to have this thing we said—that the thickness of a line on a character's face could ruin the expression. That's true in all of filmmaking. A light in the wrong place can disrupt it. Anything can take away that magical thing.

James Cameron will look at some scenes 30, 40, 50 times. He'll pick a flower out of a corner because he thinks that the color is distracting. He's a guy who is totally aware of every last thing going on in the frame.

Most of the great filmmakers do things instinctively. Years ago, when I was in college, I saw a movie called *I Never Sang for my Father*, with Gene Hackman, and Melvyn Douglas. We watched the movie and after the movie I said to the director, "I found it very interesting that in every scene where Melvyn Douglas confronted Gene Hackman, you put something between them. In this scene you had a park bench, in this scene you had a kitchen table, this scene you had the island in the kitchen, in this scene you had the mother's coffin. You literally always had them separate, speaking over things." And he looked at me and said, "I didn't realize I did that."

The Intersection of VFX with Production Design

In the ideal world the best scenario is that the production designer has supplied some concept paintings of the major effects moments to give a sense of the scope, the feeling, and whatever it is, whether it's floods or ghosts or explosions.

In the old days, the fun was in being inventive and coming up with ways to make it sell. It's the greatest thing to hear the stories of people like Richard Edlund (multi-Academy Award winning special effects cinematographer of *Star Wars, Battlestar Gallactica, The Empire Strikes Back*), about how they came up with some way to do something. Richard Edlund has a story about taking a Polaroid of the Millennium Falcon, cutting it out and sticking it on a piece of glass and that's how the Millennium Falcon went off into space. An eight-dollar shot and it worked great. In the old days you said, how are we ever going to do this? How are we going to make this storefront in the middle of Chicago blow up? And someone comes up with, why don't we make a Styrofoam store front? Nowadays they wouldn't allow anybody to do that. You'd have to build the Millennium Falcon digitally then light it . . . In a lot of ways now, it's become a trap because the potential of digital effects means you can literally do anything.

An Example of the Story and Design Being Really in Synch?

The opening 25 minutes of *Wall-E* are a revelation. Because that has almost no dialogue at all. Literally every single cut of every single scene conveys a new, essential piece of information and it's all wordless. By the end of the first 25 minutes you completely understand what happened to the world, why it's screwed up, who this little guy is—and you LOVE him. You are so attached to this little guy and what he wants and his longing for love that when the girl shows up, you're into that movie. That's a gem. And the screenplay (which was nominated for an Academy Award) is so perfect because it doesn't miss any of those beats. It describes everything without dialogue. It says, then this happens. Then he sees this. He notices that. In just a couple of words it conveys it . . . The hardest thing to do is simplicity.

10 Why All This Talk about Authenticity?

Art Director Priscilla Elliot

I was doing reshoots for a New York movie on a studio lot in LA, and there's a little subway stop set. They put up the light balls that decorate the exterior staircase that goes from the street-level to the subway station. I said, "Those aren't the balls that are at New York City subway stops." The people on the backlot said, "What do you mean? We use these all the time." But they were white globes, like they have in Paris, not the right colors for what they would be in New York. And the difference when you use the right colors is, it changes from looking like a fake New York street set to a New York street.

Cinematographer Bill Dill

Design has to be authentic. It's not enough for you to say, these are actors doing this and this is a set. It had better be their bedroom . . . A really good actor will walk around and touch everything because it can't be a prop, it's got to be a real book. Their book. They can't lift it and be surprised at its weight. We're really sensitive to that. I learned that from Jim Henson. I shot him for *60 Minutes*. Jim Henson carried Kermit (the Muppet) around in a trumpet case, and he only had two rules. He said, "You can't show Kermit in the case, and you can't show Kermit without his legs." Now, as soon as he came out of the case and had his legs on, Kermit was alive! Kermit watched me do the lighting set up. He's talking, they're talking and Kermit is watching me do the lighting. I said, "Watch your eyes, lights coming on," so what did he do? Just like people do, he looked directly in the light. And I put my hand over (to shade him).

He reacted to the light coming on and the sound man put the mic on and he reacted. We totally bought into the reality of it. Henson explained that. He said, "Look, Kermit is just about five dollars of felt and a ping pong ball cut in half. The thing that makes Kermit real is the fact that he's real to me."

People who make films talk a lot about authenticity. Clearly, everyone knows you're making a movie or television show. Even if it's "based on a true story," it's going to be fictionalized or changed—it's not a piece of journalism. Why then the constant harping on authenticity? Here's a quick example—a prominent actress I worked with once said that she didn't care much about her costumes—but she cared about her character's shoes. She said that when she first met with the costume designer, the piece of wardrobe it was important for her to weigh in on was her character's footwear. She stated very seriously, "I build my character from the shoes up." The only time I've ever heard of this woman being "difficult" was when a costume designer tried to push her into wearing the "wrong" shoes. She said, "It told me that the designer didn't understand my character." "When I have to *be* this person I prepare. I create her story, whether or not it's relevant to the script. I know whether she likes chocolate or peppermint, and how she felt about her first kiss. I know what kind of shoes she'd wear." (In "real life," I never saw this woman in anything but flipflops and ballet slippers. This was not a vanity call.) End of the story: the designer, being an intelligent person and a savvy Hollywood survivor, quickly found a different pair of shoes for the actress to wear.

One more story, because it was a problem so easy to overlook—and so easy to fix. A popular actor was given a messenger bag to carry on his shoulder. The character was meant to be a hip, successful advertising guy. The bag was so great-looking—heavy canvas with leather straps—that the actor asked where he could get one. Perfect for carrying scripts, and this guy was sent a lot of scripts. The problem wasn't that he didn't like the bag. And it wasn't that he didn't think it was right for his character. The problem was, the bag was flat. The actor, known for his lack of star attitude, picked up the bag, said a line—then stopped the scene. He looked at the director and said, "I'm supposed to be a busy copywriter. So busy that I'm late for my meeting with this girl. Why is my bag empty?" That bag was filled in less than 30 seconds. The point is, yes, it's make believe and yes, these people are paid to act. But it's so easy for the whole facade to fall to pieces—a detail that doesn't feel right can even take everyone on the film, and everyone watching the film, out of the world of the film. Then it's very hard to pull them back in.

Cheating Reality

Lee Ross

There's a way to do everything. On *Tombstone*, I made fake cow patties with foam and fake chew spit for the saloon walls. I have one giant road box of sand, there's literally a bucket in there that says "real dirt". I use cat litter. I throw it out on a road for texture.

For rust—I use water-based paint. I did a sunken ship. The under hull of this rusted out ship had to look huge. We built this 85-foot long ship on the stage. At the end of the ship there's a big hole and we did a forced perspective so the ribs of the hull get smaller and smaller and go on forever. I went to a specialty paint seller where they have this very atomized particulate, almost a metal. Activated with a chemical, it oxidizes and literally creates rust.

I also use patina solutions. And for metals there are bluing compounds. I use acrylics to create a pattern that looks effective to camera. I just did an elevator that was supposed to be brass. I made brass out of a metallic powder and acrylics.

Rachel Kunin

I did a series called *Longmire* for television. I was lucky, I could have a full-time ager/dyer. Sometimes things on television look brand new because they are, so you wash them first to make them look more real. There are companies that do stone-washing and you can do a light stone wash, which means that it just softens them up. And you tea dye. [Tea dying is a process used to age textiles, to take the brightness out of cloth, and to stain it, if that's what's needed.] If I want something to look aged, worn, less high-end, I might go for a warm tack [dye]. It will look a little more vintage, more sepia. But let's say there's a lab coat. I don't want it to look dingy. I just don't want it to be so bright. Then I go with a cool dye.

Topstick is double-sided tape which was originally developed for toupees but has been used in the costume department for decades, it's a must have. You use it for last-minute hemming, collars that need to be controlled, a blouse that puckers when someone is moving.

For bangle bracelets you glue them together with museum wax, the same stuff you use for earthquakes. It doesn't damage anything, but it holds things together. That's so there won't be a problem for sound.

Hundreds of tiny details, just to help that authenticity—to keep the audience from suddenly realizing that something isn't quite perfect, and they're at the movie instead of in it.

The Responsibility of a Production Designer

Alec Hammond

We want to take the audience to a place where, even if it is a strip mall in Encino, it feels vibrant and alive with exactly what is happening inside, with exactly the perfect environment, volume, space, juxtaposition, relationships between the characters. It should be the thing that tells you everything that they don't, and sets up the conflict between the people in that space.

To go back to the olden, olden days, an example is *Carnal Knowledge*. Where every single opening that you look through has another opening behind it. The whole movie, there's a window behind a window, there's a door behind a door and a window behind that. You constantly get these framing devices that are used beautifully to compose but also to suggest things that are just beyond, things that people aren't seeing. To suggest them in a way that even if you don't know intellectually that there's a frame behind the frame, it affects you as you're watching the film.

One of the tools we have in cinema is that it's a completely immersive experience. The fourth wall instantly goes away and you're within the movie. You're moving through it either as a character or as a fly on the wall, so you get to experience this world. If we think of the audience experience watching it, in addition to the thing that it's telling us intellectually about the characters, a designer can serve the story throughout in a different way.

Period Films

Line and proportion tell a lot about period. The thickness, thinness, spacing of things. If we're lucky enough to work on shows of different periods, you end up having to be an architectural historian but also a people's history historian. You look at a door and when you understand why it's constructed the way it is—you learn a ton. If you look at the different kinds of early doors, then at more complicated doors you'll learn about how much money there was. You'll learn about what natural resources there were around where that wooden door was made. Nobody thinks about that. It makes

(continued)

(continued)

everything deeper. You can go into that deep dive about how things were built and why they were built that way. Then it also allows you to step out and say, "OK, and does it look good? How does it tell the story?"

The Budget

Alec Hammond

When you start a project and you don't have a lot of money, at the beginning you can't think about the fact that you don't have money. Because there are many different visual strategies you can employ to fully design whatever script has whatever action and whatever director's vision—if you go back to what is fundamentally important about the design in relation to what visual story you're telling and how. And you don't worry about, "Oh my God, I only have $400." "Or Oh my God, I only have $1,000, or I have $5"—or I have none. You have to set up what is the visual story and how are you going to tell it. Obviously, there are financial ramifications for that. I was just working on a $150 million movie and we had CG characters and it was (set) in a different world and we had to design everything. Can you do that with zero dollars? I don't know that I would try. But I started that design the same way I started *Donnie Darko*, which is, what is the script about and what is the fundamental thing that you're trying to design?

The Contender, which I did years ago is a good example. It's about the first woman to become Vice President of the United States. There's tons of stuff that happens in that film. There's 30 speaking roles. At the end of the day, though, that movie is about personal sacrifice for a larger ideal. That is what that movie is about. Every single thing in that film revolves around that. If you come up with what is the beating heart of that script, the Jodie Foster beautiful idea, then that I can design. I'm not worried about the Oval Office. I'm not worried about the Senate Hearing Room. I'm worried about the visual environments that supplement and help the idea of personal sacrifice in relationship to a larger ideal. When you do that, it doesn't matter what's (literally) on the page. I know the writer wrote "Arlington Cemetery." But it's the idea. In terms of Arlington Cemetery, we built it for no money. We went and got a class in Civil Engineering Surveying at Virginia Commonwealth University to come out and make their final project the laying out of a thousand tombstones. We had no money to make the tombstones, so we cut and shaped white foam. It cost $1,000. I was there with them for three weekends nailing pieces of rebar into the ground which we got donated. None of the headstones had any names on them but it didn't matter. This character was a woman who was thinking about her place in the larger idea. She is willing to give up being the first female in the history of the United States to become Vice President because there are things that are more important. She stood up for her principles. Having that scene set amidst those who have sacrificed for principles and even more than that, in a military cemetery where the generals and the privates have exactly the same gravestone, everybody is the same in death, all of those ideas went to it being the right place, so we said, great. We'll figure out a way to do it. *But* if you don't have the idea that "that's what the movie is about," that's what the design pivots around . . . then you don't have any strategy.

Same Setting, Different Problem

After *Flightplan* and *Nonstop* I became the airplane person because I think they're the only two nose-to-tail aircrafts people have done completely from scratch, that I recall. I thought it was great when I got hired to do it the second time because I learned a lot during *Flightplan.* We came up with a lot of solutions that hadn't been done before and we came up with ways to shoot an airplane. Here's an example of when the base idea of those two films is almost completely diametrically opposed. In *Flightplan*, the way the visual world has to justify the base concept of the film is that plane has to be large-ass and complicated enough that a reasonable person could believe that a little girl could get lost (on an airplane in flight). If it doesn't do that basic storytelling function, game over. You walk into that plane and after the first three shots, if later on, as she actually disappears, you think there's no way they wouldn't have found her by now, you're dead. The movie's over. You've sapped it of all of its action.

In *Nonstop,* it's exactly the opposite problem. It's Liam Neeson. Somebody threatens to blow up the plane in mid-air and he has to find out who it is. You walk into this plane and from one vantage point you have to see every single one of the possible suspects because if you don't and you think someone could be hiding in

(continued)

(continued)

a bathroom, again, game over. Because then the question is why aren't we looking rather than (the movie's intention of): here are the likely contestants for blowing up the plane. Which one is it? In some ways the set had many things in common, but those two things were completely different.

Outside of that *Flightplan* . . . had an extra layer of visual metaphor. In some ways that entire film is an externalization of Jodie Foster's character's internal emotional state. When we're in Berlin, it's a frozen, empty, unpopulated wasteland. At the beginning of that film, her husband has just committed suicide. The only other person in her life is her little daughter, and they're leaving. They're fleeing someplace that resembles the inside of her mind. That was a directorial idea, and it was a brilliant one. And that was designable. For me, it was "Oh my God, awesome! Now I can design." Completely 100 percent design.

He (the director) gave me the strategy to design, because it was such a clear expression of the beginning part of the film. And then the same cool tones, the same clean lines, the same sophisticated design sensibility was then applied to the plane because Jodie, being who she is and who that character is, was one of the designers of the aircraft. So you got to have the aircraft, in a way, become her body, the outward expression of who she was. The other thing we were able to do with that plane, which was nice because it was so large, we were able to change the character of the rooms you were in to match the action of the scene. Because you have a completely contained world, you have to use that containment to your advantage. There's a moment where she (Jodie Foster's character) is losing her mind and she thinks that all of the flight attendants think she's made up that she has a daughter. They don't have any record of her. We created a galley that was completely and utterly white. We over-lit it and there are no geographical markings, there's nothing to set where you are, she's floating in the middle of space. There's a very eerie quality to it. That was visual strategy. When you're matching it with what the scene is, just augmenting it. Because when you come out of the theater whistling the scenery you're in trouble. It's about the story that's happening in front of the scenery. Sometimes we as the designers forget that.

We got to do a lot of fun visual stuff in that because of the contained quality of it. I could talk all day about the difference between *Nonstop* and *Flightplan* but a really good example is, Jodie Foster is, I don't know, about five feet two and Liam Neeson is about six feet four or five. There couldn't be two more different sized actors I'd ever worked with to design the same (kind of) basic tube to fit both of them. For camera you want to [be able to] go between the seats and the overhead bins but as soon as you have a 30-inch camera between a seat and the bin, that bin for her to put her luggage in is really high. If the director wants her to put her luggage in, are you going to bring a step stool? And with Liam, the airplane has to swell. He's got to pass by the cart that comes down the center aisle. So somewhere in between the super-creative externalization of Jodie's internal state and the very practical—she's got to be able to reach into the overhead bin—is where the production designer lives and breathes. It's the bridge between the creative and the practical. Our job is to do both. If you have an airplane that is perfect in terms of what it looks like and all of a sudden Jodie can't put her luggage in the overhead bin you've failed. It doesn't work. The verisimilitude of looking at that plane becomes off. People won't necessarily recognize it initially but it will affect them, so you have to thread that needle very closely. That's why in some ways it's very much a craft. It's a collaborative art form but it can also be very much a technical exercise. The art part is the most important, but you don't get to do it very long unless you're good at the practical.

Section 3

Your Low Budget Film or TV Project

11 Putting All This Together

Now we know that everybody breaks down a script. Everybody cares about the story and the characters, and everybody does their homework (research). How does this apply to you? You aren't making a big budget extravaganza. You're trying to make an indie movie or student film. You have no money and a tiny crew, but you want to have a coherent design.

On a low or no budget movie, the team is smaller. Clearly, on a bigger budget there are dozens of people involved in the process of storytelling through design, and they all have to work together effectively. There may at times be conflicts between certain disciplines, but everyone seems to be comfortable with some degree of conflict, in part because there is a clearly defined hierarchy.

One of the ironies of working on films with big budgets vs. small indie projects is that on big films, which are highly unionized, the lines of communication are not only clear, they're drawn in indelible contractual ink. People help each other but are careful to work within the occupational boundaries proscribed by their unions. On smaller films, the good and the bad is that people often wear more than one hat. They take on multiple areas of responsibility. If you are a department of one, sometimes you are so overwhelmed that you just want to get things done. You think you can't spend a lot of time and energy on the thinking/discussion part of the process. WRONG. You've got a huge amount of ground to cover—but in the end the point is that you want a well-designed movie, or why put yourself through any of it?

On a low or no budget movie, the positives of working with a tiny team are:

a) easier, more direct lines of communication—you usually don't have to go through tons of channels and political red tape to get answers;
b) because one person is fulfilling more than one set of responsibilities, often the team is more able to turn and re-work things when they need to be altered;
c) although there is far less money, usually only one or two people are spending and tracking the money, so there are fewer surprises.

Rather than mourn your lack of budget and manpower, figure out the logical way to combine positions.

How It Can Work

The production designer can (and on very small projects often does) take on the responsibilities of art director, set designer, props, and graphics. These positions are often combined because they require a sense of design and the ability to draw—or at least to draw well enough that what is drawn is recognizable. In this case, the overworked production designer takes it all on. On a low budget film, the production designer is always faced with the age-old filmmaking challenge—cheap, fast, or good. On low budget projects (this includes student films, where the budgets for art are notoriously low), the designer is expected to deliver all three.

Often, the designer also takes on the responsibilities of not only being the construction coordinator but the entire construction crew. Not all designers know how to build well or quickly. It's essential that whoever is working with tools, ladders, lifts, etc. understands how to do these things safely or you'll have a much bigger problem than not having the set ready in time. If you're planning your crew, it's safer and more reasonable to assume the designer will design, but not necessarily construct. That's a conversation you'll have to have. Exceptional design is more important and often less expensive than building. Sometimes you may have to find rather than build the sets, but you can alter them so that they are perfect. Unless the designer has lots of help, think about either finding a construction person or finding practical locations that the designer can turn into something brilliant.

Saying Yes

If you are the designer on a low budget project, your biggest concern is usually not whether you can handle the creative part of the job. It's being in two places at once. As the designer you may be looking for locations while at the same time shopping for dressing or aging a wall. The designer who finds himself or herself in these situations can be tempted to be the hero and suck it up. You might say, "I can handle it all," but it's your responsibility to be knowledgeable enough to do the homework and honest enough to come clean about what can and can't be done with the time and the money allotted. Your desire to sacrifice yourself to make everyone else happy can easily turn into you taking the brunt of things not being as good as they can be, or not ready when they should be—because you said you could do it!

Expectations are everything. If you say you can do something, people count on that. If you first go through the process of figuring out whether you can get things done with what (and who) you've got, then you let the producer and director know that what they want isn't feasible, then you're being professional. You should always come up with alternatives, and you absolutely must let them know in plenty of time.

Something to remember: for anyone who is not a member of the art department, the art department is one of the least understood departments on a project. If you haven't done it, you don't know how complicated it can be to build and paint a structure and make it look good. You don't know how much it costs to buy nails and lumber. If you're a designer on a very low budget project, you can pretty much count on the fact that no one else on the crew has any idea what it will take to create, erect, and dress a set, or to make good-looking signage. It's almost always time and money or time or money. If they don't want to hear the realities of what is required, you may not want the job. This doesn't mean you become the "no" or "not my job" person. You should be the source of suggestions and solutions. But if there is no place to meet in the middle, you may want to pass. Again, don't agree to anything you can't do, and don't decide at the last minute that you can't do whatever you agreed to. That's unprofessional.

If you are the designer-decorator-costume person, try to look at each step of what needs to be done. What part of the job is creative and therefore really your purview, and what is administrative? One of the priorities for a designer under these circumstances is to speak up if you need help. Sometimes that help may just be an extra PA to run errands, to pick up materials, or dressing. That person can get signatures for a location if they are needed. That person can hold a ladder during construction. That person can be trained to help with on-set dressing continuity, depending on how tiny the project.

What doesn't usually work is the production designer as location manager. The designer should scout with the location manager, guide them, stand there beside them, but the designer should not be the location manager. It's a different skill set. Location managers are persuaders, negotiators, budgeters, schedulers, facilitators, and they deal with contracts and fees and insurance. On small films, the financial and logistical location responsibilities should fall on the shoulders of the production manager or line producer. This doesn't mean that the designer should not accompany the location person on every trip involving design and decision making about creative matters, but once the location has been chosen, it's time for the art department to get back to art and away from deal-making and paperwork. They should start thinking about how the locations will be painted and dressed.

What *might* work on a tiny project would be the designer taking charge of the costumes. This should only happen in the selection stage. The designer shouldn't be responsible for getting the actors in and out of wardrobe. A tactful PA can do that. You'd do better having someone do triple duty as hair/make-up and wardrobe than sticking the designer with getting cast camera ready. Again, because people who don't do the job tend not to understand the job, it isn't unusual for people to stack responsibilities on those jobs. In their minds it makes sense because it's about the look of the actors. But if you're the designer and you're moving furniture and wall-coverings into place, hanging curtains, tending to greenery, and tracking prop rentals so you aren't charged for extra days, the last thing you want is to be tethered to the dressing room making sure the actors feel good. Learn to teach people what you do!

If you are on a budget so tight that you can't pay help to alleviate the load, seek out nearby schools or local theaters. Many people who now have big credits started in art or film schools or in theater programs. They have the transferrable skills you'll need and they are used to working on shoe-string budgets. They can build or paint or handle costumes and create graphics. They may be great additions to the crew. You'll want to work with them again because you speak the same language and have the same passion for storytelling.

Clear communication is the key to success at all levels but especially when you're dealing with a low budget project. Communication isn't just letting people know what you want them to do. It's asking them for suggestions. People are doing three things at once, and they're in a hurry. What you lack in funds you must spend in prep time, careful attention to detail, and in sitting down and going through everything. This applies to experienced crews with a generous budget as well as those with no money. If you listen and are open to input you may find that a local PA knows more about a town or a place where something can be found than you do. Harness their enthusiasm. Make sure there are no questions. Check back. Root for the people on your crew. Get them on board. Don't take advantage of them. Get down in the dirt with them so they don't feel used. Even if they are volunteers, they should feel that they are part of the family. If someone has a concern, follow through.

Be accessible. And if anyone has even the slightest hint of a worry about safety, stop what you're doing and give it weight. Film locations and stages can be treacherous. There's electricity, there's construction, there are myriad ways to get hurt—or worse. You MUST take that seriously. Nothing matters more. Don't be afraid to halt everything to investigate, and don't let anyone scoff.

When you are collaborating with the director or producer, be honest. Be straightforward and don't assume anything. Let them know what you're going to do and the resources you need to do it (including time, which is often the most important resource of all, especially when you are working with people who are changing their minds at the last minute). Show them anything you can. If you can't show them, describe things. Diagrams don't work if the person you're working with isn't good at looking at them and making the leap from diagram or blueprint to life-sized three dimensions. Your idea of small and theirs may not be the same.

Ever see the comedy *Spinal Tap*? The over-the-top rock and roll band thinks they are getting a towering 18-foot tall replica of Stonehenge as set dressing for their concert stage. Instead, the person responsible writes down "inches" instead of "feet," and the band is publicly humiliated—again.

Alec Hammond

When you're a young designer you may be the head of four or five departments and just the physical practical work of getting something to screen can take up all your time. Your actual time for thinking and experimenting on how you design the film, and how you discuss something with a director about designing the film, is something that may take up 2 percent of your time on a small independent movie. And that's the part (the discussion) that takes the most practice.

12 Planning Your Project
Building It, Finding It, or Both?

This chapter is a walk through the general process of what will/should happen on a film, whether on a large scale or on a very small independent film.

> **Production Designer John Chichester's Broad Outline of the Design Development Procedure**
>
> 1 Read and break down the script. List every set. Every set, interior or exterior.
> 2 Research the subject of the script.
> 3 Make a preliminary determination with the producer and director as to which sets are to be locations, which are to be built, and the extent to which locations are to be modified, as best you can.

Breaking Down a Script

How exactly do you break down a script?

Every scene is assigned a number and, as you probably know, they run in order so that Scene 2 follows Scene 1, Scene 3 follows Scene 2, and on and on. You may not know, however, what warrants a new scene number, so here are reasons the scene number will change.

A new scene number is assigned when there is a change of location. A change of location can be from Interior (INT.) to Exterior (EXT.) of the same building, but it's also a change of location even if the set moves from INT. Ann's house—living room to INT. Ann's house—bedroom.

Here's an example:

Let's say the script opens with the slug line:

EXT. Chicago City Street—Bank Entrance—Day
JILL (23) rushes through the crowded street, late. She is dressed for business, but everything is a little off. Her hair is messy, her blouse is

not fully tucked into the waistband of her slacks. She checks her cell, almost slams into her brother, ALEX, 28, who calmly steadies her then gives her a big bear hug.

CUT TO:
INT. Muldoon's Bar and Grille—Day
Jill and Alex, laughing and sharing photos.

JILL
I can't believe we're finally living in the same city!

We've now gone from Scene 1 (your first set or location, the Exterior of the Chicago Bank Entrance) to Scene 2 (a new slug line, a new location, the Interior of Muldoon's).

To complicate things, as the scene continues, the screenwriter has written:

CUT TO:
INT. Muldoon's Bar and Grille—Evening

A new slug line, the same location. What changed? The time of day. Now we know that Jill and Alex have been sitting in Muldoon's for hours, which leads us to the reason that Scene 2 (the daytime scene) is over, and Scene 3 is beginning.

A new scene number is assigned when there is a change of time or condition. Going from day to evening counts. Even if nothing else changes. Because there will be a lighting change, there may even be a set-dressing change. As it gets darker the Bar and Grille waitstaff might light candles on the tables, put tablecloths out, or the inside lights are on—and if you can see out the windows, it will be dark. If the script sets out to tell you that Jill and Alex have talked the hours away, there's a reason a point is being made of that. As a visual storyteller, you'll want to show it. The slug line might change from day to night, night to day, one location to another, one time period to another, or one weather condition to another. The screenwriter could have written that while Jill and Alex catch up inside, through the window we see it's begun to rain or snow. That would a new scene. A scene is intended to be a single filmable unit of the script.

Your break down, whether for locations, art, or set dressing, would read:

1   Ext. Chicago City Street—outside Bank Building—Day.
2   Int. Muldoon's Bar and Grille—Day.
3   Int. Muldoon's Bar and Grille—Evening.

As you go through the script you would note every scene, every location, day or night, and every set within that scene. For instance, if in Scene 3 Jill excuses herself to go to the Ladies' Room at Muldoon's and we follow her in to see her standing at the mirror—that's a new scene, Scene 4. It's a new set. Even if the script reads Muldoon's, your set list would read, INT. Muldoon's—Ladies' Room—Night. Because the Ladies' Room might be shot in an entirely different location, or on another day.

The next thing you need for your break down is a sense of how long you will be shooting in each set. If you're a location person, you need to know how long you'll need to rent the location. You may need a location for four days. When you find the perfect place, maybe the owner says you can use the interior for only three consecutive days, a Monday, a Tuesday, and a Wednesday. Can you move the scenes that are currently scheduled for the fourth day? Can they be in the parking lot or on the street outside, so you still see the established building? Would that work? What about using the hall outside the community room? The director, the designer, and the assistant director, who has done the schedule, would be involved with this part of the discussion.

Another consideration, if you're the production designer. If you see you're in Muldoon's for a total of 13 pages of the script and a lot of action happens there, you'll want to decide with the director whether finding a practical (real) location is the right way to go. Maybe it would be better to build Muldoon's on a sound stage or in a warehouse. Maybe you'll want to find the Bar and Grille but build the Ladies' Room.

There are several build vs. find pros and cons coming up but, for now, take a look at those 13 pages. If there is already a schedule, you'll know how long the director intends to take to shoot those pages. It could be four days if the only thing that's happening is dialogue. If while Jill and Alex are sitting and reminiscing, and day turns into night, there is some more complex action—interaction with an unexpected old friend, a conflict between other bar patrons, a song and dance, or a fight, those 13 pages could easily take seven days to shoot. Shooting for a film averages somewhere between two and three pages per day but that's an average. It's all about what is happening in the scene and what kind of shots the director intends for those 13 pages. That will affect the lighting change-overs. One of the factors that surprises most filmmakers accustomed to very small scale or student films is how long everything takes to do correctly and effectively. If you are taking on the location responsibilities, this information is part of your process. You're asking people to lend you or rent you their property and even if they do want to help or make that money, they'll want to know how long they'll be inconvenienced.

Breaking down the script also solidifies things in your mind. As a location manager, designer, or decorator, you'll read the screenplay first for story and an overall impression of mood, theme, and the characters. In other words, you're the audience. When you read a screenplay the second time you notice the little things you'll need—you're reading as a film-maker. Hopefully, you'll visualize the story as written and think about the geography of the sets. Is Scene 2 inside or outside, and what if the characters start outside then walk through a door? That may be broken up into two scenes later, or it may be shot as a continuous scene, meaning that the camera will start exterior and move interior with the actors.

If you are the director and acting as your own designer, or you're the designer working with a director, it will be great to have a conversation about the intended camera movement in the location. Why do this so early in the process? First, you'll need to have an idea how much space is needed in order to find or dismiss potential locations. Second, the dramatic content and the way a scene is shot are tightly interwoven. Maybe the entire idea of the Jill and Alex scene in Muldoon's is that one of them is being stalked. In the scene, the plan is to make the audience aware that someone is watching the pair. Although we aren't supposed to know why at this point, the director's intention is for us to feel uneasy. Maybe the director will position the camera so there's a POV (Point of View) shot through the doorway of an adjoining space in the Bar and Grille. Or maybe the camera will be hand-held (meaning not mounted on a dolly or a tripod but on the camera operator's shoulder.) When edited, a hand-held shot is another way of establishing someone else's POV because it's a little shakier and might mimic the way it would feel if we're seeing the two through someone else's eyes. It also is used for a more documentary/news/real feel. Maybe it's a Steadicam shot. This means that the camera operator is wearing a specially balanced harness that stabilizes the camera, and they themselves are holding it, rather than the camera being mounted on a tripod or a dolly. The operator is moving along (sometimes behind) the actor. The use of this kind of shot can give the audience the feeling of being *with* the subjects of the shot and being part of the action rather than watching and being a passive observer. How much territory does the director plan to traverse for the stalker shots? If none, then the camera will be placed at a distance where the stationery POV shot will work. But if the plan is to follow the actors from exterior to interior and walk with them, maybe more space is needed. The plan for the shot often dictates the size and shape needed for the location. Sometimes the director unfortunately doesn't have a plan or will adapt the plan to the space. Then a bigger space is better because it opens up the possibilities.

Back to your set list. You'll have interior/exterior, day or night, the script name of the location—and then your notes about the action that takes place in that scene. The notes can be brief. (Stalker POV) or (conversation) or (desperate search). But you'll have that information ever-lurking in the back of your mind, as you scout your locations, or dress them, as you meet with your team and with other teams. You'll be amazed at how that will serve you when creating your distinct and appropriate visual design. The script is your bible and everything else will follow.

Researching the Subject of the Script

Research doesn't have to mean looking at historical artwork or what robes were all the rage in turn-of-the-century Japan. This isn't school. Research is coming up with the character's backstory, taste, and level of education through hints in the screenplay, even if you're the only one who has that in your head while you or your team is coming up with ideas. Would this person have a kitchen with bright red walls? Would anyone? Your character might live in the big city but be a small-town kid at heart. You job is to supply clues that reveal character, so that the impression creeps up on the audience rather than broadcasts the news.

Your film is a comedy about an uptight, single 35-ish year-old renowned law professor living in New England. She trades houses for the summer with a free-wheeling, cynical, type-A 35-ish movie executive in Los Angeles. Through a series of misunderstandings and complications, the professor tries on the movie executive's business and love life and the exec teaches the professor's classes and they fall for each other. The film is basically a classic rom-com fairy tale about figuring out what and who you want in life, and realizing that you are the one standing in your own way. We've seen variations on this story dozens of times.

Research in this case may start with, what is the life of this kind of celebrated professor? How many hours per day do they spend on campus vs. at their desk at home? Do they travel to lecture at other universities around the country or around the globe? Are they like doctors and lawyers, displaying their diplomas on their office walls? What do they wear when they're working? At some schools, the law school professors dress as if they're addressing a jury or a team of investment bankers, at some they wear jeans. What about at your character's school? If the school is made up, it's probably based on someplace real. If the school is right in the city, the law school professors may dress up and their office may be more formal and lawyerly than if the school is in the country. That should start the thought process of: where in New England? Is it clear in the script? Are they in Boston, Massachusetts or Storrs, Connecticut? And does the professor walk to work, or commute on the train, or drive in heavy traffic? This is all a conversation with the director and the director may have definite ideas about it or they may think whatever you come up with is fine. New England could be brownstones and your commuting professor might commute to a woodsy stone cottage near a lake.

More subjects to research: what do professors do when they're not teaching? How do you figure this out? Start with your own experience. Did you go to college and did you have a professor you could call and interview? If not, is there a local college of the type that's in your movie? Get on the phone and start asking questions. Most people are delighted to talk about what they do. If you can't find someone then start asking people you know who they know. Don't wait until the last minute.

This takes time and you'll want to think about things once you have answers. When you get those answers, don't stop—ask more than one person. Ask them for stories about their working lives. The same method will apply to your movie exec. The good thing about some highly visible jobs is that people give interviews and people write books about their professional experiences. Start reading! (I know you're a visual person and trying to make a movie, but I don't know anyone in the industry who doesn't read a lot, whether for pleasure or just for information.)

How much money do your characters make? There's lots of stuff online that lists professions and their average salaries, but average doesn't exactly describe either of your high-level characters. Again, you'll have to read. If the average professor at an Ivy League law school has an income of $150,000, but your character is celebrated and published and a big deal, their income could be more than twice that. Major movie executives' salaries vary hugely—but it is safe to say they will be living pretty well. Especially if you are dealing with a world you don't know much about, you'll want to be sure you get it right because some of the visual decisions that will be made for your characters will realistically be based on their financial circumstances and, if you get it wrong, some of your audience will close their door on the suspension of disbelief that many movies—and particularly rom-coms—depend on. (This doesn't apply to just romantic comedies. I remember sitting in a theater watching a suspense thriller and the heroine, who is not supposed to be wealthy, and whose husband has just been found murdered, unlocks the front door to her very large New York City apartment. As we see this woman in mourning, crying, walking down the hall of a very nice, multiple-room home, the audience began to stir, then to laugh. Someone in the crowd shouted, "Forget the husband! I want the *realtor*!" The entire theater began to laugh. The film-maker had lost the audience over a bad location choice.)

Imagine the lives of these people. Does this professor live in a house, a condo, an apartment? Is it meant for entertaining or is the person more reclusive? (If it's meant for entertaining, there should probably be a big table somewhere.) Regarding the movie executive. Is the executive all flash and Hollywood-ish, or is he a fish out of water in his own life? Does he have stacks of screenplays and novels piled up every place? Posters of films he helped get made? What do we need to know about this person and his life-style? Does he have more than one phone? Maybe he's hyper-organized and his office and home looks as if the maid's just left. Maybe he has two massive flat-screen TVs. Does the executive have an oddball collection that lets you know his inner self? Could this collection be a good fit with a collection the professor has? If the exec is not happy with his own life in Hollywood, maybe his house holds absolutely no clue as to what he does for a living. There could be artwork, sports memorabilia. What if he is a frustrated writer and there are bookcases overflowing with poetry, classic novels, and all sorts of non-movie material, and posters that glorify something other than film.

Once you conference with the director, you may find that he or she is excited with your "clues" as to the characters—or disagrees entirely and has their own take. Either way, that discussion is usually appreciated by the director and ends up in the frame. And whether you go with your concept or with the director's, the audience experience will be enhanced because they'll know more, thus be more invested, even in a sweet little romantic comedy.

Deciding about Locations

Let's decide that our professor is a country mouse, to contrast with the showbiz-ness of the executive. She could live in a quaint, charming house in a gorgeous natural setting. Or she lives in a very cool, historic idiosyncratic brownstone in the heart of Cambridge. She *has* to live in a place that's great in some way for the story to work—otherwise why would the executive want to trade a house in the canyons of the Hollywood hills (or at the beach in Malibu) for the summer?

Those are some of the secondary decisions about locations.

The primary decision is one that combines the creative and the nuts and bolts part of the visual storytelling process—where will the movie be shot? It could be shot in Los Angeles and New England, as written. It could be shot mostly in Los Angeles on location and on stage, but with a few days in New England to get enough footage to be convincing. When you look at your set list, you may be surprised to see that there are fewer true exteriors than you'd think—or there could be lots of walking and talking along the streets of either city, and lots of unquestionable landmarks that are mentioned or used as plot points.

At this stage, a preliminary shooting schedule will have been done by either the production manager or the assistant director and a major question will be, how much of the action takes place in each location? Is it half and half? How much of the action takes place exterior? This is very important because you can fairly easily dress/build an interior to look like somewhere else and, if you're careful and spend some time figuring out what you see out the windows, you're OK.

Business Basics and Design

Let's assume that the screenplay is in good shape. This means that although there may not yet be a final shooting draft (scenes are often rewritten 20 times before they are deemed ready enough), there is a draft that is close to final. The producer, or production company, or studio needs a preliminary budget because the budget total has tremendous impact on how the movie is made, or if it is made at all.

If this is an independent film, everyone has to be clear on how much money has to be raised to prep, shoot, and finish the movie in post-production, and sometimes how much money must be raised for marketing. Whoever is raising the money must approach investors with facts and figures.

If this is a film being produced by an established company, some of the same factors are in play. Companies sometimes have a budgetary range that they "do"—meaning they have a monetary comfort zone. Smaller, and they may not think it's worth their while. Larger, and they worry about profit (although pretty much everybody is worried about profit). The classic formula is: a film must earn the production budget multiplied by 2½ or 3 to break even or get into the black (see a profit). If the production company has an ongoing distribution agreement with a studio for marketing and distribution, they will involve the studio in the money decisions. If their studio or company isn't interested in the film or the budget range, they will re-think. They may look to additional or alternative arrangements for financing. Or they may not make the movie. In any case, they do need a ballpark figure to answer the question of what this thing is going to cost.

Budgets and the Producer and Screenwriter (and Sometimes the Director)

Often, these two are the motor behind the project at this early juncture. They've done the heavy lifting of developing the script. Or the producer found the screenplay, and put up some money to take it around and try to get it fully financed. The producer will want to attach a director and leading cast (have them commit to working on the film) so an attractive finance-able package can be presented. If the screenwriter is also the director, as sometimes is the case, then they will start to go after the star. If they can interest a known actor who has had proven box office success at the appropriate level (indie, small budget, mid-budget), and they can use that actor to obtain a deal for the appropriate distribution platform (cable, theatrical, streaming, or all of them), then they can really start to move. Part of moving ahead includes having an idea of how much money is going to be needed to make the movie—how much they'll need to ask for. That means a first draft (or first pass) of a budget will be necessary.

If you are a writer-director just out of film school or are making your first-ever movie, you probably won't know how to do a real budget on your own, even if you're just looking at $250,000. You'll want to find (at the low end) either someone who studied producing and has been trained to create a professional budget, or (at the high end) a production manager or line producer who has worked on lots of low-budget films to do one for you. If your cousin has made 15 films for Paramount and you are making a project for under a million dollars, they may not be the right person to do this. They're used to thinking and working at a different scale. They may not be as schooled in what can and can't be done at a bargain basement level and how. Although the 'people skills' don't change, the hands-on allocation of resources can be very different.

As mentioned earlier, a budget at this stage is an educated estimate. Often it's done without much input from the people who will have to live with the amounts of money estimated. What this means for the visual design of the project may be that once someone is hired (or volunteers, or interns, depending on the budget) as a production designer, a location manager, a costume designer (or all three), or cinematographer, the plan may change. Money may have to move around from one department to another. Things that were expected are re-thought. Again, although pre-production and discussions are crucial at every budget level, the less money you have, the more time should be spent on them and the more time should be spent looking at story, and what MUST happen and be found or created to make the story work. If you are the production designer on this project, you and everyone in the art and set decoration departments will be constantly prioritizing. If you are a director working with a production designer and they aren't prioritizing, then it's time to talk.

Now Back to Our Rom-Com

Maybe you'll want to build.

Budget plays a major part in the final plan. If you are making a film and you have limited money, do you build on stage or in a warehouse, do you find the location and use it as is, or do you find an existing space and alter it so that it becomes your perfect shooting location? What is the thought process that should go into making this decision?

When the designer meets with the director to show photos, the designer might walk the director through what would be done to make each location work, or the discussion might be why none of the locations work, and there may have to be a different solution. Perhaps the decision should be to build the interiors of one of the houses for maximum scheduling flexibility. Or to find a house in an outlying area of Los Angeles and "New England it up." What about the practicalities of shooting the scenes? What if the DP is noted for working with a jib arm (a piece of equipment that is basically a small crane). The rooms in a practical house might not be big enough to accommodate that. Do you hire someone because you like their style then put them in an environment where they can't do what they do? How much time do you spend in each house? Perhaps the crux of the film is the relationships between the lead characters and their environments and that's how they learn a) who they are, b) who they want to be, and c) that they want to be together. If so, the interiors might be so important that you'll want to be sure that the confined space of a normal room won't adversely affect the blocking (positioning of the actors) or the camera placement.

For the screen, the only thing that matters is what shows, so sets are built to stand, but not to last. They can be skeletons with false fronts.

The building materials are flimsy. There is no ceiling or a removable ceiling because you want to accommodate lighting from above. The walls are removable so that the camera can set up at any angle and a dolly can move freely. Parts of the set can be separated so that you can have the living room space adjoining the hall for a continuous shot, or you can have them separate when the director wants to go in for an angle that might be impossible in a real house with a typically narrow hallway.

So you'll want to build. As a matter of fact, why wouldn't you want to build almost every set? Who needs the trouble of obtaining location shooting permits, restricted hours, obtaining the signature from the resentful people on the block who aren't getting the big rental fees but still are forced to put up with the intrusion of the film? On a constructed set you can control everything.

Not so fast. There are pros and cons to constructed sets, just as there are for shooting practical. Here are some pros for interior sets:

1   You control the light and darkness.
2   You won't get rained, fogged, or frozen out.
3   You have virtually no shooting restrictions involving time, other than your overtime budget.
4   You have easy access to sources of electrical power.
5   You can design, paint, and blow up whatever you want, and it can look the way you want it to.
6   You have space and parking and bathrooms and a place to cater (the work environment plays a large part in morale, and morale has a huge impact on productivity).

Here are some cons:

1   Building usually costs quite a bit more You aren't only paying for the labor and materials it takes to make the set, you're paying for the stage or space that houses the set. Unless special activities are planned or the location is not findable or you're shooting in the location for several days, it's generally less expensive to find someplace real. Building takes time, and time on a film means money. Unless there are specific conditions that prevent the use of an existing location, it can often be preferable financially if your efforts are concentrated on a known entity, a place you can see ahead of time, where there are no surprises.
2   Although you have superior control, you might lose realism. Despite the best work of the design team, sometimes a built set feels like a set. You may not be able to put your finger on what's off. It could be the way the light comes through the windows, or the way the doors shut. But a poorly designed built set can be a bigger miss than a practical

location and can feel like a 1970s or 1980s sit-com apartment, or a stage play. It's not always a tangible thing, but subconsciously the audience can tell, and it takes you out of the story. If you're thinking maybe you can shoot exteriors on a sound stage and solve some of your travel or landscape issues, using green screen and Computer Generated Imagery (CGI), you might be able to do that. That can work, or it can fizzle. Using those tools, when the work is done by experienced people and you have the time to light and shoot the scenes in the painstaking way necessary, it's fabulous. But if you don't have the money or the time or patience, it doesn't work and then has the look of an old monster movie.

3   Finally, there is sometimes an inertia that hits a shooting crew when they are in the same set day after day after day. Theoretically things should be easier and proceed faster, but often the energy level isn't there, maybe because the sense of urgency and moving on isn't hanging over everyone's head. A few days or a week at a time seems to work better. There are exceptions—for example television soap operas and multi-camera sit-coms are always on a stage—but it's something to consider.

More Factors in the Choice of Practical vs. Build

When does the movie, or at least the scene, take place? Current day, the recent past, medieval times, the future? Where are we? The US? Beijing? New Orleans? Are we talking high-end Manhattan, artsy Taos, Las Vegas, Amarillo? Urban, suburban, the Cape Cod shoreline?

Some questions:

1   How important is the location to this story?
2   Does this kind of space even exist?
3   What kind of scenes take place in the set and what is the shooting plan?
4   Are there a lot of scenes that take place in this place? How much shooting time will be spent?

In the television series *Mad Men* we see the evolution of an ad agency, Sterling Cooper & Associates, over several seasons. The series progresses from the early 1960s until 1969. The offices and halls change as styles change. Most seasons the change signals that we're moving ahead in time without the dialogue announcing the shift. Early 1960s conservatism morphs to Kennedy-era youth-focus, then to hip drug-era. The furniture changes, as do the wall and window treatments, and the colors and materials. In one episode, an interior staircase is built between the two floors of the ad agency. For shooting, this creates the opportunity for conversations and activities to be followed from floor to floor, where before that all had to be choreographed for a walk to and from an elevator. This design change (pointed out as part of the new décor of Sterling Cooper), is in keeping both literally and figuratively with the changing times, from the repressed late 1950s, early 1960s, to the openness of the late 1960s. It helps to support the changing eras by the dismantling of the previously closed-in space. Although shot in Southern California, *Mad Men* is about Madison Avenue and is really a New York story. The production design and set decoration are key to the storytelling. Since this was an episodic series, the episodes constantly return to the established location—the agency itself. This set was incredibly important. Hundreds of scenes take place in and around this set. This type of office space may have already existed in Los Angeles, but you couldn't have shot in it with the ease, frequency, and access of a built set. Not unless you bought the high-rise. And real estate costing what it does in Southern California, that wasn't a likely solution. What kind of scenes take place in that set? Major scenes. Sterling Cooper is meant to be a busy, modern, advertising agency, and there are glass walls dividing all but the private executive offices. Interaction in the halls, the offices, and conference rooms can be observed, staged, and shot through those walls. There's a great deal of movement from office to hall to kitchen space. Building those sets makes perfect sense.

Conversely, as mentioned previously, *LA Confidential*, a fantastic-looking period film set in the 1950s, surprisingly was shot almost entirely on location. The designer and location manager found locations in and around Los Angeles. The practical locations completely bring the audience into the old-California setting of the movie. Even the one major constructed set was built on a location rather than on a sound stage. That set was constructed in part because of the action of the explosive gunbattle that literally destroys the built location.

Watch old episodes of the television series the *West Wing* and current episodes of *Madame Secretary*. Clearly the makers of those TV series were not going to have access to the White House and the Secretary of State's offices, but these places are much photographed. Since we have seen the Oval Office countless times on the news it's not as if the production designer could say, "no one will know if we aren't authentic."

Another issue is the way the shows are shot (the kind of camera activity that takes place). These were/are not action shows but in the case of the *West Wing*, the camera was frequently in motion. The tone and pace of the show was fast, full of scenes of brisk walking from place to place to keep up with the lightning-quick repartee of the cast. The pace and design served to underscore the sense of urgency in a location (the White House) where decisions of monumental matters of state are made. Those hallways were constructed on stage.

How much time is spent in the key locations and, specifically, what has to be done? On a practical location, you can paint and dress and alter the look somewhat but, in the end, you're in an existing structure. You probably can't move the walls, make the set bigger, raise the ceilings, or change the configuration of the doors and windows. You sign a contract that you'll be in the location on X day and you'll be out on Y day. If you want to return or take longer than was originally stated, it's a negotiation and the place might not be available when you need it.

On a television series, it's customary to build the recurring sets. With a tight weekly shooting schedule (could be eight to ten days per one-hour episode), the art department and the rest of the crew can't worry about access to sets that have been established as ongoing locations (the police station on a cop show, the newsroom on a show about broadcast journalism, the high-tech *NCIS* headquarters and morgue). A built set for recurring locations (called a standing set) can be available at the last minute if needed for cover if weather is interfering with the shoot. The pattern of being on stage four or five days, and on location out on the streets for three or four days is common on episodic television. In many ways it's the best of both worlds. You have the convenience and comfort of knowing that despite the vagaries of weather and time of day, you have a location that will be available—and you can combine that with the visual variety and realism of practical locations.

If you aren't making a series or a bigger budget film, and you don't have a lot of money to build? The rule is pretty much, the less money you have, the more advance planning is required. If you don't have money it is more imperative than ever that everybody is clear about what is needed to best tell the story.

Let's think about a bar. What is the purpose of the scenes that take place in the bar, and how long are we there? It could be a single day shoot and we introduce a character who strides into a bar and picks a fight, or the scene could involve a couple who meet through a dating site and are having their first date. The script could describe a reporter's assignation with a source, or old high-school buddies having a sodden ten-year reunion.

Or it might be that you're working on a screenplay called "20 Drinks". There are 20 scenes in this bar. We follow the evolution of the couple's relationship from first meet to the romance to the break up? If that's the scenario, you would consider the most significant story elements.

1   The couple must be drinking. Do they have to be in a bar at all? Could it be a café? Cafés are easier to find and/or build than bars and usually cheaper to rent. The script might call for a bar that serves alcohol because of the action of the patrons and because meeting at the bar works with the essence and theme of the story. That's fine,

and in this case, you probably shouldn't even consider an alternative for a second—and certainly not out loud. But if there is one scene in a bar and it's not part of the theme, maybe it doesn't have to be a bar, if you can't find one you can afford.

2   How old are this couple? Do they have money? This leads into . . . what type of bar should this be? A shabby hometown hangout with old wooden chairs? Photos of local high-school sports heroes tacked to the wall? Tufted faux leather booths? The walls weathered, and the tables scratched? That's one kind of bar. If the couple are in their forties and have money, the bar might be upscale and glossy. Greenery and etched glass windows, Deco style. In both instances, is it necessary to see the mirrored walls and shelves of a traditional bar? Rows of bottles and a keg or a more elegant set-up?

Dissect the concept of the locations. The filmmakers control the frame. Allow the information you have about the story and characters to create their reality. For a blue-collar bar you might find a VFW or an American Legion or Elks Lodge. Many of them have bar set-ups and if you shoot during the day you'll probably have far less of a location fee than if you had to compensate a bar owner for the loss of several days business.

If you shoot in a real bar, you want to be mindful of windows. It's usually cheaper to rent a bar during the day. The owner may let you use the location from 5am to 5pm for less because there are hardly any customers during the day. You may want to look for a bar that either has few windows or that has windows you can cover from the outside using Duvetyn (a black fabric that Cinematographers use to block the light).

You're looking for a location that has most of what you need to facilitate the way the scene will be staged, but you also must keep an open mind. It's possible you'll find a space that needs very little done to make it right, or that has the right configuration (doors and windows and walls in the right places), but the space might be brand spanking new and you don't want new. The location manager will have to ask the owner of the place if it would be possible to age (paint and give texture to) the walls, or hide them with posters and pennants and neon bar memorabilia, or plants and artwork. A set decorator can do that and come up with the right rentals for tables and chairs.

On micro-budget projects, I've seen students use a veterinary hospital for an operating room. I've seen filmmakers erect scaffolding and lengths of pipe in a parking lot, hang lush, brocade curtains, lay down faux marble flooring, and shoot the parking lot as a formal dining room at an estate. It cost only $300. The set decorator put weights in the hems of the curtains to hold them tight and straight and it looked like very elegant

Photos 12.1 and 12.2 Approaching the Enlistment Center and signing on the dotted line.

fabric wallpaper. A veteran production designer saw it and didn't bat an eye. He was impressed that the team had come up with the money for such an elegant mansion.

On one student film, the team didn't want to spend a lot of money on a World War II enlistment center, so they created a sequence, setting up the frame so that they controlled exactly what the audience saw (see Photos 12.1, 12.2).

This was accompanied by the sound of marching—and it was very clear that the hero had enlisted.

In one instance, a production designer on a micro-budget feature searched everywhere in vain for a location that was scripted as a fancy resort hotel. The scene called for two people eating and arguing. The plan was to shoot from one direction only. The designer wanted to allocate her budget strategically—there were bigger, more important sets coming up. With the director's blessing, the production designer found these elements:

1   a stucco wall with Mediterranean-looking tile trim;
2   a metal outdoor table and two chairs;
3   a bright, immaculate over-sized beach umbrella;
4   a friend's swimming pool.

The scene was shot in close enough to see the two actors, a bit of the umbrella, and a corner of the pool. It worked.

The usual process when shooting is to get a shot that establishes the geography of the set (the master), and singles (individual shots of each key actor). You'll want to have enough coverage (different angles) and sizes (close-ups, mediums, etc). Your editor needs that footage so there can be a back and forth as each actor has his or her say. If there's a handheld shot of the old girlfriend entering through the front door while the two old boyfriends are drinking, you'll have to think about all this when you're scouting.

Altering an existing space is almost always a less expensive option than building from scratch on stage if you can manage it. Even if you have some money, it can work better to find your location and, if it is not quite right, adapt it. The appearance and tone of a building exterior can seem like a totally different spot with a change of paint, new trim, some bushes and window boxes, and awnings.

If you want a street with lots of storefronts for a "walk and talk," a mansion, an artist's loft, a suburban duplex, an ultra-modern highrise, a shopping mall, or a brownstone, whether for a day or a week, there's no need to go through the time and expense of building. There are great-looking locations to be found and for a low-budget film, finding a location is usually the answer.

Unless . . . the action involves destruction (a fight, a fire). You might not be doing this on a practical location. Unless you have a lot of money. Most property owners won't allow you to do it. Though you may be tempted otherwise, you do have to tell them what you're planning and even give them the script pages for the scene. If they agree to let you shoot the scene on/in their space, you still face the issue of perhaps not have enough space to stage it effectively. If you have breaking chairs and flying glass (FX glass of course), you want to make the most of it, and many practical locations won't work for your epic battle.

Location Manager Brian Haynes

There are certain bars in LA, very accommodating, I could shoot there for days, blow the place up and they would be fine with it—as long as I'm willing to pay a lot for it. But without that premium fee—no.

If you have gun play, if you have fire, explosions, etc. and it's an important story point, and you have very little money, you're going to have to decide where that activity will be staged. Those all-important discussions and meetings will be about a) whether the stunt/effect is so important that you want to pull money out of other areas to afford it, or b) could there be an alternative? Could it be done at night, at a distance? Could it be exterior in a parking lot? Could it happen off-screen, with sound? Sometimes seeing nothing and hearing a lot has more impact that seeing the little puff of smoke or half-done effects that you can afford.

John Chichester's Design Development Procedure for Locations

1   Make an art department pre-production schedule. Working back from the first day of shooting, based on the information you have as to when sets are to be shot, create a workflow chart as to labor and materials.

2   Make an initial estimate of the time it will take to build each set or modify each location. On larger films this pre-production schedule would be created in consultation with your construction coordinator and your set decorator. They would create the schedule for their departments, you would concentrate—or your art director would concentrate—on the art department and how much design time and staff it would take to create the designs. Once you have made this budget, typically producers will expect you to abide by it unless there is a big change in how the film is to be made. The costume and property budgets are also created at this time.

3   Scout locations. Once a shortlist is made, take the director to the ones that could work.

4   Once the locations have been chosen, draw a plan of the locations, in scale, with all the notes as to what you are going to do there to modify the locations for the film, including main furniture pieces. Distribute this plan to the director, producer,

cinematographer, location manager, decorator, and construction coordinator. Make sure the location manager gets approval for this plan from the owner of the location. Once this is done, design the details for the locations: signs, new architectural elements, paint, whatever it may be you are doing.

5   Determine with your staff (if you have a staff) how long you will need at the location to achieve your ends and to put the location back to what it was before you got there. Make your request of time to the location manager. Do this for each location. A calendar can help a lot with this, showing you where prep time between locations can overlap, and where you may need more labor and transportation on those days as a result.

6   Make or acquire what you need, load it in, and set it up, shoot it, and strike it.

13 Shooting Your Film on Distant Location

As there are so many visual design decisions, the discussion about shooting on distant location (a location where the cast and crew would stay overnight rather than commute back to their homes) has to work creatively, financially, and logistically.

The Cost

It's expensive to work on distant location. Unless there's a large and experienced local crew where you're going, the budget, in addition to a normal film or television budget, has to expand to cover hotels and travel for everyone. The budget will also include per diem (daily expense money, to compensate for the fact that they will have to spend money on the meal they're not eating on set, on trips to the laundromat, on those many small costs incurred because they're not home). On student and micro-budget projects there may not be per diem and people may share rooms, but it's still more expensive than shooting at home, wherever home may be.

Even on small features, the cast and crew might number 30 people. On a large film there may be 60 people, with additional cast and manpower coming and going for specific scenes.

Let's do the math:

Bulk-rate discounted hotel rooms: these can average $30–$80 per night.

Travel: if flying crew in . . . depending upon where, let's assume a low rate of $300 round trip per person; if people choose to drive their own vehicles, reimbursing for gas . . . let's assume about $200.

Paying crew per diem: the expense money is required on any union film and paid on any but the most micro-budget film—let's assume a range of $20 per day per person at the low end to $60 per day per person. If the cast are members of the Screen Actors Guild (almost anyone whose name would help the producer raise money is), then the minimum per diem is approximately $75 per day.

It adds up.

The Logistics

If you're shooting a union project (usually anything above a million dollars), you likely won't be able to bring most of your West Coast crew to work in the East Coast and vice versa. This includes most of the art and decorating department. As mentioned, people prefer working with their own well-oiled team. It helps the speed and efficiency of production. When a new group has to be found, hired, and broken in, there is always a bit of getting used to each other. On a small budget, with a short schedule (low budget films must have fairly short schedules because each day has rental, personnel, and even food costs attached), tensions and conflicts may arise just because people aren't used to each others' styles.

If the film is shooting in locations where they don't make a lot of movies or commercials, the equipment needed may have to be traveled in, and if anything goes wrong, there is unlikely to be a spare of whatever it is conveniently available. If you're shooting on an Alexa (camera), the nearest Alexa to rent may take two days and shipping fees to arrive, and what do you do while you're waiting?

The Good News and the Bad News

Bad News: If you're shooting, for instance, in a small town in Kentucky, the nearest prop house may be in Nashville. Or Chicago. And there probably won't be a lot of people who are qualified to help you, so you'll have to raid the nearest film or theater programs and cross your fingers, or you'll pay to bring people.

Good News: If you bring people, housing them and paying expenses will probably be less expensive in a small town in Kentucky. If you bring on local people, they will probably be happy to work hard for you. You may find fantastic props and pieces of set dressing in local thrift stores and you may be able to borrow things from residents, which probably won't happen in a big city or production center. Your budget may go further than expected and the experience itself may be wonderful.

Your location may be unique and yield authentic and incredible visuals that you just couldn't find anywhere else

The Takeaway for Producers, Directors, and Those Who Suggest Finding the Locations "Away"

1   Make sure that it's worth it to do the traveling and deal with the potential downsides.
2   Scout thoroughly before you make your decision. DO NOT rely on photos or what you are told by the local film commissioner or film office. (More on that in a minute.)

3   Remember that you can shoot on location for only what you really need, then you can return to your home base and that can help your budget/production logistics.
4   Figure out if you can get away with establishing shots of your distant location. These shots are exterior shots, can usually shot by a much smaller (less expensive) crew, in only a day or a couple of days, and are edited into the film to set the scene and establish your location.
5   Investigate the use of stock footage. Stock shots are establishing shots that someone else has taken, and you can license them for your use. If you need an exterior establishing shot of the Golden Gate Bridge, you don't have to go to San Francisco to shoot it. There are hundreds of those already. You can go to a stock footage website, do a search for "Golden Gate Bridge, 1950, at sunset." Chances are you'll find something for a couple of hundred dollars.

Tax Incentives

These days, everybody is talking about tax credits and production incentives. They're assuming that if they shoot in Canada, Louisiana, New Mexico, or Georgia, they'll save a lot of money. Although this is very much in the producer's wheelhouse, if you are a filmmaker in any department and at any budget level, there are a few things you should know before a distant location is determined.

1   Tax credits and incentives were created for the purpose of economic development for some states and that can be a true boon for a filmmaker, but you must understand the reason these exist is to encourage the spending of money and to encourage local employment. This means that in many states, you earn these credits and incentives based on how much money you spend in the location and how many local people you employ. This can mean that a Marvel movie may find it more advantageous to shoot in Atlanta than you do. Your little project may not qualify for all the breaks you're counting on receiving.
2   There may or may not be enough crew depth (groups of qualified people) to support more than one project at a time. If that Marvel movie is in town, they will get the A list—and there may only be one A list local crew. Obviously, the more production that goes on in an area, the more top tier crews there will be. Sometimes the B crew is fine. But you should make a point of checking out everyone's credits before you commit to choosing an incentive location purely on the basis of money.
3   Tax credits and incentives are often political tools and, depending on who is voted in during the last election, everything may change. Be sure that whoever is investigating shooting in an incentive location understands what the deal really is and whether it is expected to change in the middle of your production.

4   If you are looking at shooting out of the US, be sure your production understands the visa and shipping restrictions and timelines. They can be convoluted, and you have to know what to expect for your art department workflow. (If you're the designer on a US film shooting in a country like Canada you won't have to worry about bringing anything, because there are so many films shot in Canada, they have all the support equipment and vendors you'll need—but you yourself might not be able to work there because there are designers available who are native to the country, and they come first.

5   For your art budget, keep in mind that currency fluctuates, which means that the currency exchange rate may be $1.20 to the US Dollar in May, but $1.10 in July. Again, things add up, so give yourself some wiggle room.

14 Your Process

Action

Your screenplay opens with an action sequence. Your lead character is a surgeon being abducted by terrorists.

> *INT. HOSPITAL EMERGENCY ROOM*
> *WAITING AREA—NIGHT*
>
> Quiet. The only sound is the second by second movement of a malfunctioning wall clock. Click, click. 11pm. A few random people waiting to be seen. A SECURITY GUARD chatting with the receptionist at the front desk.
>
> The double doors to the inner examination area swing open. DR. MARIE BARRY (35), pretty, exhausted, blood-spattered scrubs. She heads to the front desk, as if to say something. Then—a deafening explosion rocks the room. Thick smoke fills the area. Chaos. Doctors, nurses, waiting patients running, shouting. Alarm blares.
>
> *INT. HOSPITAL EMERGENCY ROOM WAITING*
> *AREA—NIGHT*
>
> MASKED MEN smash into the room, automatic weapons raised. One of them grabs Marie. The security guard makes a move to help her but a second masked man waves his weapon.
>
> Marie struggles. The men back out of the room quickly, yanking Marie with them and using her to shield them. One of the men raises his gun and peppers the walls with bullets. Plaster goes flying. Everybody dives for the floor. When the guard looks up, the masked men and Marie have vanished through the hospital emergency exit.

We've seen this kind of thing before, it's a standard action scene. Let's break it down to its essential elements and cover the questions every department involved with the visuals would want to ask.

This is the first scene in the screenplay. The director will expect the opening scene to set the tone for the film. He or she wants the audience to feel shock, confusion, and to experience Marie's fear. How does the director see the scene playing out? The director may have something in mind, but unless it has been decided for sure where shooting will take place and the location is already known, the director will want to see what's out there.

The first discussion with the production designer might be, do we find it or build it? Imagine the possibilities. Here are some questions:

1   Where in the hospital is this Emergency Room?
2   Are the kidnappers able to go right from the waiting area to the front door of the hospital and out to the street?
3   Do we want to see the street through a glass front, as is the case in many hospital Emergency Rooms?
4   What kind of neighborhood is the hospital in?
5   What comes immediately after this scene? In Scene 2 are the kidnappers pushing Marie into a vehicle that's standing by, or is the plan to cut to inside a van with blacked-out windows, or to cut away completely to a different location? (That question will probably be answered by reading the script.)

This all may determine the requirement for a location.

As written, one might expect the area outside the waiting space to be connected to a corridor. That way it can quickly become a scene of turmoil, with smoke, and people running, and terrorists having enough room to shoot a broad swath of wall and still get out the door. The shooting space can't be small. The director and production designer will discuss specific configurations. If the director is one who expects the designer to take the lead, the designer will go through the action, what is required, and possibly sketch out his or her idea. Do you want to "cheat" the connecting scene? Cheating a shot means shooting from a specific angle or editing the footage in a way that manipulates reality. In this case you might shoot one angle, then either move to a different location or to a sound stage, but plan it so that it appears as if it's a single location. One caution—the Designer shouldn't decide that the scene will be shot in a way that limits the camera movement before the director is ready to narrow the options. The designer can suggest and try to persuade, but the final decision rests with the director.

If you're based in a place where films and television shows are shot all the time, there is sometimes either a shut-down hospital used for filming, or standing hospital sets. But if you're shooting elsewhere, a real hospital may not be willing or able to allow production on the premises, especially for this type of sequence. Actual working hospitals worry about liability. When you're dealing with people's health, possibly life and death situations, production is a dangerous nuisance. There's crew and equipment and distractions. The hospital is practically inviting a lawsuit if anything goes wrong with a patient. Most of the companies that insure hospitals and the hospital legal staff would probably nix the proposal instantly.

The art and location departments will be thinking ahead. What practical location could not be a hospital but might look like a hospital if properly dressed? There may be a building that can be decorated to look right. There is an institutional look to old hospitals that can be found in other types of buildings. Worth a try. If you do find a place, will the property owner let you stage the mayhem the director is going for?

What about a completely empty, out-of-use building that might have the right size halls and spaces? A set designer and construction crew can handle the swinging double doors. The set decorator can lay flooring, change the color of the walls, and set up a counter for the front desk. Computers, files, the clock on the wall, hospital gurneys, bulletin boards with helpful healthy pamphlets can be displayed. That could make the space feel real and give it character.

Regarding the smoke effect and automatic weapons (either props with blocked barrels and no moving parts, or real but shooting blanks), will a practical location work for that? Is the idea to construct false walls and breakaway windows set with tiny explosive charges synched to the gun shots so they splinter and shatter? How many takes (tries) will be necessary to do that so that it looks good enough? Will there be false walls and windows built so the re-set time between takes doesn't take all day? On a film set, the cast and crew is on payroll from the first moment of the day (their call time) until they are finally wrapped (dismissed), so every bit of down time can get expensive. The last thing anyone wants to do is to see a crew standing around waiting.

What Does the Director Want to See?

If he or she wants to "see the world," that means a complete multi-sided set is needed. If the set has to visually connect with a practical building serving as the Emergency Room exit to the street, the transition must be constructed also. This might require a large space because of the stunt and pyrotechnic effects and the crowd of people scrambling for safety. Will the sequence be lit from above and is there a special piece of camera/grip equipment that will be mounted from a lighting grid? Or can the sequence be achieved by using a lift parked just outside the set wall?

Once there is a vague idea of how the action will play out, and there are plans, the construction crew takes over. Working construction on a film or television project is obviously not the same as building a house. Nothing is meant to last, not even the sets for TV series that are used for months at a time. When the series is cancelled it takes very little time to strike them and sell off/trash the materials used to build them. The construction crew (the coordinator, who is in charge of the department, and a group of carpenters, painters, possibly welders, greenspeople) know how to make temporary structures that are safe and that will look real. The construction coordinator is responsible for ensuring safe building practices, and understands all aspects of construction. When the walls and windows are shattered by the kidnapper's bullets, he or she must plan accordingly. Maybe squibs (tiny explosive charges) will be embedded in the plaster that covers a few of the flats that make up the hospital wall, so when the effects person triggers the squib remotely—bang! You have your shattering plaster/spray of bullets effect. Maybe (less expensively and what you might do for your micro-budget film) the kidnappers shoot their weapons in the air just to scare people while they make their getaway. In that case, the gunmen shoot, the pops of the guns and flashes are added in post-production.

In the script, it says there is smoke when the explosion rocks the building. There are a variety of ways effects people create smoke. There are smoke pellets, smoke machines, and foggers that create haze. The issue is that you will want to be able to predict how thick the smoke is because you want to be able to see the chaotic aftermath of the explosion. You must be sure that the space you're shooting in can be ventilated. Otherwise you'll have hacking and coughing actors and crew and you've created a safety hazard. You'll want to be sure the clean up and re-set is quick, so that you get more than one take every couple of hours. If there are panicked people running around you will want to be sure that there are places to run built into your set. These things are dealt with through discussion, diagrams, more discussions, and walk-throughs. Everyone who might be involved, either because they'll have to deal with the decisions made, or pay for them, has to have a complete understanding of everything planned, how it's planned, and what their part will be in making it happen. This group will include the director, the producer, production manager, production designer, art director, assistant director, prop person, armorer, stunt coordinator, set decorator, effects person, and the costumer. Why the costumer? Because the actors must be able to move freely and fast, the costumes must be flameproofed, and if blood is supposed to show, that should be considered when choosing the color of the wardrobe.

Let's accept that after all that input, the plan becomes to build the Emergency Room area and the exit corridor. The director will meet with the production designer to discuss in detail what the action of the scene will be. If there is an assistant director and a director of photography is already hired, they'll be in the meeting. The job of the AD is to create a shooting schedule and run the set, making sure that the schedule works for the plan. Without knowing the plan, that can't happen.

The production designer comes up with the design, using all the information he or she has. The planned action can dictate everything, down to how big/long/high the set should be. The production designer will sketch or design the set on computer, or will meet with the set designer who will convert the production designer's conception to blueprints. Assuming everyone with a say agrees with the plan, the next step is to find a site where the now-to-be-constructed set will be built.

Stages

In cities where there's a lot of large-scale production (New York, Los Angeles, Atlanta, Chicago, Orlando, Toronto, Vancouver) there are many sound stages. These are large, hanger-like buildings made specifically for production. In most cases, they are sound proof so dialogue can be recorded without interference. There are usually no posts so there's a clear expanse for building and lighting. Rails hang in a grid from the ceiling to enable lights to be arranged and rigged from above. Often a stage rental includes (for a price) the use of dressing rooms, offices, workspaces, and parking for trucks and crew vehicles. Stages are heated and air-conditioned. If the stage is at an actual studio, there is a commissary (restaurant), and perhaps props, costumes, set dressing, and lighting and grip departments nearby. This is convenient but it's also expensive. One day's shooting on a studio sound stage in Los Angeles can easily run to $5,000. The stage usually is rented at slightly less for building days and striking (tear down) days, but even at one half the shooting rate, it adds up. Then there are facilities costs. The stage manager or contact are billed hourly, at usually time-and-a-half after 8 hours and the typical shooting day runs to 12 and 13 hours. These costs don't include the labor or materials you'll need to build your set. You are paying for the rental of the real estate and everything else is an add-on.

Projects with budgets in the hundreds of millions dollar range don't worry about using the big stages in LA or Queens or Brooklyn, or those all over Europe, because the cost is in proportion to the overall budget. For those projects, availability is often a factor. Needing several stages over the course of several months means that you're hoping that other projects with the same needs haven't got everything tied up. You would rather not be on one stage in Burbank, another in Hollywood, another in Playa Del Rey. Many television series have standing sets that are used week after week for a portion of filming and are bread and butter income to the studios. They're not going to bump them.

When none of the major stages are right or available or the right price for a project, the production finds a warehouse. In production centers there are converted warehouses that are set up as rental stages. They fulfill the basic need of a roofed expanse, and they have lots of room for truck, motorhome, and crew parking.

What about projects like yours, with small (or smaller) budgets? There are stages and warehouses that cater to projects with financial limitations. Often even student films can find a semi-affordable space to build their log cabin set, if they keep the rental days to a minimum, or they make the commitment to allocate the bulk of their budget to the rental of the space.

You know about the Universal Studios tour. You may have visited and taken the tram through the back lot and seen the facade-only areas used for some exteriors. There's a New York street with brownstone frontage, which can also be a Boston or Montreal or a European street. Other back lots have sets that are outdoor market stalls that can be dressed as Morocco or Brooklyn. There are "movie ranches" where you can rent and dress "locations" of pre-constructed army barracks, Mexican villages, Western towns, and urban streets. In Los Angeles some shutdown hospitals and school are used only for shooting. There are facilities housing mock-ups of 707s, police interrogation rooms complete with mirrored glass, 1950s diner sets with red plastic and chrome soda fountains. These standing sets are great—the only caveat is that they can look generic—because they are. That's what they offer. But if they're used as a foundation rather than as a finished set, and the designer and set decorator come in and do their magic, these standing sets can save you time and money.

15 Practical Matters
Location Agreements, Permits, Insurance

The visual aspects of shooting on location aside ("on location" in this case means shooting anywhere but on a sound stage), there are business and legal matters involved.

If you're dealing with locations, whether on a project where you are the key creative "decider," or purely as someone helping out in the production department, here are some of the essentials that will help you to avoid getting into trouble.

The Location Agreement

For every location, whether interior or exterior, assume you need a signed location agreement. This includes property you use, even if you don't actually shoot it (a parking lot, for example).

A location agreement is a contract between the project and the property owner, allowing you to a) use the property, and b) show the "likeness" of the property in your film. Note that these are not the same thing. You may have a property owner who is OK with you setting up equipment in their driveway. That doesn't automatically mean you can use an image of their property in your movie. This is a binding contract and your agreement should account for either (if you really do just want to use the driveway), or both, if that's what you want. In this case a verbal agreement is meaningless. Don't be casual about this. Property owners aren't. Your signature or your producer's signature on the agreement counts and if you're ever taken to court, you want to be sure that you've kept to the terms of your agreement. (If you want to use existing signage or the address of the place, that should be spelled out also.)

There are examples of location agreements online, and if yours is a school project or you're working for a production company, they will probably have their own version of a location agreement, pre-vetted by their attorneys. But read things before you sign—you, not the company or school—are liable when it's your signature at the bottom of that form. Understand what you're asking for, what permissions you're getting, be sure everything is covered, and don't sign anything until you do.

One more legal matter—the person who signs the location agreement MUST be either the property owner or the official designate of the property owner (for instance, a property management company). That means your friend can't say, "Sure, you can shoot in my apartment!" unless he or she owns the building. It is necessary in that case to have two agreements—one with the renter and another with the owner of the building—and if you don't, you're there illegally. If you're there, you need permission to be there.

When negotiating for a location, it's important to know how long the space will be needed. Remember that shooting is only part of the process. There's prep and strike. The conversation with the production designer or set decorator should include the prep and strike schedule because your location rental begins when the production walks in the door, not when shooting starts. It ends when you are done and every bit of equipment, trash, and material is gone. The property owner doesn't care when you finish shooting—they care about when anyone will be at the property and when everybody will be gone.

When you're going to shoot, be sure that you have time-stamped photos or video of the property so that you can be sure when you're asked to pay for damages or repairs needed, that these were caused by the filming and weren't there before you ever knocked on the property owner's door. And once you're done shooting, there should be a walk-through with the property owner and they should physically sign off that everything is as it should be. When dealing with a location, restoration (fixing, repainting) should be done immediately. The property owner doesn't want to wait until it's convenient for *you*. It's not up to you to decide something "isn't that bad." If the production is responsible for whatever it is, the production is responsible for bringing it back to its original condition.

A contract with the property owner states the fee and the conditions of the agreement. Some property owners figure, "in for a penny, in for a pound" and give the filmmakers the run of the place. Some agree to exterior only, or interior only. Depends what you ask for and what you need—but everything should be written into the contract or you don't have it. If the art department is going to move the existing furniture out, it should be noted, and the fee for storage will be delineated in the contract. If the property owners are going to move out for a few days, then the production will be paying for their hotel as part of the location budget (and the hotel will be predetermined, so people won't be expecting The Ritz and getting Motel 6). If the pets are going to go with the owners, there may be a deposit added onto the hotel fee. If they are going to be staying at a pet hotel, that cost will be covered in the agreement. (Even if the owners suggest the pets can stay in the home if you have someone take care of them, don't agree to it no matter how much you think it can save you. If the pet is fed the wrong thing, gets out of the house, or in any way is harmed, not only will you have that on your conscience, but you will be facing an ugly and emotional lawsuit. Pay for the pet hotel if that's the owner's choice for housing but they should choose the place. Make sure the hotel accepts animals and pay whatever deposit. Take the responsibility for a living thing off your to-do list.) If you are planning to use the backyard to feed the crew, that should be noted. Any work done to change the house paint, holes for picture hanging, should be noted. Some location managers are very loose about putting all these details in writing. They may think that the more there is in the agreement, the more skittish the property owner will be about signing. They also may think they can deal with some of the details once the crew is there and everyone is basically stuck. Not a great policy, and almost guaranteed to engender bad will. The best policy with property owners is always, no surprises.

Remember also that property owners don't want to upset their neighbors. A location agreement for one house means just that—the house next door is off limits, unless you've got an agreement for their property also. Don't want to pay for that? That's OK, but if your cinematographer decides the night of filming that a light absolutely must be hung from the roof of the house next door, it's a little late in the game to start your negotiations.

Shooting at a business can be different than dealing with a house. With certain types of businesses you may be expected to compensate the owner for loss of revenue. Some businesses may be willing to let you shoot, but will want you to pay for an employee to be present, to watch out for the interests of the owner. If you're shooting at an apartment building or a multi-occupancy business building, you will need sign off not just from the tenant but from either the authorized property manager or the owner of the structure. It can take a long time to track these people down, but the owner, not the tenant, has the last word. If the art department wants to alter the interior or exterior common areas of a multiple-occupancy location, be prepared for a lengthy process of negotiation, notification, and restoration.

If your location is a public park or a sidewalk, or an otherwise public area, there is no owner, per se—but the city, county, or town must give permission for you to shoot. What about if you only want to be on the sidewalk in front of a store? Will you be blocking customer access? Will whatever you're doing interfere with business as usual? Remember than anyone can say no—just because. They don't owe you the ability to "do business" on their street. And if they are forced to allow you to be there without you paying them a location fee, they may feel justified in making it as difficult as possible for you to shoot. (Every time you begin recording sound some very loud music may begin to play and the cappuccino blender may start up, just coincidentally.)

There are locations where it might be extremely expensive, or very difficult, even impossible, to get permission to shoot. Since September 11th and the tragedy of the World Trade Center, many cities will not allow film crews in major airports or harbors. Not that they think you're a terrorist—but a shooting crew takes up a lot of security manpower that may be better used on other things. You might be able to shoot at a smaller local airport or a private terminal and cheat it so that with a combination of signage, stock footage, and shooting a corner of a much smaller version of a baggage carousel, you can cheat your British diplomat arriving to a cheering crowd. You can do almost anything if you isolate the elements your audience needs to see for the story to work.

Permits

A permit is not a location agreement, and a location agreement is not a permit. A permit is a legal document that gives the production permission to shoot in the city, town, or county. That includes exteriors and interiors. A permit is usually issued by either the local filming office, or by the town, city, or county government. It's up to the municipality as to whether you can shoot there at all. You need a permit for every place you shoot, or you will be shut down. This applies whether you are shooting interior or exterior. It also applies if you are shooting in a public park, on a public roadway, or on land regulated by any government body. Assume that you need a permit to shoot pretty much everywhere. A permit is the way a local government signifies that you have met their requirements and have been permitted to "do business," however fleeting, within their boundaries. Requirements vary wildly from place to place, even from one town to the town next to it. A permit application will ask for information. What is the exact location? If there is no street address, you might have to say, "the southeast corner of Patriot Park, next to the tennis courts." You will commit to an area. Once you decide, you'll stick to that area. What day or days do you want to be at that location, and from what time to what time? There are local regulations that limit the hours public areas can be used. What kind of lights will you have? Permit fees vary from place to place (sometimes it is free, usually it's in the $100 range, occasionally it's much more). The person in charge of permits may tell you:

a) that where you want to shoot has been shot too often, the residents are tired of it, and there is a moratorium on permits in that area for a year. (There goes your location. Try to always have a second choice.)

b) that it is too close to residents to shoot as late as you want to shoot. It's a quiet neighborhood. You can be issued a permit from 7am–7pm, but you've got to be "tail-lights" (packed up and driving away) by 7pm. (Depending on the time of year, that may mean you have 2½ or zero hours to get that nighttime shot.)

c) you can shoot there but you have to obtain signed agreement from (50 percent, 70 percent, 90 percent) of all residents and businesses within 500 feet. Once you turn in those signatures they will issue the permit.

d)   you can do what you want but you'll have to shut down the street and hire police to stand at each end of the closed street to direct traffic. (In Los Angeles this can be $75 per hour for an 8-hour minimum. In Valentine, Nebraska, it can be a courtesy donation). Or, because you're shooting indoors in a hotel or factory, you'll have to have a fire safety officer there with you. (Police and Fire are also accounted for in the location budget.)

e)   there will be no problem, and everything will be smooth and easy.

The secret to getting permitted to shoot is to do your homework and leave plenty of time. The permit office, like a property owner, is under absolutely no obligation to help you, so be very nice! Manners make a difference.

A last word on permits: permit offices have different timetables. The requirement to submit your application to one office might be ten business days in advance of your scheduled shoot and the next town over, it's two days. Whether you're filming on public or private property, they will want to see that your project is carrying the correct liability insurance, so if somebody trips on a cable, they will sue you, not them.

Insurance

Here's what you need to know about insurance: it's expensive and you've got to have it. Sorry, but that's the fact. Every project you make needs to be insured to protect your locations, your cast and crew, your equipment, and everything and everyone else from loss and damage. There are standard Producer Packages for film, and every time you rent equipment, props, set dressing, wardrobe, or a location, the production will be required to show proof that there is an insurance policy in force, covering the project. Insurance will also somewhat protect the project and the people involved in the project from personal liability and law suits.

Ways to Get Help: Film Commissions

Every state in the US, every province in Canada, and many countries the world over, see filming as a positive. There is money to be made, and a great-looking project can boost tourism. Miami was always a tourist destination, but the series *Miami Vice* gave it extra glamour and raised awareness. The TV series *Nashville* had a major economic impact on the city of Nashville. Most places have some kind of film office. The intention of those offices is to help you while helping themselves. Places want you to come make your project. They want you to stay safe, legal, not bother people, and have a great experience, then leave, with a minimum of fuss and trouble for you and for their citizens.

The best film offices or commissions have knowledgeable representatives who understand the needs of filmmakers, while caring greatly about the welfare of their constituencies. They have the benefit of history (who shot there in the past, what were the problems) and contacts (if you want to shut down the Golden Gate Bridge who can help you get an answer, what crews live in the area and did they work on local, or international productions).

In Los Angeles there is so much of a demand for filming locations that the city and many nearby city and town governments contract out their process to FilmL.A., a not-for-profit public organization. FilmL.A. provides permit processing to filmmakers, works with communities, and assists filmmakers on production planning.

Jamie Burton-Oare, Filmmaker and a Community Outreach Liaison with FilmL.A.

FilmL.A. acts as the link between the production company and the community in which they film. We also act as an advising agency to the city and LAPD (the Los Angeles Police Department). LAPD is the approver or denier of permits—they enforce the permit. We coordinate all the way from pre-production to post-production and serve the community even after. My specific job is Community Liaison, and I am one of three.

Our office will let the applicant know what the location requires. That could include a public safety officer, a fire safety officer, etc., and the applicant has to fulfill all those obligations in order to receive the permit.

In addition to that, FilmL.A. represents the city in all community needs related to filming by addressing anyone who has a concern or a question specific to that permit or filming in general. Our goal is to facilitate a film-friendly environment for all parties—the resident, the filmmakers, the city, and county, and businesses.

The Things Filmmakers Should Know

I am a filmmaker also, which gives me a unique perspective. The more you shoot and work, the more you realize the impact filming has on an area. Filmmakers should realize that when they film at a location, they're coming into someone's home (or home territory). As a filmmaker, you think about matching your location to your vision and getting it done. But if you re-frame your thinking and

(continued)

(continued)

realize that taking the time to consider the community and jumping through the necessary little hoops to satisfy everyone affected, it will save you from jumping through bigger hoops at a later time. The more you communicate and involve the residents, the easier your day will be.

[Even with all the filming that constantly goes on in LA] people still are pro-movies and they still get a kick out of being a part of something. If you communicate well in advance and show them the respect they are due, you'll be surprised at the ease it will offer you.

FilmL.A. has a production planning department. A filmmaker can call and get direction on various locations. You could call that department as well as our department (Community Outreach) to obtain the temperature of specific locations and neighborhoods. Like, if there's been a lot of filming at one location you might want to suggest an alternative location because the climate is better at the moment. Additionally, location managers use LocoScout, a list that offers suggestions.

Burton-Oare's Personal Experience with Shooting with a Very Low Budget

I was shooting a feature film and the spine of the film involved actors hiking in a park where the Hollywood sign is located. I found out how expensive it was to shoot that park, that I'd need a ranger who would be paid by the hour—and at that time, I decided that I would shoot my actors in the street alongside the park, instead of them in the park.

I learned that you may be able to shoot certain angles, and FilmL.A. allowed me to permit that location (the street). It was the same effect, but I had to adjust my shot. Also, I couldn't afford to go to New York, so I found an apartment building in LA that looked like it was in New York. It didn't have palm trees and I made it work, it looked like the Bronx.

I was teaching at an LA Unified School District school and I needed a mental hospital.

I turned a nurses' office at the school into the hospital. It also served as a casting location for another scene. I had to look for a location that could have multiple uses. Necessity is definitely the mother of invention.

Location challenges aren't an excuse not to make your film. You have to be creative.

Other Ways to Get Help: People

Who has shot in your target area or even at your location before? Call them. They'll probably be willing to share their experiences. If you're in a place where lots of filming happens, start networking and getting to know how the local film office work. If there's very little filming where you are, things may be less formal but that will just make everything easier. Whether or not you're a film student, if there's a reputable film program near you, the people who teach there have probably made at least a short film or two. Take them to coffee. Don't worry that your project is tiny and theirs was a national commercial that aired on the Super Bowl. Believe it or not, there isn't much difference when it comes to the legal, permitting, and insurance aspects of production. A tiny project will pay less, be less visible, but the basic requirements will be almost the same.

David DeGaetano

Advice to young filmmakers—be flexible. A lot of people come in and they're set on doing a particular thing in a particular way and that's just going to severely limit what can be done and the quality. If they can remain flexible, turn around, look at another way to do it, they'll probably save some money and end up with as good of an effect. Don't be locked into an idea. That's the creative part. Being able to look at different ideas. Be receptive. In terms of communication, if they're a new filmmaker and there are more experienced people on the crew, make use of the crew's experience. It will save them some grief.

There's a lot to be said for the new filmmakers because of their energy and the creativity and it doesn't always have to be done the way it was. It's good to experiment, but there's a lot to be said for the old folks who have done it for many years.

Here's an interesting location story where a little research might have helped:

There is a neighborhood in Los Angeles that encourages production. The style of the architecture and the configuration of the main shopping area is not typical for LA. It's not even typical for the West Coast. The neighborhood looks like small-town middle America. When a film can avoid leaving town and still get that look of someplace else, an area like this one is in demand. Television episodes, feature films, student films—everybody wants to shoot there. An inexperienced location manager on a low budget film did what he was supposed to do. He had several days of exteriors to find and the film was set in the mid-West. He settled on a price with the local film office, and obtained the proper permits. The day before the shooting was scheduled, when it was too late to find another location, the production company was ambushed with demands for cash payments from all the local merchants. Although the shooting was to take place on the street and was not going to block incoming and outgoing customer traffic, the merchants decided that it was an inconvenience that they should be compensated for. The local film office wanted to keep their merchants happy so although the production had a signed location agreement, they didn't intervene. The idyllic small-town location became a nightmare. Months later, when one of the outraged producers told the story at a party to a few veteran location managers, they all laughed. "I could've seen that one coming," one of them said. "I don't shoot there unless it's a big project that can afford that dance. Happens every time."

16 How to Be Your Own Location Manager

What if you have a scene where your actors are walking and talking and passing storefronts? You want authenticity on a budget. The only challenge is, your story takes place in 1968 and it's now 2018. There are a few things that you can do.

Back to Basics: Research

What does the screenplay describe? Is this a named and known city street that's a real place? Is it anytown USA? Why is the scene set in that particular location? Is there a specific purpose or it is flexible?

Some examples: the scene takes places in Haight-Ashbury, in San Francisco, during the hippie era. The Haight is an actual neighborhood, so the first thing to do is get online, go to the library, look at magazines, and take a look. Forget that it's in San Francisco. You can't see the skyline or the Golden Gate Bridge. Think about the basic characteristics of the location. You'll see three-story, wooden, or stone Victorian-looking apartment buildings, or shop storefronts with Victorian-tinged accents. You'll see awnings, and a lot of 'psychedelic' style signs in the windows. The streets are wide, with two lanes going in each direction and there are broad sidewalks.

Now, how much of the film is set there? Is it the one exterior scene only? You probably can't afford to travel to San Francisco, shut down the street to traffic (and you would have to because modern-day vehicles wouldn't work with your story). Assuming that you need that walk and talk, can you find a stretch of buildings that work wherever you are based? Look for the same general age, same general style, and think about dressing the storefronts with the awnings and signage, using appropriately dressed actors, and limiting your shots, staying fairly close in? Can you shoot at night? In this sort of situation, darkness and focusing your audience's attention where you want it focused via how you light it, can be your best friend. You may think you can't make this work, but as you will see in a later chapter filmmakers have been able to find an area of a mall-ridden suburban section of southern California's Orange County and turn it into a street market in the Middle East.

What if it's a small town, in anywhere, USA? Back to the library. Have your discussions with the screenwriter and director (and if you are the screenwriter and director, really think through where you want your movie to be set). You may not want to name the place in the script, but you must have some place in mind. It can't be this amorphous town. What's the source of the economy of the town? What kind of shops would this economy support? Find a place that fits into your vision and research it—there are generally photos and materials that can be found that give you an insight as to whether there would be cute little shops that sold yarn and knitting needles, nautically themed souvenir stands, or drive-up feed stores and tackle stores. Thinking about this will help you with one of the least expensive ways to sell a location—graphics. Signage is eye-catching and can have lots of personality.

Details to look at—street lights, and the configuration of parking. If your location is a crowded city, usually parking spaces will run alongside the curb. If your story is set in a small town where space is not at such a premium, you may look for diagonal parking. Quaint, homey towns may have parks with gazebos in the middle of downtown. Is there a place near where you're based that might not be small at all but might have those pieces, so you can have your actors walk alongside the park, and shoot them facing in a way that you can avoid seeing the cars across the way? Can you rent a gazebo and put it in a big yard, if that's what you need?

What Do You Really Need to Tell Your Story?

Back to Haight-Ashbury. Find the older parts of the nearest cities and towns. You're looking for 1968 or earlier. Chances are, you can find someplace that existed then. Drive around. Keep going. Take your phone and film the areas, duplicating the walk you think the characters will make. What do you see? What would you have to hide? If the height and materials of the buildings work for your location, you're way ahead of the game. If you're a good persuader, you can probably talk shopkeepers into dressing their windows with your dressing as long as it isn't for more than a day or two. The advantage you may have of not shooting in a production state with incentives is that people haven't been overrun with movie crews and aren't used to charging exorbitant fees. They may think it's just a nice thing to help you and charge very little.

Can you find a way to shoot in only one direction? Is there an old office or apartment building that you can dress as something else? Is there a way to avoid seeing cars, or, if you see cars, not seeing many? Seeing many may mean you have to block off the street for your use and that can become expensive. If the background actors (extras) are dressed in the correct period and passing the couple in the other direction, you can place only one or two cars that are of the period parked along the way, and you can have your actors positioned so that they share the frame. That will go a long way to convincing the audience you're in the 1960s. Some details to remember: not everybody in 1968 had cars from 1968, most people had older cars and much older pick-up trucks. Picture cars can be towed to the curb, they don't have to actually run. There are loads of vintage car clubs. Especially in cities where there is not a lot of production, local collectors tend to be pleased when you want their baby in the movie.

Don't get hung up on titles. If you need a school, you might come across a different kind of building where you can create classrooms that you can shoot during the week and you can find a school exterior to film over two Sundays. Do you need a radio or television station? Check to see if there is a cable access station available to rent.

While you are scouting, be sure to visit potential locations on the day and time you'll want to shoot there. You might not want to be shooting next to the church with the bells that chime every hour, or the car repair shop. Your empty park may be mobbed with families having barbecues on the weekends.

If filming is in a city where there's a lot of production, an experienced location manager will have a sense of what the average house/office/restaurant/bar/store/golf course charges to rent. But in a place where filming is more of a novelty, it's one big question mark. Will the community happily host the project and make it easy, or will property owners be planning on a big payday? Researching the few past productions that have shot in the location may be of limited help. It depends upon how long ago the past productions shot there, and whether the impression the production left was positive or negative. Was the experience fun and profitable for the residents or did they feel abused?

Another less talked about consideration is the subject of the project. Might it offend the residents or local government? You may have trouble finding houses and government cooperation shooting a movie about sex or racism or political corruption in areas where those are hot-button issues. It might not be blatant, but people don't like controversy. They probably won't give you a break on the site rental fee.

Speaking of government cooperation, what can you do if your film involves the military? Well—is it positive or negative? The Armed Services has a film liaison who will read your script and, depending on the prestige of the people involved in the project, how the service is being portrayed, and what the state of the world is, it's up in the air as to whether you'll get help with locations, props, and vehicles, etc. Even filmmakers making positive films set in the military may have to shoot their military scenes in other countries because the troops and bases are too occupied with actual, rather than fictional, defense. Military cooperation is something that should be dealt with far in advance or there should be an alternative, equally affordable plan B in place.

It is much more difficult to shoot residential areas late at night or early in the morning. This even applies to shooting interiors. People don't want to be disturbed. They don't want you keeping them up or waking you up. Look at your schedule.

Stores and restaurants don't want to close for you. They don't want to turn away customers. They may agree that you can shoot at their location if they can continue doing business while you're there. Try to avoid this. Film crews need freedom to set up and shoot. You will disturb them, and they will disturb you. If you disturb them enough, you'll lose your locations. If you are paying for the location and have a contract, it can still end up restricting your shots, distracting your actors, and creating enough tension that you just want to finish up quick and get out. That can damage your project. (If you love the look of the restaurant, offer to shoot during their slowest time and to feed your crew with their meals as part of the deal. If you don't need to see the kitchen itself, you'll be shocked to see how easy it is to find an empty space and create a nice dining space by renting café tables, linens, china, cutlery, and glassware from a catering company. You can dress the tables with candles and flowers. It's actually more difficult to create a diner or less 'fancy' restaurant than one that is at the higher-end.)

When you scout, try to have at least some of the pertinent people with you. It can save a lot of time if people aren't going off in different directions.

This is *all* much easier if you have money. But you'll be astonished by what you discover when you really commit to spending the time and remaining flexible. Sometimes you'll find something completely different than what you're hunting for and it will be much better.

Decide the General Area Where You'll Want to Shoot

For instance, towns within a 20-mile radius of X city. The reason this will help you is that you can check out the permit situation in the various towns and areas in your location zone, in advance. For instance, if you need to shoot night exteriors in the summer, that means you'll be setting up at 7pm, finishing about 6am. Some areas will just not allow that. Some areas will allow you to shoot but require you to have police around you at all times. Can't afford it? You may want to look elsewhere. Some cities require you to file for permits several days in advance. If your location fell through on Tuesday and you need to find a new location to shoot on Friday, you'll know not to waste anybody's time.

The Approach

How do you ask someone for a favor? When you want to use someone's house or business (or even a city street), that's exactly what you're doing, whether you're paying or not.

1   Put yourself in the other person's shoes. If a total stranger showed up at your door how would you feel? The first chance is the only chance you'll have. You don't have to wear a suit and tie or khakis and a polo shirt—if you do, it's possible people will think you're selling something or belong to a religious group and won't answer when you knock. But be well-groomed. Don't wear any kind of cap, hat, scarf or turned-up collar that hides your face. This seems obvious, but the key is to look nice, not scary in any way, and not overly cool. Cool may say creative to fellow filmmakers, but it can also say you don't care to strangers. Would you let somebody who doesn't care use your house? For safety's sake on your behalf and for reassurance on the part of the property owner, try to scout in pairs, either a male and female or two females. Two guys can seem threatening, especially if they're big.

2   Have a neatly printed flier with the name of the project and your contact information. It's good idea to leave a flier at the front door in advance so they know ahead of time that you may be coming by. Try to have more than one contact number on the flier. People don't love leaving messages. If you can't answer, hopefully your location partner will. If the project is for school, say that right away on the flier and in person. The contact number for the department at the school should be available so the property owner can check you out. If the project is independent, then be ready with references. References ideally aren't friends, they're people you've have worked with in a professional capacity. Ask them ahead of time if it is OK.

3   Don't scout locations or approach people until you have insurance. When you're speaking to home or property owners, let them know that the project is insured. You can bring a blank copy of your insurance company's Proof of Insurance Certificate with you for them to look at. That's reassuring and shows that you're responsible, professional and prepared.

4   Do *not* knock on strangers' doors after dark. That may be convenient for you but a knock on the door at night is not going to make you any friends.

5   Don't try to come in the house. Make your first impression standing at the door.

6   At the risk of seeming simplistic, know what you're asking for and be conscious of how you're asking. That means, after "hello, sorry to bother you," and introducing yourself, you say the equivalent of "we are working on a low budget independent film (or we are film students from X University) and looking for a house/office (interior) (exterior) to use that is the same (size) (style), (built in the late 1950s, early 1960s), like yours." Say something nice about the house, but don't go overboard. You should be friendly, businesslike, and polite. You don't want it to feel like a scam. Then, "would you possibly

be willing to consider allowing us to scout your house/office?" Tell them the genre of the film. If it's supposed to be where the monster lives, or you talk about serial killers, they are not going to be thrilled. Not just because you see their house as a creepy crime scene house, but also because they are imaging the bloody mess you might make. "Suspense thriller" can go a long way further than horror. Be honest but tactful.

Depending on their interest, you will either be asked further questions, asked in, told to come back later, or given a flat no. If it's an outright no, apologize, thank them for their trouble and go. On a low budget film, you probably don't have the resources to overcome a definite no. If they say to come back later, set a real appointment and be *on time*. Even if they aren't, to win them over you've got to behave perfectly. That may tip the scales.

If you get in the house and it's not right, thank them profusely and tell them you don't know if it's what the director is looking for, and if it is, you'll call them by the next day. Be appreciative, then follow up. Call when you said you were going to, let them know that it isn't what is needed and thank them again. You never know when it might be the right place. And (again, should be obvious good manners) never talk about someone's house or things in any way that feels unflattering.

If you get in and it's pretty good, tell them your shooting dates, that you may need X days for prep and restoration and that you'd love to bring the director—or designer—by to see it. If they are willing, then make an appointment (this means knowing in advance when the relevant people will be available) and again, doing what you say you're going to do when you say you're going to do it. More potential locations have been lost through a property owner being annoyed and inconvenienced than because of an insurmountable rental fee.

If everyone likes the house and you are ready to lock (get an Agreement signed) the location, meet again with the property owners. (The person who meets with the owners should by now have a pleasant relationship with them. That person should be at every meeting, should be the point person for all activity, and should be the one the owner can call about anything, any concern, any question.)

Explain what they should expect, including the number of cars, trucks, or trailers that will be parked on their street. The number of cast and crew. If you're hoping to use their bathrooms. If you hope to plug in to their electricity. If you will need to unplug their refrigerator or freezer so your mics won't pick up the motor hum. Do you want to use their furniture or move it out? Where will you move it and how will it be secured? Are you going to hang anything on their walls or remove anything?

Are you planning to move the family out, put them in a hotel? A seedy motel won't work, regardless of your budgetary limitations. Don't forget your tech scout, your prep, pre-rigging if any, the wrap out, and any restoration.

Restoration can be simply paying the owner's cleaning person to come or finding a cleaning service, or it can be repainting a wall and replanting a trampled flower bed. But I've seen first time filmmakers incur a completely avoidable $5,000 charge because they scratched a vintage parquet wooden floor and had to pay to have an entire room re-done because a quick fix wouldn't match.

Professional film crews use layout board (oversized rectangles of thick cardboard used to protect flooring). A good policy is to budget for and plan to have a PA whose job it is to deal with layout board when you're moving things around. Being careful helps but doesn't always prevent problems. Ask the owners if there is a place they can lock and store anything delicate or valuable. Explain that you don't suspect your crew are thieves, but people will be moving in and out and doors will be left open occasionally. If they want to lock things up but don't have a place to do it, check out a short-term storage place—and pay for it, but make sure you don't have the key or combination, and when you're helping move things in and out, be sure that the owners are with you and watching.

Another good idea is not to allow food in any house you're using. That restriction should be asterisked and printed in bold on your call sheets. Rather than overflowing the property owners' trash cans or dumpsters, be sure in advance that someone specific is tasked with removing garbage and rubbish from the property and taking it to the local dump. Figure this out ahead of time so it can be part of your pitch to the owners.

Money

Once it is evident that the owner is willing to let you use their place, the negotiations start. Hopefully you've already established that you are a low-budget movie. *Tell the truth*. Don't say you have no money then show up with a ton of high-end equipment and trailers. People aren't stupid, and they can decide to kick you out, signed agreement or not. When you look at a location, talk to the owners a little about the project. If you're passionate about it, your enthusiasm may help. If you have no money at all, is there anything you can do to persuade them to agree? I've had students offer to fix things, paint something that needs it, or in one case, to make a short promotional video for the property owner's website. That ended with a long-term income-earning relationship. Be sensitive. If the owner is concerned about the disruption of his or her routine, ask how that can be mitigated. Don't *tell* them, *ask* them. Listen to them. If they understand you aren't the next Hollywood epic, sometimes they'll come up with a fair price—especially when you are a student or just out of school. People like to help.

The Tech Scout

The tech or technical scout is the day that every key crew member dealing with locations does a walk through with the director and talks about the shots and activities planned. This should be done well in advance of shooting because the result of the tech scout is often a flurry of reconfiguration and revised plans. This is also the time when your electricians decide on their source of electricity (generator? You will need to notify the permit office and often the local fire department). This is when the designer may change his or her mind about taking down the curtains or when the gaffer decides you may need a light rigged in a tree. In other words, things change, and the property owner—and whatever governing body may be involved—must be made aware of the changes.

During Production

It's important that the person the property owners have been working with is at the location when the day begins to "open the set," and preferable that they are there the entire time. If they can't be, they should have someone there who has met the owners on multiple occasions, so they're comfortable leaving their house (if they are leaving). The original contact should be checking in a few times a day, both with the set and with the owner.

The Walk Through

Once the shoot at the location is done, the person dealing with locations should do a walk through with the owners to check for damages and to discuss how they will be remedied. Whatever is decided, the problems should be handled immediately. The ending is as crucial as the beginning. These folks either become your references or see you next in small claims court—or worse.

Finishing Up

Send flowers or passes to the local multiplex. Send a thank you note. Send thank you notes to everybody. They don't cost anything, and they are noticed. Give thank you credits at the end of your film. If good things happen for the film (accepted into a festival, wins you an award) let the location owners know and thank them again!

Last Words about Dealing with Location Logistics

You know the expression about it being easier to ask forgiveness than it is to get permission? Forget it. Ask for permission for *everything* in advance. People will tell you that they're going to "shoot guerrilla," meaning go for it without asking or following the rules. Sounds much easier to do things on the fly. In professional circles people who work like that are called "loose cannons." They're considered liabilities, not rebels. They cause problems and cost a production money that could otherwise be used for something that showed on the screen.

True story:

There once was a cinematographer who worked all the time. He kept busy on big cable and episodic television projects. He was very loyal. The same grip and electric crew had crewed for him on several shows because he'd been rightfully given the option of choosing his team.

A member of this grip crew was referred to by his fellow grips as "Destructo-Man." He was talented, but he didn't much care about damaging locations. The damages were as small as a chipped banister, or as substantial as cracks in the plaster walls from rigging. This grip also used quite colorful language when shouting to his crew-mates out in the grip-truck that was parked in front of the property owners' house. This was not a terrible person. He was funny, charming, and capable. But after a while, the word got back to the cinematographer that although he was wanted on projects for a production company he'd worked for in the past, his grip crew was not. He was angry. He was embarrassed. Then he found a new grip crew. His team had made him look bad in an industry where it's all about how you leave things once you're gone.

17 What You Need to Do What You Want

Demystifying the Budget

If you're working in the art, set decoration, construction, or location departments, at some point you will be expected to provide a budget. If there's a department head, they will be doing this, but if this is your first time as a department head or you're heading several departments at once, it will fall to you. If you are a low-budget filmmaker making a bare-bones project, you may be fulfilling several of these functions—and it's important to use the process of making a budget to help you get organized.

Creating a budget can be onerous, especially when you are a more artistic, less mathematically talented person. But truly, it's not higher math, it's more elementary school arithmetic. This plus this multiplied by this. The value of doing a budget, in addition to coming up with an idea of how much money you'll need, is that it forces you to think about every item, and how the action you're dealing with in your design plan dovetails with other elements and departments. Everything costs something, whether it's time or money or both. If you're trying to achieve something, budgeting forces you to pull it apart and figure out what you'll need. Your screenplay calls for a rock concert. Is this going to be a major concert in an arena? Can you use a local auditorium and dress it to feel more rock and roll? Are you only seeing backstage, the stage, and the first couple of rows of seats until the shot falls away into darkness? A budget will help you know what to look for that's workable, what you really need rather than what you want. Don't feel bad—even on films that have budgets of $200 million this process of elimination happens—it's just on a bigger scale. As a producer friend once told me, "The main difference between my film school shorts and the films I work on now? More zeros."

Your rock concert scene—if you manage to come up with a way to get your wished-for big crowd—what will the shot be? Is it an exterior? Could you use a drone? Will you want to have more than one camera for that one day? Do you need someone with a Steadicam wandering through the crowd so that footage can be edited in to give the feeling of an even bigger, more chaotic gathering? Fine—but there will be money involved. Not necessarily a lot of money—and that shot with that design may "sell" your entire scenario and be worth it. But you need to plan, and that brings you back to the budget . . .

Budgets look like spreadsheets, because often that's all they are. Every detail is listed. People, equipment, materials.

People

Labor is estimated in terms of people multiplied by time.

Take a look at one of the labor accounts, set decorating, on a low budget, non-union project:

Set decorator/Leadperson:

Prep 15 days	× 1 person	× 10 hours	× $11 per hour
Shoot 20 days	× 1 person	× 12 hours	× $11 per hour
Wrap 2 days	× 1 person	× 10 hours	× $11 per hour

Set dressers/Swing gang:

Prep 10 days	× 2 people	× 10 hours	× $9 per hour
Shoot 20 days	× 2 people	× 12 hours	× $9 per hour
Wrap 2 days	× 2 people	× 10 hours	× $9 per hour

On-set dresser:

Shoot 20 days	× 1 person	× 13 hours	× $9 per hour

Why is it laid out this way? Because the set decorator, who in this case (not much money to pay) is doubling as a Leadperson, will need three five-day weeks to look at the locations, meet with the designer, plan the dressing, shop, and get the first couple of locations read. They'll need two people to pick things up, and to prep and dress the sets. (Prep days are customarily ten hours.) On your shoot days, while those two people are readying the next location with the materials and pieces that were selected and collected, one of your set dressing crew, the on-set dresser, will be staying on set, to help with the dressing continuity. (Shoot days are generally figured to be 12 hours and the on-set dresser is budgeted here at 13 hours because the set has to be shoot-ready at the beginning of each day, which may mean they have to move things, polish furniture, hang curtains with or without the help of the others, who may be miles away at the next day's location. As shooting at each location is completed, two of the crew can be returning the rental stuff that is no longer needed, getting it off rental. Once the project shoot is completely done, there is nothing for the on-set dresser to do, so the crew number may be back down to two people, one returning or selling off purchases, and one taking care of repairs.

This is one scenario. On a film with an even shorter shooting schedule, the temptation is to skimp on prep to save money—but the mistakes made, the way things can go wrong when everything is rushed, may cost you more in the long run. On a school project no one may be receiving any pay, but figuring out the day-to-day mechanics will help with the logistics. If people are being paid (maybe this is a $500,000 micro-budget, but there's still some money) the production should be certain that anyone working is getting at least minimum wage. The days of interns on productions with million-dollar budgets are pretty much over. If a crew member is doing a real job, the production can be sued for violating federal or state labor laws. (This is becoming common lately.)

For a budget, virtually all labor is expressed in this way, whether accounting for a department head or the humblest production assistant. For art, construction, and set dressing, prep includes pre-production planning, scouting, design, decision-making, meetings, purchases and rentals of materials, and possibly the transport of those materials. For some activities, prep may mean building, painting, assembling, manufacturing. Prep is also when you try to predict/guess what things will cost to do before you have all the information. (All the locations may not be found or solidified. How can you be expected know you'll have to paint the white walls when you don't know if the walls are white?)

Shoot is the actual production period. Wrap is the clean-up and close down period when items are returned or fixed, or sold.

In addition to labor, a budget will list sets, divided by Interior or Exterior. Bob's House Interior will have its own budget line, even if the decision has been made that it will be the same location for both interior and exterior because there may be different strategies for each.

Payroll

Unless this is a school project, you're probably paying people something. And if you're paying people, you're an employer. If you are an employee, being paid, you still should understand this because it affects the way you are paid and, as mentioned, there are labor laws that affect both employers and employees.

People must be paid for overtime. Unless you are considered a manager (someone who plans other people's time, a department head), you and your crew will be paid X amount per hour for hours 1–8, time-and-a-half for hours 9—12, and double time for anything after that. That means if someone is making $10 per hour and working a normal 12-hour shoot day, they would be paid $80 for the first 8 hours, and $60 for hours 9–12, so $140 per day. If they worked a 13th hour, they would be paid double time ($20) for the final hour. That would be a $160 day. There's no getting around this, and as either a boss or a worker, you should understand the way it works, because it's the law.

On low budget films, sometimes people will say, they'll pay "a flat," meaning a flat fee. But unless the flat totals out to be as much as an hourly would with this fee structure, they aren't following labor laws. That doesn't mean you should run out and call the cops, it's just something to know. I know of very few people who haven't started out working on one very low-budget film for "almost free." The idea is not to do it more than once. After that, you've got some experience and they should pay you, even if it's minimum wage. Unless, of course, it's your own film—then it's fine.

Fringes

In addition to understanding the concept of how pay works on a project, there are two more things you should be aware of. One is payroll fringes. In the US, if anyone is being paid more than $600 total for a project, the employer (the production) must pay payroll taxes. These are FICA (social security), FUI (Federal Unemployment), SUI (State Unemployment), and Medicare. If people are being paid in a lump sum check (for instance you might hire a food stylist or a Steadicam operator for a single day, they give you an invoice and a check is written), they are paying their own payroll taxes. But if someone is working the entire length of a project and they are paid a total of more than $600, then it's the employer's responsibility to cover those things. (The employee also pays into these funds. If you want to know how much, you can just look at your paycheck and see how much is deducted.)

If the project is a union project, the hourly pay will be higher, and there will also be a **Union Fringe**. This is the amount the employer pays into the union for the union employee's benefits, which include health insurance and a pension fund.

Finally, there is (or should be) **Workers' Compensation,** which is insurance that covers some medical expenses and some wage replacement if a worker is injured on the job.

Other Paycheck Items You May See (or Input) in a Budget

If you are a member of the art, construction, set dressing or costume department, you have tools that you use as part of your work. Often you own your own tools and there is no need for the production to supply them. For furnishing your own equipment (anything from paint brushes to ladders, to sewing machines) you will receive a small **box rental** or **kit rental**. This way, the project doesn't have to accumulate these things, and you get to use what you feel are the best tools for the job, rather than the cheapest the production can find.

If the responsibilities of a crew member include doing a lot of driving around (for example, a location manager can easily put thousands of miles on their car looking for locations), they will often receive a **car allowance**. They will be reimbursed by the production for gas (and should keep receipts), but the car allowance is meant to offset the depreciation of their vehicle. Crew members don't receive car allowances for going to and from work, or for doing errands in the usual course of their job, although they may be reimbursed for gas. But if a crew member is constantly driving for the production, they will expect an allowance on any but the most micro (favor for a friend) projects.

The budget pages at the end of this chapter represent an example of what the budgets may be for a super-low project with a non-union crew, and a larger (but still small) project with a union crew. You can easily see the difference.

So that's it for crew. Now for the rest of the budget.

Art and Construction

As we've seen, the size of the art, construction, and set decorating crew can be quite elastic, and on small projects the roles are often combined. It still helps your plan to divide the expenditures so that you're sure that everything is accounted for and nothing is double counted—this is how:

The designer's set list reads **Exterior, Bob's House** – 1 day.

This will be a location, so there will be a note next to the listing: (see Locations). But the Bob's House that's found may not be perfect and in the script, Henry hides in the bushes near the front walkway. The 'found' house may not have bushes that are big or thick enough. Maybe there will need to be greens added. The designer doesn't know yet because the location hasn't been found, but to be safe, the set decorator and production designer have decided to put $500 into greens. (This is a low-budget film so the set decorator will be taking responsibility for that department.)

Interior, Bob's Kitchen – 10 pages.

If shooting in a real house, the trick will be to find an INT. Bob's Kitchen that works for the character, and for the camera.

The camera needs space, and the kitchen has to be lit without seeing the lights in the shot. That set is 10 pages, a hefty portion of the schedule. The project calls for a spacious kitchen, preferably one with an open plan so the director and cinematographer have options and can move the camera easily.

If both interior and exterior are going to be found, the costs will be reflected in the location budget section.

If Bob's Kitchen is being built on a stage or in a warehouse, there will be rentals and purchases. This could include a stove with an exhaust fan, a fridge, a sink built into countertops. The big items will probably be rented, unless the right pieces can be found in a used appliance store.

What's the action in the kitchen? Is anything being cooked? If it's necessary to see water really boil, your choices are cheating it (a close up locked off shot of boiling water that can be shot elsewhere and edited in), a digital FX shot (a lot of work for not much pay-off), or having the FX person rig the stage set so there's a usable water and gas line. "Furnishing" the kitchen will be the set decorator's job—unless the budget is so small that the production designer is also the set decorator.

If building, at least one wall is needed. Sometimes three, depending on the shots. That wall must be painted. Will the floor be in the shots? If so, the bare cement floors on most sound stages and warehouses must be covered. There are printed papers that can be laid on the cement that photograph as wood or tile or brick. There's linoleum.

Both labor and material costs go with building a kitchen on stage. Crews are paid by the hour. How long does it take to build a kitchen, and the walls, and to cover the floors? On a traditional film or television budget form (which can easily run upwards of 40 pages), construction costs are still ultimately considered to be art department expense because the decisions as to what to build fall under the purview of the designer. The designer consults with a construction coordinator and get the costs from him or her, but on a small film the designer might *be* the coordinator and will have to estimate. How many people will be needed to build the set and how long it will take them? What quantity of materials (wood, nails, screws, etc.) will it take to build? Will the walls be painted? Tiled? How many people will that take and for how long? And the opposite—-how many people and how long will it take to dismantle the set and dispose of the materials once shooting is complete?

What kind of **signage or graphics** will there be? That's an expense that can be easily researched and included. You may deal with an outside contractor or purchase existing "real" work (before you do this you must get a legal release in order to use any outside art, graphics, company names, or logos and it can be a long process so that's a big prep item).

Priscilla Elliott

If there's no money, think about graphics. That's the top layer of everything. You can use graphics—they're relatively cheap—to sell a place. We did Boston as Virginia in 1976. This was in 2008. We had a supermarket. We found a local Virginia chain. We got their signage, and we added fake product from the 1970s. We printed and made all this stuff.

You want to do LA, you find something that's branded. That's a cheap way to sell a city, or a place. Graphics can do a lot.

Until the locations or decisions to find or build sets have been solidified, the budget is an estimate, full of "allowances." An allowance is a pool of money set aside for a budgetary item or a few of them. You don't know exactly how the money will be allotted but you know you'll need it sitting there until more information is available. For instance, the production designer might know that to build a school locker room, it will cost a total of about $5,000.

They might not be sure how that's split up, how much the lockers will cost to rent, how much the benches will be, how much the actual labor will be—but he or she has done locker rooms before and they know from experience to set aside about $5,000. So, they'll add that into the budget under the INT. Locker Room set, as an allowance, to be assigned in more detail once they have a better idea as to how large the space has to be, and whether there has to be a bank of shower stalls in the background. Once things have been firmed up, the budget is tweaked and is expected to be quite accurate.

Locations

The location budget will itemize every location, interior and exterior, and all costs associated with each of these. This will include:

Personnel

The location department usually consists of a location manager, and assistant, and sometimes additional assistants and production assistants. Location managers usually have the longest prep time of almost everyone on a film because (unless the entire film is being shot on a stage), without the locations, no one can really do much.

Site Rentals

A site rental is the daily fee you pay for use of the premises. That daily fee is multiplied by the number of days scheduled to shoot at the location, including the required prep days (the art/construction/set decorating departments will decide that), and the number of days it will take to pack up and vacate the location. If you're shooting five days at a house, how long does it take to move everything out, load it on the truck, move all the dressing in and make it look the way you want? That's the number of days that matters. A site rental for a house could be anywhere between a couple hundred dollars to tens of thousands of dollars, depending upon the house and where you are shooting.

The site restoration budget line includes estimates for touching up or completely re-painting walls, re-seeding or replanting trampled upon yards, sanding a floor, or just getting a cleaning crew in, depending on the planned action and the unforeseen circumstances of wear and tear that happens when a film crew of 20–50 people with a job to do, moves furniture, cabling, and equipment into housing meant for a family of four.

Permits

The price of permits varies according to the city, town, even the state where you're shooting, but generally they are not a major expense, anywhere from free in some places to a few hundred dollars.

Parking

It's preferable to have your camera, grip, electric, art department, dressing rooms, motor homes, and cast and crew parking all together in one place—next to your location. Crew will be running back and forth to their trucks all day. You'll be moving your cast from their trailers or wherever they will be getting costumed and made up, and it's best when between takes, they get away from the set but remain close. It's great when you can break for lunch, cross the street, and the caterer or the picnic tables are right there. You don't lose time, it's more pleasant and everybody is easy to find for whatever discussions and decision might arise. Unfortunately, what is ideal is often not possible or affordable. The location manager is responsible for finding adequate parking—and in some cities, where parking is at a premium, a large portion of the location budget will go toward parking, a cost that will neither end up on screen or help tell the story. It is, however, a reality. Often a project will have a base camp, where the key trailers and the catering is, crew parking where cars are left, and vans with drivers or PAs who do constant "rounders" between the base camp, the set, and crew parking. That's three rentals for every location.

Holding Areas

When you have a big extras (background actor) day, a crowd scene, families in the bleachers at a little league game, those people need a place hang out when they're not in front of the camera. The location manager has to find a space to put them. (Holding areas generally provide shelter if the weather is bad and help keep your background cast from wandering around so they're where you want them when you need them.)

Holding areas often share a space with the base camp. If the location manager finds an affordable and large parking lot, that often becomes the catch-all area for almost everything.

Police, Fire

As noted earlier, the permitting authority may require these people as a condition, but even if they don't, there are times when a project needs police on site. If you're shooting outside and there is a weapon visible, you want every passerby to know that there is not a crime in progress, and a police person observing will indicate that. If you are shutting down streets for driving shots, you'll want/need police to make it safe for the public and for the crew. If you are shooting stunts or practical effects with pyrotechnics, you'll want a fireman there.

Park Rangers or Location Monitors

Some locations require the shooting crew to have someone acting as liaison from the crew to the property. They want to be sure that everything is safe, no one strays from where they should be, and they want to keep an eye on the time, so if the production has paid for 12 hours, they're out at 12, not packing up at 13. Rangers and monitors can be very helpful sources of information, and can make your shooting life far easier (or harder) than it is already.

Security

What kind of neighborhood are you shooting in and where are you parking your trucks full of all that expensive equipment? You may want security for your cast and crew parking, or standing near the set, or wherever your loaded trucks spend the night.

Equipment

This includes pop-up tents for shade and shelter, porta-potties for places with no bathrooms, traffic cones to mark off parking spots for loading and unloading, or portable AC units for those old houses where there is no air conditioning when you're shooting in August and your cast and crew are sweating buckets.

Courtesy Payments

This is a nice way of saying, gratuities—which is a nice way of saying that every location manager has a little slush fund that he or she uses to pay off the public when they complain, when the director wants them to move their car out of the shot, when their Christmas decorations show, and it's supposed to be July in the movie.

Stage Rentals

Sound stage or warehouse rental is also a location expense. This includes the facility itself, and all requirements. There are sometimes fees added on to the basic cost of filming at these places. This could be for additional parking spots, electricity, a stage manager, janitorial services, the use of an office, dressing rooms. The deal one makes with some stages can include all these—or not, and the add-ons after the fact can be a shock.

Set Dressing

Back to the set list. In addition to personnel, the set dressing budget will include anything that might cost something.

There is a category for drapery (curtains), which on a bigger film are often made rather than purchased. Same with upholstery (chair, couch coverings). A set decorator will often find pieces of furniture in second-hand stores and re-cover them to look new or luxurious. There are fixtures (lighting fixtures).

Purchases and rentals are broken out by set. Again, these are estimates based on what the decorator thinks will be spent, but as locations are set and it becomes evident what work has to be done, the estimates become hard numbers. That empty rectangular space might be transformed into a family room/dining room. That's a lot of dressing. Carpets, curtains, lights, sofas, chairs, tables, entertainment unit, bookcases. If the family is supposed to be well-off and this is a big budget film, you could easily be talking about $40,000. If it's a micro-budget or student project, maybe $800 for everything. It's all elastic—and don't be fooled into thinking you can't communicate wealth with little money. It's where you put the money, how you think through and find the furniture and beg/borrow the curtains and rugs. A film that has an empty loft location that's supposed to belong to a sad, spoiled party-girl socialite decorated the room with a lot of stuffed-animals adorned in sparkly (fake) diamonds and a lot of mirrors. That told us more about the character's life than an expensive couch.

A Hypothetical Location Budget

Let's look at a micro-budget cheesy thriller. The kind you watch when nothing else is on at midnight.

Jill, an advertising copywriter, is working in Chicago at a prestigious agency. Her brother Alex, an attorney, has now also moved to Chicago and is at a major law firm. The siblings are close, but Jill has always been the wacky baby sister, with an overactive imagination, and a history of unstable relationships and getting and quitting jobs. And Alex begins to date Jill's boss, so Jill is feeling particularly touchy and paranoid. The plot involves Jill being stalked and abducted by a psychotic office-mate and, of course, no one believes her. Finally, she outwits the stalker, there is a chase, and of course, the stalker dies, pushed from the elevated train station, and Jill is safe. Not a work of art but fine for our purposes.

When looking at a micro-budget project, as with any but the most spectacularly funded film, a decision has to be made about where to put your money. In the case of this film, the sets and time that is scheduled to shoot in the sets are:

Interior Jill's Apartment/living room	1 day
Interior Jill's Apartment/bedroom	½ day
Interior Jill's Apartment/kitchen	½ day
Exterior Jill's Apartment Building	1 day
Interior Jill's Office Lobby	1 day
Interior Jill's Office	2 days
Interior Jill's Boss's Office	1 days
Exterior Jill's Office Building	1 day
Exterior Chicago Streets	3 days
Exterior City Park	2 days
Exterior Elevated Train Station (El)	1 day
Interior Muldoon's Bar and Grille—Dining area	2 days
Interior Muldoon's Bar and Grille—Ladies' Room	1 day
Interior Stalker's Apartment	3 days

A total of 20 shooting days and we'll say your micro-budget is $225,000.

Here's the discussion. At first, the idea is to find everything, build nothing, save that construction money. But what if the scene in Muldoon's Ladies' Room is crucial, it's where the first bit of action happens, it's where Jill is ambushed and abducted. No filmmaker is going to want to have to make that work or be exciting in an ordinary restaurant/bar bathroom. Not if there's a struggle. Everything else can work in existing spaces, but possibly not that. So maybe, even though you're only spending one day in that location, it would be better to build it and have some major stunt action. That's a directorial/cinematographer discussion. Or maybe you'll want to put money in the stalker's apartment. You're there for three days and it's got to be creepy. Or maybe you really want to go to town action-wise when dealing with the El, because that scene takes place at night and you can get some scares and surprises out of that and that's one of your two big stunt scenes with the guy falling from a great height.

After consultation with the production designer (who has consulted with the director) the decision has been made that the location manager will find everything except the Ladies Room, which will be built on stage. The location manager has been asked to find the most decrepit place possible for the stalker's place, maybe an industrial space that hasn't been renovated so that when Jill is being chased there are lots of possibilities for hiding, big dark industrial equipment, catwalks, etc. The location manager has also been asked (by the assistant director, who is responsible for keeping the company on schedule, and the line producer, who is responsible for keeping the company on budget) to see if there are any locations that can be consolidated so every day doesn't have a huge company move (which can result in the loss of production time, which means it will cost money).

The location manager has also been asked to come up with a rough budget for his or her department. This is the start of the budgeting process.

The location manager will immediately decide, "I don't have to think at all about the Ladies' Room" because that's now an art/construction/ set dressing project. However, the Ladies' Room is connected (story wise) to the restaurant, so there will have to be some discussion between departments—you don't want to end up like your characters are inhabiting two different locations when it's meant to be the same place—and they are also finding and paying for a stage, or in this case, probably a warehouse or empty space.

Then there is Jill's Apartment. There are three rooms (and 2 days scheduled for interiors, 1 day for the exterior of the building). But the exterior scene is not scheduled to shoot the same week as the interiors so there is not much point in thinking that the interior and exterior locations should be the same. Rather, the exterior of Jill's building is scheduled to shoot the same week as the exterior Chicago streets. So the location manager will try to find someplace in the same general neighborhood as those streets—and maybe the park. The location manager begins their plan. There is the creative concern—these places not only have to look right but because this is a micro-budget project, Jill's Apartment may have to be used as is, meaning the owner's furniture is not moved out, the owner not relocated to a hotel. That makes the search more difficult.

For Jill's Apartment (Interior) the location manager is going to come up with an estimate. They will figure ½ day to prep the location, 2 days to shoot the location, ½ day to get it back to the way it was. In this case, since there's not a lot of stuff moving in or out, that seems reasonable.

They decide that they can probably find Jill's Apartment (Interior) for $500 a day for prep and wrap, and $750 a day for the shoot. They know also that there has to be a place very close by to use as basecamp—to park the equipment trucks, set up the basecamp (where portable toilets, a trailer for the actors, and catering for the crew will be.) In a big city, parking can be very expensive, and this is for two days. (On prep and wrap days, the set decorators will park in a regular spot.) They'll figure $500 per day for that (which is VERY inexpensive in most neighborhoods). Then there is the cost of the permit from the city, and a little money set aside for gratuities (meaning money to soothe an angry neighbor).

Added up, Jill's Apartment (Interior) on a micro-budget may total $4,100. Or maybe the location manager will find someplace less expensive (that may come with a big parking lot) in a slightly outlying area. In any case, that's the thinking behind one key location.

The location manager continues planning and researching and scouting. As locations are found and approved, the guesswork will go away, and eventually there will be a reasonably accurate number.

A location manager native to the area where the shoot is taking place may have already known places that might work well, but if they and the production designer are committed, they will want to find the miracle location that works perfectly. Then comes reality—there may be the great location that everybody loves and that is affordable, BUT it's in a really dangerous neighborhood. Then the cost of security is added to the budget and becomes part of the cost of the perfect location. You may need a security guard where people walk from the set to the trucks, a security guard to be with them when they leave the set and get to their cars when they go home. And if you're in the area for more than a day, and you're parked on the public street or in an open, unfenced lot overnight, there may be the need for security to stand guard on the trucks once the day's shoot is over so there is equipment when the shooting company returns to work the second day.

Those three days Exterior Streets and the El may seem to be inexpensive (and may be) but, whether interior or exterior, there is the cost of a city permit. And if they are part of a chase scene, there will have to be police there, either for crowd control or so that people understand that there is a film shoot and that a deranged guy isn't really chasing a desperate woman. In some film-friendly cities, the services of the local police are free. In some, they're expensive. The location manager will add in the cost if there is one. And again, those city streets—you may want to mount a light on a building, block a doorway. There is more gratuity money budgeted for those days.

The ad agency and law offices may be tough to find because the type of offices needed are fairly high-end, usually with views of the city, and those don't come cheap. That kind of company not only usually doesn't care about earning a paltry location rental fee—they feel that the disruption of a film shoot would cost *them* money. Maybe those will be scenes shot in different offices in the same building, over two weekend days, and the production will have to pay a monitor (someone to watch over the property) in addition to a site rental fee.

Eventually, the location budget (the locations themselves and all the attendant expenses) may top out at $20,000. Or more, or less, depending upon the film, the number of locations, and the circumstances. On short student projects, it may be $1,000—but at least you're not paying anybody!

What would be the differences if you're doing a bigger (but still small) film—maybe for $1,000,000? You can see that there are larger amounts

Table 17.1 Micro-Budget for Locations

Set No.	INT./EXT.	Set/Location Name	Site rental	Pkg/locat	Pkg/bscmp	Police/Fire	Trash	Security	Permit	Rentals	Stage build	Stage Shoot	Stage Strike	Reloc	Expend	Gratuities	Total
1	INT.-1 day	Jill's Apt/Livingrm	1,750	1,000					300							200	3,250
2	INT.-1 day	Jill's Apt./Bedrm/ Lobby	(See above, assumption is same location)						see above								
4	INT.-1 day	Jill's Office Lobby	500	500					300								1,550
5	INT.-2 days	Jill's Office	1,500	1,000					see above								2,500
6	INT.-2 days	Jill's Boss's Office	1,500	1,000					see above								2,500
7	INT.-1 day	Alex's Office	750	500					see above								1,250
8	INT.-2 days	Muldoon's B&Grille	2,000	inc.	inc.				300								2,300
9	INT.-1 day	Muldoon's Ladies' Rm		(2 days build, 1 day shoot, 1 day strike)							1,000	1000	500				2,500
10	INT.3-days	Stalker's Loft	2,250	1,500				450	300							100	4,700
11	EXT.-1 day	Jill's Building/Street	permit only	500		300			300						100	100	1,300
12	EXT.-1 day	Jill's Office Building (LOCATIONS)	permit only	500		300			300						100	100	1,300
13	EXT.-2 days	Park	permit only Free	from park dept.		600			300						100	100	1,100
14	EXT.-3 days	Chicago Streets	permit only	1,500		900		450	300							300	3,450
15	EXT.-1day	Elevated Train Stop (LOCATIONS)	permit only	500		300		450	300								1,550
																TOTAL	29,250

Personnel and construction are part of art/construction budget.

Table 17.2 Low Budget for Locations

Set No.	INT./EXT.	Set/Location name	Site rental	Pkg/locat	Pkg/bscmp	Police/Fire	Trash	Security	Permit	Rentals	Stage build	Stage Shoot	Stage Strike	Reloc	Expend	Gratuities	Total
1	INT.-1 day	Jill's Apt/Livingrm	2,500	1,000					300					relocation	5,000	200	4,200
2	INT.-1 day	Jill's Apt./Bedrm/Lobby	(See above, assumption is same location)						see above								
4	INT.-1 day	Jill's Office Lobby	500	500	400 holding	300			300							100	2,100
5	INT.-2 days	Jill's Office	2,500	1,000					see above								3,500
6	INT.-2 days	Jill's Boss's Office	2,500	1,000					see above								3,500
7	INT.-1 day	Alex's Office	1,250	500					see above								1,750
8	INT.-2 days	Muldoon's B&Grille	2,000	inc.	inc.				300								2,300
9	INT.-1 day	Muldoon's Ladies Rm		(2 days build, 1 day shoot, 1 day strike)							1,000	1,000	5,00				2,500
10	INT.3 days	Stalker's Loft		(4 days build, 3 days shoot, 2 days strike)							2,000	3,000	1,000				6,000
11	EXT.-1 day	Jill's Building/Street	permit only	500	400 holding	300			300							100	1,600
12	EXT.-1 day	Jill's Office Building (LOCATIONS)	permit only	500	400 holding	300			300						100	100	1,600
13	EXT.-2 days	Park	permit only Free from park dept.	permit only	600				300						100	100	1,100
14	EXT.-3 days	Chicago Streets	permit only	1,500	1,200 holding	900	450		300						200	300	4,850
15	EXT.-1 day	Elevated Train Stop (LOCATIONS)	permit only	500	400 holding	600	450		300						100	100	2,450
																TOTAL	41,950

Personnel and construction are part of art/construction budget.

allotted for each location, there's more for parking (when you have a little more money you can pay more for convenience). There's money for a
"holding area." On a micro-budget your background actors (extras) may
be wandering around the parking area. Depending upon the season of the
shoot, there may be outdoor heaters or air-conditioning units rented for
some of the locations. And you would move the real-life occupant of Jill's
fictional apartment out to a hotel and pay the expenses. Mostly, additional
money gives you additional options, and can make things more comfortable.

Art Department Budget

When you are making a micro-budget film (this is true for any film, but
particularly when crew and money are in short supply), you are going to
decide where you should put your money. What are the most important
sets, whether because of something that is written in the screenplay or
because there is an important piece of unwritten information about a
character, an emotion. On this film, the decision to build the Ladies'
Room means that proportionally a lot of money will be allotted to that
set. The production designer will hopefully know the way the sequence
in the location is planned, therefore know whether there will be two
walls or three, whether there will be no ceiling, or a removable one. How
large will the set have to be? That will all play into the construction cost.
The set decorator will be renting bathroom fixtures—how many stalls
will have to be outfitted—or can there just a door and you don't see the
toilets? Is there a window? The decision to build that Ladies' Room can
really impact the limited budget—but the decision may have been made
that it's worth it to do that and skimp on dressing in other areas. In
this particular example, the designer and decorator have come up with a
combined number of $2,100, not counting the space itself.

For Jill's Apartment Interior, they've decided they will have to find a
place where they can use at least the bulk of the furniture that's already
there. On a very limited budget, they've decided that the way to dress Jill's
Apartment to reveal character will be with a combination of artwork,
family photos of Jill and Alex from when they were children (which will
entail asking the actors for their own photos once they are cast, having
them copied, then framed and displayed), and some small pieces of dressing that tell us a little about who Jill is and where she's been. If the walls
are a terrible color, maybe they will paint and then will have to paint it
back to the original color once shooting is done.

For the offices, they are counting on the location manager finding the
right look and maybe doing some painting, adding some plants and small
desk items from thrift shops, etc. Maybe they will create samples of work
from one of the ad agency's award-winning campaigns, blow them up,
and hang them on the walls. For Alex's office, they may create diplomas
or purchase/rent a few shelves full of second-hand books about case law.

There are several exterior locations where they're just planning on using graphics or signage. Maybe to make the chase sequence through the park that climaxes at the El, there will be more obstacles for Jill and the stalker to dodge and avoid. One of the least expensive ways to heighten tension is to create close calls and things to hide behind.

The Stalker's Loft—that's another key location. They've asked the location manager to find a great, intricate industrial loft space with lots of texture, and they plan on dressing it with tons of debris, and creating all kinds of hidden-camera photos of Jill (the object of the stalker's obsession), papering the space with them, and filling it with stuff that we've seen Jill discard and seen him grab and take home. They're going to spend a couple of thousand on filling that space, painting it a color they feel will lead us into his disturbed mind, and literally burying part of the space with his psyche.

If they have more money, here are some changes they might plan to make:

1   Jill's Apartment—change out all of the furniture, repaint, change the curtains, give her a flat-screen TV in an armoire or other big pieces, maybe higher-end lighting.
2   Jill's Office Lobby—probably not much of a change.
3   Jill's Office—again, rent furniture, curtains, framed copies of ad copy for products.
4   Jill's Boss's Office—possibly moving out the existing furnishing, moving in higher-end furniture, better light fixtures, plaques created on the wall attesting to the awards the company has received. Trophies.
5   Alex's office—more of the same.
6   Muldoon's—if it's perfect, they'll leave it alone. If not, maybe there will be different table settings, candles, table linen.
7   The exteriors may get altered slightly—especially the train platform of the El, where the climax of the action happens. Maybe something will be constructed that will enhance the stunt.

These are just a very few examples of the thought process you will go through in order to arrive at a way to best use the funds that you have. Whether you are a student making a short or someone making an extremely low budget project, the resources will vary, but you will work better, more efficiently, and more creatively if you go through this kind of set by set, scene by scene analysis, always asking yourself and your team, exactly how can we accomplish what we need to, to best tell this story about these people, with what we have? Planning and communication are the most important aspects of pulling together any project—and they are free.

Table 17.3 Art Department Micro-Budget

Set No.	INT./ EXT.	Set/Location Name	Rental	Purchase	Drapes	Fixtures	Construction	Materials	Paint	Labor	Greens	TOTAL
1	INT.	Jill's Apt/Livingrm	200	200					100	200		700
2	INT.	Jill's Apt./Bedrm	200	200								400
3	INT.	Jill's Bldg/Hallway										0
4	INT.	Jill's Office Lobby		100							100	200
5	INT.	Jill.s Office	300	200								500
6	INT.	Jil''s Boss's Office	400	200	200						100	900
	INT.	Alex's Office	400	200	200						100	900
7	INT.	Muldoon's B&Grille		100								100
8	INT.	Muldoon's Ladies' Rm	700				450		150	800		2,100
	INT.	Stalker's Hide-Out	300	500			graphics (500)		150	800		2,250
9	EXT.	Jill's Building/Street	(LOCATIONS)									0
	EXT.	Jill's Office Building	(LOCATIONS)									0
	EXT.	Park	(LOCATIONS)									0
	EXT.	Chicago Streets	(LOCATIONS)									0
	EXT.	Elevated Train Stop	(LOCATIONS)									0

TOTAL 7,350

Personnel (See Labor for Crew in addition to regular crew)

Table 17.4 Art Department Low Budget

Set No.	INT./EXT.	Set/Location Name	Rental	Purchase	Drapes	Fixtures	Construction	Materials	Paint	Labor	Greens	TOTAL
1	INT.	Jill's Apt/Livingrm	1,000	750	300				100	200		2,350
2	INT.	Jill's Apt./Bedrm	300	200	200							700
4	INT.	Jill's Office Lobby	200	100							100	400
5	INT.	Jill's Office		200			Graphics 500	300				1,000
6	INT.	Jill's Boss's Office	500	200	200	200	Graphics 500				150	1,750
	INT.	Alex's Office	500	200	200	200					100	1,200
7	INT.	Muldoon's B&Grille	1,000	500								1,500
8	INT.	Muldoon's Ladies' Rm		(see micro-budget)								2100
	INT.	Stalker's Hide-Out	1,000	1,500 (includes photos)			1000		200	1,000		4,700
9	EXT.	Jill's Building/Street		Signage 500								500
	EXT.	Jill's Office Building (LOCATIONS)	–	Signage 500								500
	EXT.	Park	200	Signage 500					200	200		1,100
	EXT.	Chicago Streets	500	Signage 500					200	200		1,100
	EXT.	Elevated Train Stop (LOCATIONS)	300	Signage 500			500		400	600		2,300
											TOTAL	21,200

Personnel (See Labor for Crew in addition to regular crew)

18 Learning the Craft
Starting Out

It's not that unusual for someone to aspire to a career as a director, a writer, or an actor—but unless you happen to be one of those people who sits through the list of names at the end of the movie, or someone in film school, it's rare for someone to know about all these design-based roles. They just aren't as public, and they certainly aren't considered the glamour jobs.

Where do these people come from? Many of them stumbled into their careers. They started in architecture, theater, art, interior design, or fashion. Or they wanted to work on movies and the department that needed bodies happened to be art.

How Lee Ross Became a Scenic Painter

I was a philosophy major and a musician and eventually found myself working in set shops. I was making $8 an hour, then I saw an invoice of what the shop was billing (maybe $35 an hour) so, at 25, I ended up on the paint crew of *Tombstone*. They went through two crews and for one reason or another they didn't last. Then a producer came up to me and said, "Hey Kid, you work hard. You're now head of the paint crew."

Production Designer Brendan O'Connor

Coming out of school you have big dreams. You were the designer. You were the head of the department. You were the creative decision-maker. And coming out of school, you have to turn all that off. You have to step back and change your attitude and realize you're still learning.

(continued)

(continued)

I had always known that I wanted to do film and television design. In high school I took every art class under the sun and was working in drama club doing set design for the school plays. I loved being able to incorporate all these artistic mediums into one installation. Production design really takes every medium. It's photography, it's painting, it is micro-level fine arts skills, but on a larger scale because everything is fake. We're on a sound stage, recreating this world.

At grad school I was lucky enough to be able to really do a production design project, which is not something a lot of kids have the option to do. We spent $11,000 creating a medieval village out in the middle of a cattle field (see Photos 18.1, 18.2, 18.3, 18.4). It wasn't perfect, but I was happy with it.

That propelled me along because I was able to put that in my portfolio, and I ended up getting the Television Academy internship for Art Direction where they place you with designers on TV shows. It was the summer right after I graduated and I used that opportunity to meet as many people as I possibly could. That's how I met the designer from *Shameless* on Showtime. I was able to go to the set, visit Warner Brothers studios, do a tour, get a little bit more of an insight of how the office works. I was able to get hands-on experience as an intern. I went to the set of *Dexter* and to a couple of other smaller shows, daytime soap operas. I got a really well-rounded experience with that program. And it was keeping up those relationships, making sure to check in. I kept in touch with the designer of *Shameless* every six months. I knew that she had an

Photo 18.1 Field with overlay establishing Medieval period and location of *The Devout*.

Photo 18.2 Nighttime establishing shot of Medieval village, built entirely on location in Southern California.

Photo 18.3 Medieval village center.

Photo 18.4 Medieval village house.

(continued)

Art PA (Production Assistant) position and I knew I wanted it. It was about a year after school and I was PA-ing on a small feature. I got the email from the designer saying, "I'd love to bring you in for an interview." I went in. She said, "you're overqualified, you're going to be bored, you're going to hate it."

I finally convinced her to hire me. I was with her for Season 4 as a PA and I went on with her to a pilot for NBC where I was doing a lot more than PA-ing, I was doing a lot of computer drafting because I had the skill set, I went to school. It moved me up quicker. That pilot ended, and I got a phone call from a producer out of Boston who randomly found my information on Production Hub [website]. He really liked my work on [my school project] *The Devout*, my medieval village, and he had a million-dollar feature with Darko Entertainment (they did *Donnie Darko*). We built a motel room set on stage and there was a backlot street that was previously used on the TV show *Las Vegas* that we turned into a Mexican street and we converted a couple other places on the lot to a strip club and a gambling backroom.

We wanted it to feel as authentic as possible, so it was figuring out what the storefronts should be. It was a border town. We did a souvenir market. We didn't have a huge budget so a lot of it was graphic design, coming up with different storefront signage, and posters. We made things not look new. I kept thinking the street was too high-end and I had to bring it down. I covered up part of a sign with fabric and rope. You come up with details that help sell the textural aspects of it, doing phone card posters that have been aged and painted on and beat up. I think the broad strokes of choosing that, especially when you don't have a lot of money, can be done with graphics. Bringing in an artist for a couple hundred bucks who will do a mural on the wall, a free-hand Virgin Mary on a Mexico street will help sell a sort of textural cultural correlation. A lot of it was layers of paint and water and age effects.

Coming out of film school and having the opportunity to be at the ground level of development of a project—my thesis project—I was involved in every aspect of it. You have to be. If you're not willing to do a little bit of everything, there's not enough people on the project, and it's not going to get done! You don't have any money. You've just got to do it. There's no bitchin' and moaning. You've just got to roll up your sleeves and do the best work that you can. If that means that you and the DP are building a lighting grid or something together in order to help that department, you want your sets to look as good as they possibly can. If you're able to do that—work with people and communicate—that's super important.

Starting a Career in the Art Department

You are your own business and you have to look at yourself that way. You have to use your skills and make sure you are represented to the best of your ability, whether that's your portfolio, your website, the industry sites where you can have your portfolio. Make sure they're updated and show only the best of your work. A lot of that is making sure that you have the skills. Drafting and graphic design are skills that will sell you. You have to show that you're comfortable with that, at least to fake it to get in and sell yourself so people can say, OK, this kid can do it and learn on the job. Because it will be a starting position and school is all theory. Until you're out and doing it in the real world you have to keep building that skill set.

If you don't have a job, give yourself one. If people need help with their resumés lay them out for them in Illustrator. Learn the different programs to keep those skills fresh. My first year, I didn't turn down a project. Whether it did pay or didn't pay. I just wanted to get the experience and meet people. One project that I did for $100 a day was this little short film with a crew of USC grads. It was a cute little children's fantasy film, it was shot in a warehouse downtown and it was fun and young and I was able to create a cool treehouse environment. I didn't make any money on but I met a lot of really great people and one of those people I continue to work with, I continue to hire her, she's now my on-set dresser. It's being in the trenches together.

You're going to eat ramen for a little bit. You're not going to be able to go out to the clubs, you're going to have to make sacrifices. But I think it's important if it's the job you want to do, do it.

Another thing is persistence. Keeping up with people. Being low key. Understanding that people are working and if they don't respond to your email right away it's because they're working, it's not because they don't care. Don't be a stalker. But every three months it's not bad to make sure your name is back in their in box. You never know when a project is going to end and the next project is going to begin.

(continued)

(continued)

And once you're working you shouldn't get pigeon-holed into one type of movie. You should be able to understand every set. It doesn't matter. Your aesthetic has to be flexible. It's funny because producers might say, this person's done a lot of comedy, so they understand comedy sets. What's a comedy set?

The Politics

It's important that you're learning at a story level and understanding that yes, it really is about the story, it really is about the characters. Art is so subjective. It really does come down to making sure the work you're doing is best for the story. And if something needs to change because of scheduling or whatever, hopefully you're not compromising the story because that's really what you're trying to sell. If you're in preproduction and you're budgeting to build a set and unfortunately that set is cut because of budget and you have to shoot it on location, you roll with it. It would've been fun, it would've been a nice portfolio piece, it would've been great. But get it on the next one. You've got to be able to take it and roll with it and understand it's what's best for the story and the production.

John Miller: Words of Wisdom for Students Who Want to Make Films That Don't Look Like Student Films . . .

I've noticed that film students are afraid of close-ups. Everything is a medium close-up. That's a safe distance. People are afraid to get up close and personal. With a close-up, you're invading someone's personal space. I am a fan of extreme close-ups because they're extraordinarily effective—as long as you know when to use them. Students tend to think that everything is about information. It's never about information. Again, its's about emotion. As soon as you get that, it changes the way you shoot, it changes the way you design things. Once you realize, this is an emotional experience that I'm putting people through, you're good. Film is an emotional experience, not an informational experience.

On Locations

One of the things young filmmakers do, if they need an office, a classroom, whatever, they'll pick the most affordable, convenient one. But if it's a vanilla nothing office—is that what your film is supposed to be about, this vanilla nothing world? How is our sense of this character reinforced by this vanilla office that you picked? They say, it's not really, but it's what I could get. But if you keep looking you'll probably find something good that is affordable.

19 Doing What You Want with What You Have
Student Films

Student short films have the double whammy of not very much money and a not overly experienced crew. The temptation is always to pare down and suppress ambition because often ambition on these tiny films can't be realized. But it's interesting when you see someone create something really visual, transcend "using a friend's house" as a location, and come up with a good-looking project that overcomes the "smallness" while perfectly supporting the story. As demonstrated by the examples below, you can do a lot with a limited budget if you spend time planning and you are committed.

Jon Milano's graduate school thesis film, *Straw Dolls*, about the Armenian Genocide in 1915, won a student Emmy. The production team shot the exteriors at Big Sky Movie Ranch in Simi Valley, California. Lauren Israel and Rebekah Schey were co-production designers and built the exterior of a farmhouse for the project. They researched with books about the Genocide and with the descendants of Genocide survivors to be sure that the details were accurate.

The team matched the exterior of the farmhouse with a three-wall interior set that was built on stage and worked with the cinematographer, Justin Alpern, on the roof design so that he could light through the roof boards (see Photos 19.1, 19.2, 19.3, 19.4). Although, as noted earlier, shooting at a movie ranch can be very expensive for a micro-budget or student film, it was decided that for this film, the terrain and the freedom to shoot in all directions was essential. That's where the bulk of the budget went.

Jon Milano

We started scouting four or five months in advance and went to every scenic location in the 30-mile zone. (A zone within 30 miles of Hollywood. Shooting beyond the zone would mean it was necessary to house the cast and crew overnight.) Cost was a major factor as was selling 1900s Armenia in 2015 California.

Photo 19.1 Establishing the cruel round-up of Armenians in 1915.

Photo 19.2 Establishing exterior of Armenian farmhouse to match interior build on stage.

Photos 19.3 and 19.4 Soldier searches for potential prisoners. (continued on next page)

Photos 19.3 and 19.4 continued

Brenna Malloy's thesis film *Rocket* has screened in over 40 film festivals in eight countries. In 2016, *Rocket* won a Student Academy Award, and awards in China, the UK, and multiple festivals across the United States. Malloy directed and co-wrote the project. *Rocket* is about a young female dirt track race car driver, set in the late 1940s and 1950s. Here is some input from Brenna and her team about how the visuals of the project came together.

Brenna Malloy

My first inspiration for the visual design was the painting *Prom dress* by Norman Rockwell. I stumbled upon it as I was getting close to pre-production and the shooting draft of the script. This painting could very easily be the backstory of our protagonist; a teen girl in her childhood bedroom in the late 1940s, searching for her self-identity, caught between tradition and her own personal truth. I stared at this piece for hours and hours in the early days of prep for *Rocket*. I am in no way an art historian, but to me there is something about Rockwell's use of color and texture to tell universal stories through the lens of the American experience that I find profoundly moving. The tone and feeling of this painting is what I wanted to infuse into the film.

Our conversations began with the characters and their journeys. How do we portray through design Annie's journey from a happy and full childhood, to a lonely existence at the start of act II, to heartbroken, but full of hope for the future, at the end?

Our wonderful production designer Rahma Farahat, and our dynamic cinematographer Nick Ramsey, and myself had long conversations about how we were going to use color and texture to tell the story. What we were trying to stay away from was making this film look like a memory; we felt that too many period pieces have done that without specificity. There was a painting Nick and I found at the Laguna Art Museum that we felt perfectly captured the texture we wanted to capture through the camera. A lot of our conversations came back to that painting; of a barn and a front porch and the light bouncing off the old structures a certain way.

Our goal was for our two time periods, 1947 and 1959, to feel very different, but live in the same world. In 1947 Annie's world is bright, happy, and full of wonder. To reflect this, we decided to use brighter colors in the design, more reds and oranges, and really filled the frame with cars, people, and set design. When we jump to

(continued)

Photo 19.5 Ext. Annie's house.

1959 Annie lives alone, on a desolate farm long past its heyday. To reflect this change, we used more blues and grays and left the frame more empty. As Weston comes into her world and helps her find more hope, the warm colors and fullness of frame start to return. This choice of warm to cool back to warm again was the foundation upon which we built the visual design of the film.

The Locations

I grew up visiting a ranch just above Santa Barbara every year. This place is incredible, and has definitely influenced how I tell stories—using the land, and the landscape, as a character. When I first got the idea for *Rocket*, I used this ranch to visualize the story in my head. I never thought in a million years I would be able to shoot this film there and now, looking back, it is clear to me this film wouldn't have been possible if we didn't have access to this beautiful and ideal location (see Photo 19.5). Luckily, the owner believed in us and the story we were trying to tell and not only let us use his property, but he himself led the effort to build the dirt track you see in the film. A silver lining of the terrible California drought was that this rancher wasn't able to grow anything that year so he was excited to make his land useful in some way. I am eternally grateful to him and his neighbor whose barn we used for the interior scenes. One of the gifts of making this film was learning how important grassroots efforts are when making independent films. A lack of financing can be overcome by a good story and the key creatives' abilities to involve others in the telling of it.

The only location we used not on or near our main ranch, was the exterior of a restaurant in rural California that still had a 1950s look to it. Our producer Sarah Hulsman scouted multiple options within driving distance from the ranch and found a great one that let us shoot out in front for a small fee.

Costume Design on a Period Film

I remember in early conversations with Rahma and our costume designer Jeff Solis there was a big discussion about the clothes not "looking" 1950s but "being" 1950s. Luckily for us, Jeff is an extremely insightful designer. He also has an extensive collection of period clothes himself. He was able to find the perfect clothes for the film, without having to use reproductions. Since our color plan was to go from warm, to cool, back to warm again, Jeff designed the clothes in this way.

(continued)

(continued)

He tracked the arc of our protagonist and matched his design to her journey. He also spent a good amount of time talking to us about how a woman in the 1950s, who wasn't traditional, would dress. This opened up a great conversation with our lead actor Lizzie Clarke—where we all got on the same page about why Annie dresses the way she does, and how this choice can possibly evolve as Annie and Weston grow closer. Like most design choices in period piece films, costume can make or break the credibility of the film. Thanks to Jeff, our characters fit right in to the world we created around them.

Rahma Farahat, Production Designer

As the script was developing into what it is now and we were starting to research the period look, we talked a lot about the visual representation of the characters in the sets, and how the look changes along with their arcs throughout the film. We also discussed how to accurately portray the time period and the lifestyle of our characters, while still keeping it aesthetically pleasing for a modern audience and in tune with the overall look we were aiming for.

In the broad strokes, we made sure to use a color palette that the audience would be familiar with for our time period, using things like paint chips and fabric samples from the 1950s to dictate the tonality. We also paid a great deal of attention to the details of our sets, from things like furniture and drapes, to the little ashtrays and electrical outlets; everything on screen had to fit within our period by using a mix of turn of the century decor and 1950s accents to create a history within our locations.

We first started with the location that inspired this whole story, an area of land near the beach in Lompoc, California, with a huge field, a barn, and a cute little house that has not been touched by modern technology of the present day. We wanted to get the feeling that inspired Brenna to write this story by experiencing it first-hand. We went into the little town and imagined how the locals lived, and it wasn't hard to transport ourselves back to the 1950s. After considering a few other locations, we all agreed that no other place could give our film the uniqueness this place had to offer. While on one of our many trips to the location in Lompoc, an eager neighbor stopped by because he heard what we planned on doing and was very excited to help (something we found common with most of the neighbors).

Photo 19.6 Annie's garage (a barn that was dressed).

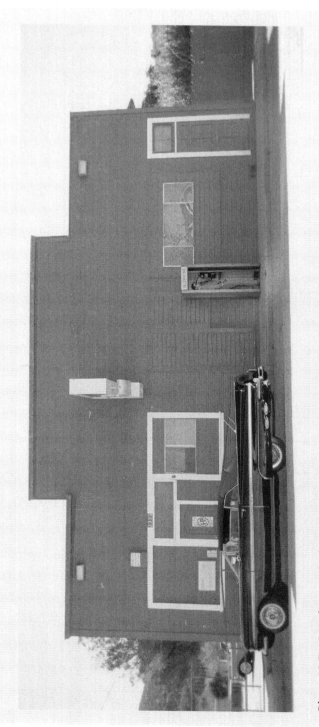

Photo 19.7 1950s barn with phone booth.

After talking to this man about our leading lady and her barn-turned-auto-garage, he took us over to his own barn-turned-auto-shop and was happy to lend us any tools and machinery he had that fit our time period (and he had quite the collection). After some discussion with Brenna, Nick, and Sarah, our producer, we realized it would be easier if we moved our location to this new barn and redesigned it to fit our look, than to move heavy machinery and the pieces we liked to our original location (see Photo 19.6).

Early on, Brenna and I discussed the color palette and how we wanted the colors and mood of each set to reflect the characters and the story. We knew we had a base color of brown (since the majority of the film takes place on a dirt race track) so we wanted the rest of the palette to accentuate the nature of our location. After a few weeks of research, I put together some boards with newspaper and magazine clippings, reference photos, possible location images, as well as an overall color palette I thought fit the best from everything I had compiled. We then went on to fine tune the colors that went into each individual set, keeping in mind how lighting would affect the look on the day of the shoot.

I believe that my most important job as a designer is to help tell the story visually, to convey a backstory and emotions to the audience without relying on acting and dialogue. In this instance, the design of the film helps deliver a deeper layer of emotions. As the relationship between Annie and Weston develops and they begin to influence each other's lives and choices, there is a shift in the environment, costumes, hair styles, etc. to convey how deep the connection between them really is. Also, Annie's garage is full of memorabilia from her father's racing days. The things she surrounds herself with help tell the history of this family and show just how much Annie is attached to the memories of her father.

Nick Ramsey, Cinematographer

Prep

As a period piece, this film is all about the design. We created an old race track in the modern day so we had to talk about everything that would be in frame. We were constantly looking away from or hiding something too modern. There were huge production challenges, but also we had to figure out a way to capture the image with modern

(continued)

(continued)

technology but make it feel like it was older. We used a combination of lenses, filtration, and color grading to ultimately achieve the look we landed on. We were recreating something that no longer existed, a nostalgia, a dream, and every detail mattered.

We made sure to only use materials and processes that they had available to them at the time, whenever possible. We were lucky to have access to an abundance of old props for our set. We were looking for age and textures.

We wanted to get rid of the all the plastic and metal of modern day and replace it with the earth tones, dirt, and wood of the time.

We certainly discussed a palette. It began as a simple conversation about period and the kind of colors we could use to help convey this. Brenna and I took an Art Museum class with Bill Dill (cinematographer and professor) and we were able to pull so much inspiration from that. There was an old painting of a farmhouse front porch in Laguna Beach that we really used to inform the feeling of the time. We constantly went back to look at this painting.

We started with our base palette and as we found our cars and locations we introduced some more interesting colors like the reds and blues.

We had to find a location big enough and remote enough that would allow us to create a race track. We were able to find an old farm way outside of the city. Then we had our own little *Field of Dreams* moment: "If you build it they will come." We got to build our own racetrack! The location was everything, full of great textures and personality.

Special Lenses and Lights Used to Underscore the Feel of the Period

All the lenses we used on the film were at least over 25 years old. We had so many action cameras, we needed a variation of different mounts. Mainly we used Zeiss Standard Speeds and old Cooke Zooms. We also played with filtration somewhat to underscore the period, but more so to convey a sense of the different times. We wanted her father's time period to feel more like a dream, so it got a little bit more filtration then the gritty real world. During the actual time period they probably would have used much harder light, but with the sharpness of modern cameras, my goal was to soften everything as much as possible. Big Soft lights and extra soft glass and filtration. I was constantly looking for ways to knock the edge off of things.

Photo 19.8 Race cars on a dirt track built for the film.

Sarah Wilson Thacker's work includes films, television, and branded content for clients such as Sony/Playstation, Google, Caesars Entertainment, and Revlon. Her grad thesis film, *The Bright Side*, a period musical short, won a 2014 Student Emmy Award and was an official selection at dozens of film festivals worldwide.

Sarah Thacker, Director

The Bright Side is a romantic musical drama set in 1941, just before Pearl Harbor. It's about two childhood best friends reconciling their feelings for each other. The protagonist, Leonard, has always had feelings for Hazel. On learning about her engagement to be married, he thinks it is his last chance to win her over. The visual design—I have always been a fan of beautiful romantic period pieces, musicals like *Moulin Rouge*—*Moulin Rouge* was one of my favorite films growing up. I really wanted to do something that was romantic and of another time and place, something that was an escape. I think romance in the 1940s was in many ways the same, but in many ways it was very different than romance today, in terms of the stakes (the war). I wanted to explore a romance in that period, through that lens. I wanted to do it through song and dance and kind of bring the love alive in that way. I started pulling from Joe Wright's *Pride and Prejudice*, that was a big inspiration, and pieces of *Moulin Rouge* in terms of how musical numbers operate, and *Scrooge* as well. I think we always knew we wanted it to be a blend of old and new, so we're marrying newer techniques with the older, more traditional, "Let's watch them dance for a minute." Let's do moving masters and marry old ways with new ways the same way we were marrying classical musical numbers with modern, alt-rock songs.

Rachel (the Production Designer, Rachel Aguirre) was a huge part of developing the look. I know we always liked the color mint green. The character's name was Hazel and we looked at different ways of bringing in greens and hazels. There was a lot of Art Deco inspiration as well. In terms of design, we really liked crisp, and clean—playing off her character.

Locations

The theater scenes and the imaginary war scene . . . they're sitting in the theater, watching a movie on an unofficial date and they start to fantasize about them being in the movie. What was wanted was to have them start in the movie theater that would play for period, one of these old classic movie houses, then they'd run out into the street and suddenly it would be a war zone outside on the street. The initial intention was for the big scene to be outside. Obviously, an exterior street set in the 1940s was a challenge cost-wise. We came very close to doing it on the CBS Radford back lot, but it was still a little too expensive when everything was said and done for us to justify it. But that was going to be the big in the streets type of musical number, at night, with lots of extras dressed as soldiers running around and firing guns and explosions and what not. That was the vision for the scene. And the film was completely different from that, but it actually worked great. We stumbled on a theater that was no longer functioning, they were about to do renovations on it at the time, the Fox Theater in downtown Fullerton. We toured it for the movie theater location thinking we would shoot the musical number on the lot and that would be the interior location. When we were in there, the theater was just a ruin and it looked like someone had bombed it. The idea came up—why don't we just shoot the whole musical number in this theatre? We can have them watching the movie and suddenly we turn around and they're in this bombed out theatre (see Photo 19.9). It saved us so much pain! And it had a gorgeous look. It was a little more dance heavy than it would have been otherwise. Neither actor was really a dancer so there was also the challenge of finding dance that was appropriate for non-dancers, movement-based more than dance-based.

We used the Mission Playhouse in San Gabriel to play the theater that they (the characters, who play actors in the film) actually act in. That location was phenomenal. I think the fact that we were students at the time was the reason we were able to make the movie that we made. People wanted to help us.

The engagement party scene was in Redlands, California. That was an old train station. We needed something like a verandah with old stone columns that was very grand and looked like it would be attached to an estate. The goal had always been to shoot at some massive estate, someplace very regal. And what we ended up finding was this long hallway corridor in Redlands that was part of an old train station that wasn't functioning anymore (see Photo 19.10). We hung a bunch of curtains that blew in the wind and made it work (see Photo 19.11). We were outside. It would have been where people waited to board the train, it was right next to the tracks.

I don't remember how we found all these locations, it was a lot of work online, a lot of time spent looking at photos and driving around. That night the design team needed way more time than we had and were only able to dress half of what they needed to. We were supposed to flip around halfway through and shoot in the other direction and it was apparent it was not going to happen, so we just turned

(continued)

Photo 19.9 Stylized fantasy World War II gun battle.

Photo 19.10 Outdoor railroad station before dressing.

Photo 19.11 Railroad station after it becomes a grand ballroom.

the people around and pretended it was flipped. There was a lot of choreography because we'd been doing it the whole night and it was making sure we didn't cross the line. [Author's note: In film, one of the first things a filmmaker learns is not to "cross the line." The line is the 180-degree arc that is set up in a shot. Unless you purposely want to disorient your audience, you will be careful to maintain the left/right and spatial relationship of the actors from shot to shot in a scene. Otherwise, when the scene is edited together, it will look as if your actors have inexplicably flipped positions or jumped from one place to another. That's very jarring for the audience.]

(continued)

(continued)

It was a cold night, and everyone was in bare ball gowns. Everyone was freezing, we didn't have the money for proper heaters like you would on a bigger budget film. That was the hardest night of the shoot—that and the ship day. (It wasn't supposed to rain that day—and it did, off and on. All day.)

Steven Snyder, producer of the project, is now a Creative Executive at Innisfree Pictures, a boutique production company with a first look deal at Focus Features.

Steven Snyder

Getting the ship for *Bright Side* was a trial and error process, but one that turned out to be very fortuitous. We kept an open mind and explored the idea of an air hangar versus a ship. As far as ships, we tried the *Queen Mary* first. That was going to be incredibly expensive, but they recommended we look into the USS *Iowa*, also located at the Port of Los Angeles. We met with a man who went by the name "Barefoot." He proved to be very helpful. He allowed us to use the ship for free. We had to get special insurance for that day, which took maybe a week or two to process. It was only $250 to add that rider, which was way less than what we had initially attributed to it in the budget. Plus, we got some rain on the day of filming, perhaps a hassle to deal with, but it added nice production value to the scenes (see Photos 19.12, 19.13, 19.14, 19.15).

Photos 19.12, 19.13, 19.14, 19.15 Using a sequence of shots to "sell" a
location when access is limited.

Rachel Aguirre was the production designer on *The Bright Side* and, after graduating, Rachel was granted an art direction internship from the Television Academy of Arts and Sciences. She is now a member of the Art Director's Guild local 800 and has recently worked on ABC's *The Real O'Neals*, Disney's *Magic Camp*, *SuperHuman* on Fox, and *S.W.A.T.* on CBS.

Rachel Aguirre

It's a student film so of course we had restrictions on time and budget, but I believe we really pulled it off. We used (almost) all period locations so the bones were there. For example, when we shot in the San Gabriel Mission Playhouse (built in 1927), we knew the architecture was already beginning to tell the story to the audience. We just had to add the details with costumes and props to show we were in the 1940s.

Luckily, living in southern California allowed me to rent from prop shops and have authentic 1940s pieces. These helped sell some of the more difficult locations. I tried to use only period objects or some that could pass as such from far away.

I worked closely with our costume designer, Michael Philpot, and our cinematographer, Ryan Broomberg. Initially, Michael met with Ryan, Sarah (director), and myself to discuss tone, color scheme, and what each character would wear. I made a board that showed my inspiration for the set and based on these notes, Michael built all the costumes. He was a rockstar! Michael would give us updates and send photos of his progress from time to time.

Ryan and I would have frequent meetings to discuss what we wanted to do vs. what we could do. Both of us had a common goal to make this film as beautiful as we could. By the time we were shooting, both of us had a shorthand. I knew when Ryan needed a foreground object or when he wanted to create a specific look.

Some Tricks/Tips for Students and First-Timers

I have so many things to say! But to narrow it down:

1   Dress for your frame. On a student film, you can't waste money dressing space in your location that you'll never see. Discuss with the cinematographer and director where exactly you need to dress. Where are the edges of your frame? Will you see into any other adjoining rooms? Are there reflections that you'll need to cover with decor?

   TIP: Sometimes just closing a door, adding and/or closing curtains, adding a foreground object, or a larger piece of decor can help hide something that is unsightly. If that's not possible consider color or lighting. See if there is something you can highlight in the frame that will allow the rest to fall back. For example: a bright yellow raincoat in a closet will pop among muted colors around it. Or a man on stage under a spotlight in a dark theater.

2   Balance. This can mean many different things, but balancing a frame is something you, your decorator, and cinematographer can work on. It's usually a good idea to make sure there isn't something too heavy (meaning large, dark, or glaring) in the shot. Balance the frame by using other objects (or people) to create an attractive vignette. This doesn't necessarily mean the frame is symmetrical. Objects in uneven numbers usually look more attractive. For example: three candles of different heights/ widths looks more interesting than four that are identical.

TIP: Sometimes if the frame is a bit complicated, blur your eyes slightly so you can only see the shapes themselves. Then try re-arranging.

3   Have options. If you're able to, have options for important pieces. For example: tour character is a powerful executive in an office. She needs a chair that tells the audience she's not just anyone in this office.

TIP: Don't lose the receipt! Keep all your tags and buy a few options you can try out.

4   Be prepared. Have an on-set kit that helps you in a pinch. The more prepared you are, the faster you can fix an issue. Some good things you should always have:

- Gaff Tape in white and black (or any black and white tape if you can't get your hands on Gaff).
- A small tool kit and power drill.
- Cleaning products and paper towels as well as microfiber cloths. Try not to get products that have ammonia in them, they damage certain surfaces.
- Mat knives and Exacto knives with a cutting mat.

5   Continuity. This is about having consistency with your props and decor. If your character is drinking from a glass of water, make sure that water line is consistent with where you are in the story. In the beginning, the water line is high on the cup, later in the scene it'll be lower, by the end it may be totally gone. But after multiple takes, the water line will start to move. Keep refilling it to match where you are in the scene.

TIP: Take a photo of the monitor at the beginning of each scene to compare when you move onto the next scene.

6   Lastly, it's cheesy—but have fun. Making connections leads to future jobs!

Ryan Broomberg was the cinematographer on *The Bright Side* and winner of the American Society of Cinematographer (ASC) Student Heritage Award.

Ryan Broomberg

Sarah, Rachel, and I had a lot of discussions about the look we were going for. Without that, it's hard to accomplish anything by yourself. It is a very collaborative process. We started with visual references. There were a few musicals that we referenced—*Moulin Rouge*, *Chicago*, and also some TV shows like *Boardwalk Empire* and *Peaky Blinders*.

Since school (and I've been out five years), I've shot several features and it's funny, I prepped more for this movie with the director than anything I've ever shot since, and that includes features with budgets over $4 million. Sarah was just so passionate about her vision and wanted everyone to be on the same page. We had this film very planned out with storyboards, overheads, and references. We have a document that shows each scene with overheads, story-boards, shot list, and a reference frame for each shot.

I remember sitting in the hallway at school with the director and AD going through each set up asking, how long is this going to take? It was good, it got me to pre-visualize technically and to get the look that we were going for. We also consistently made our day, which was great considering it was such an ambitious film.

In the "Crossfire" scene (the fantasy war scene), we wanted to create a world of fantasy mixed with reality. We had this war scene where the leads are watching a movie and they transform into the characters in the movie. We did things like using confetti instead of explosives and the look was more theatrical. We found a period theater that was being renovated, which was actually an alternative for another location in our film, but it ended up working better for the Crossfire scene. This is an example of finding things that work best from scouting and having options.

Our main theater location had all these different hallways and entryways and the stage. It gave us the look without having to do tons of dressing, which made it easier for Rachel because then she could spend time on the fantasy scene and the stage opening scene where she had to actually build set pieces. We also were able to pre-light different parts of the theater while we were shooting another area. That was one of the ways we were able to move quickly but to make it look like we had more time and money than we actually did.

The aged look—how it was lit . . . I spent a lot of time looking at movies I liked for this type of period and looking at how they were lit, which was very practical (using practical lighting) based. And coming from the far side of the talent. We never wanted it to look like artificial lighting. Our goal was as much realism as possible. We always wanted the lighting to look like it was lighting them from a lamp or for interior day they would be lit from the windows. I would have Rachel add lamps in the background to try and always have motivating source in the shot. She was always game for moving practicals around and trusted me that the continuity doesn't matter for those moments. I spent a lot of time figuring how to get that look.

We had bigger soft (lighting) sources, coming from the back. It was always very subtle and we tried to use more Tungsten lights instead of LEDs to get that warmer effect. But we did use some LEDs, we mixed it up. As far as the "softness" of the look, we did a lens and filter test at Panavision. We ended up with Panivised Zeiss Superspeeds, which are older and have a lot of character, They're really fast so you can shoot them wide open at a 1.4 with low light and it gives you that softer look.

If you use a newer lens they're normally very sharp because they're newer technology and newer glass. We figured out the amount of filtration we wanted to use. We ended up using 1/8 Black Frost.

We shot with two Panivised RED Ones. Sara wanted two cameras, especially for the musical numbers. We talked about the dance numbers—what perspective did we want? Was it from the audience or from the dancers' perspective? It depended on the scene, what was happening. The opening musical number of the movie was from the audience's point of view. We wanted it to be from further away and used longer lenses. This was to make it look like you, the viewer, are watching it as an audience member. This was also one of our bigger set-piece builds that was a huge archway with about 12 Mole Richardson 600 watt lights rigged into it on a dimmer board. We programed chase and fade up effects on the dimmer board.

This gave the scene a 1940s Hollywood spectacle feel.

Looking at Locations as a Cinematographer

The main thing I look at when going into a location is what is the best direction to look at, with composition and lighting as top priorities. Most locations have more of a cinematic perspective, which usually is shooting toward the windows. Most directors look at a

(continued)

(continued)

location for very specific things, but most directors I have worked with don't usually consider lighting, which is understandable, and they plan the blocking of the scene with the camera right in front of the windows, so it will be a lot of artificial lighting to avoid it looking flat.

I think lighting is one of the most important aspects, if you want things to look more realistic and practical based. This is one of the biggest challenges as a cinematographer, if there's a window there, let's shoot toward the window . . . When you're shooting toward the window, the shadow is toward the camera so it looks three dimensional. If you flip around the other way so that the window is lighting the room, it will look flat, and like a video project, not a movie. Obviously this depends on the scene and feel of the scene but nine times out of ten this is the case.

I feel like, with a lot of movies, you can get lucky sometimes. You can plan things but until you go to the location, you don't know for sure. When you get to the location you'll discover that you don't like something but you'll also find some happy accidents. That theater we found – to me it worked better than shooting on a backlot. But we only used it for that scene after we lost a different location.

It's not just about making it look cool, it's about telling the story. There's a meaning behind everything. When I first read a script, I try to read it as a filmmaker, not as a cinematographer. What do we need to tell the story?

On *The Bright Side* instead of the traditional doing a master then close-ups, we wanted to be smoother, smooth transitions from one scene to the next, to feel more of the period than something that would be very cut-y or jarring. We wanted to keep the shot more wide and static, do moving masters to make it feel more real. We were on the Fisher dolly most of the time and Steadicam for some of it . . . I think the biggest thing is just seeing the movie in your head. It's not science. You have to feel it.

Mian Adnan Ahmad's work is inspired both by his life-long love of movies and his life in Pakistan, where he interned at an advertising agency, worked at a local television station, then received a Fulbright Scholarship to pursue an MFA in Film School. *Heal*, his graduate thesis film, was an Official Selection of over 25 international film festivals and has won over 21 international awards. The log line of the film is, "In the midst of the ongoing conflict in Afghanistan and Pakistan, a gifted child makes an extraordinary effort for his people."

Mian Adnan Ahmad

Shooting a film set in a war-torn region between Pakistan and Afghanistan was an ambitious task to begin with, and one that very few thought would be possible, especially as we had to shoot on a shoe-string budget and remain within the US. Looking back, it was a huge team effort and this desire to tell the story with an authenticity that perhaps was not prevalent in a lot of films being made in the US at the time, about stories set in that region. Whenever we've screened the film, people are very surprised to learn that the locations are all in and around the US and even within Orange County. Then again California is one of those states which is blessed with a diverse terrain and a variety of locations which may be hard to come across elsewhere.

The locations were all within an hour's drive from Orange, with some being even less than 15 minutes away from Chapman University. They mainly included a studio set, an abandoned building, Holy-Jim Canyon (Trabuco Canyon), and the Tustin Airbase. Marcus Metsala, our producer, played a key role in finding most of the spots and we worked very closely together to make sure the spaces were workable in terms of production and telling the story. Finding them was a mix of extensive research, driving around (a lot), getting leads from friends and other people, and good fortune. Even timing was crucial and played a pivotal role in what we ended up with. For example, there are some shots in *Heal* filmed from across a river creek with mountains in the background, which play as the outskirts of where the story is set. I came across this location purely by chance when some friends of mine who were also my neighbors at the time were showing me pictures of a trip they had made to Holy-Jim Canyon. Seeing those pictures reminded me of the terrain from the rural areas back home and this started the conversation toward pinpointing the spot we used in the film. The creek was disappointingly mostly dry during the days coming up to the shoot but as we got closer to D-day, it rained and it poured and the creek filled up, to be exactly the way we needed it to be. Similarly, one of the locations we were having the most challenge with (as a financially limited student film) was finding a workable

(continued)

(continued)

space with rubble and major wreckage for scenes of the remains of the aftermath of a (bombing) attack on the village. Then just a week or so before the shoot there was a building that was demolished right next to another location we were using at the Tustin Airbase and we were able to make it work for what we needed in the film. A spot in the same area also played out nicely for a makeshift school for the children as well (see Photo 19.16). So suddenly we were able to make these three great locations at a space that was supposed to be just one.

Prepping and Dressing Orange County, California, for Pakistan and Afghanistan

It was very important to get the right kind of feel for the environment where the film was set, which was a rural village along the borders between Pakistan and Afghanistan. Things like building texture, wardrobe, spaces, colors, and writings on the walls, etc. were all areas that needed to reflect that region in an authentic way. This was an area that needed a special effort in order to take the audience "outside" the US and into the film's story. Growing up in Pakistan and from my days spent in my own village in the rural parts of the country, along with having Prajakta Ghag, our production designer, being from India, was a blessing. I feel together we brought the right

Photo 19.16 Schoolhouse between Pakistan and Afghanistan.

kind of sensibility for the story and spaces we needed to recreate. In particular the home where the lead character resides had to be made of mud and so we built a set from scratch for the interiors based on the same. The dressing had to reflect a similar environment for a basic room in the village, which was mostly bare apart from the basic essentials needed for cooking in one corner and some traditional bedding and other ornaments in the rest of the space.

There was an abandoned school near Chapman University that had been vandalized a bit, which actually ended up being used as the makeshift medical ward in the film. In this particular case the damage to the space worked in our favor and then Prajakta and her team worked on re-coloring and re-touching some of the area as needed, along with bringing in the necessary basic metal beds, etc. for the scene. But the most astonishing find at this location was a large wooden door that just lay against a wall outside the school. It was so traditional in its look and feel and resembled the wood works of doors in a South Asian rural village that it was strange to see it just lying there at this abandoned school in Orange County (see Photo 19.17).

A particular production design item that we had a challenge in finding was a traditional village bed made of wood and string, also known as a *charpai*. We felt that this item in particular could really convince the audience that we were actually there. More so the purists who may belong to Pakistan/Afghanistan or know about the

Photo 19.17 Rural South Asian village in Orange County, CA.

(continued)

(continued)

region. So it was not easy but we continued to reach out to all ave-
nues and see if it could be found from somewhere. Finally, Prajakta
heard back from someone at an event management company for
South Asian weddings who happened to have one. It looked like it
had also been recreated just for the 'look' but it did the job for what
we needed (see Photo 19.18).

Photo 19.18 Funeral ceremony.

Photo 19.19 Marketplace.

The marketplace was also another area that needed a lot of work to recreate the environment of a regular market in the village. Sort of like a farmer's market in the rural areas. Once the set was ready, then the right kind of actors and wardrobe also helped in filling up this space and giving it a realistic feel overall (see Photo 19.19).

Coming Up with the Design Concept

Conceptually the story brought two worlds/genres together: the story about a rural village affected by war in a region between Pakistan and Afghanistan, and the supernatural story of the lead character (Azeem) set in that region. Personally it was a challenge to initially convince myself that this could actually work as an authentic and realistic narrative, where audiences accept and live in both worlds side by side. I was adamant that the story and the characters had to feel "real," meaning that they had real consequences to what they did, especially for Azeem's character, as compared to being a comic-book hero in the traditional sense where the hero always overcomes the situation and moves on to the next adventure. So visually the film had to feel the same. It had to give you a slice of life in the world of these characters as compared to a stylized conventional superhero film.

It's bits and pieces like this that helped inspire or give fruition to some ideas from other sources as well. Both Dani Sanchez-Lopez (the DP) and I agreed that there would be strength and impact in keeping things simple, without unnecessary distractions, and Dani played a crucial role as a collaborator and thinker and in bringing what we conceived to fruition.

From what I recall there was no major reliance on storyboards. If any, I would say it was minimal or very basic, selectively used for some of the scenes where it was crucial or something out of the ordinary was being done. The shot list was key. After a lot of research and exchanging visual ideas/references with Dani, I initially prepared a shot list based on how I saw the film visually. Then we sat together and collaborated on finalizing the same. It was all really done at the last minute; I'd say probably a week or so before the shoot. But we had all discussed ideas and the concept before then as well so we were pretty much aligned in terms of the look and feel for the film, including Prajakta who also had some key input for how we could adapt certain requirements through the limitations we had. The three of us were also generally on the same page based on our site visits, which were all

(continued)

(continued)

mostly done by then, in terms of what we see in the frame, from the widest shot to the close-ups, etc. In some cases Dani had taken pictures of the actual locations as references for production design to use as needed for filling up the frame, etc. There was also a dedicated column in the shot list with enough space for drawing in what we see in a frame and this was our main substitute for a formal storyboard. We knew that we were dealing with the limitation of not being in Pakistan/ Afghanistan and therefore had to be very effective in terms of whatever locations we could recreate or the spaces that we could find to match what we needed from that region. So from the get go we had to prior- itize what was absolutely important to see in the frame for a particular shot in order to tell the story authentically and in the best way we could. What would be the background, foreground, the wide shots, close-ups, etc. The wide shots in particular had to be very selective and we were able to get most of these in the outdoor locations such as the marketplace and when the lead character is in the mountains or next to the river creek. For everything else it was all frame-by-frame and finding a balance between what was needed for the story and what was possible on set. Since we had access to some traditional carpet/rugs, a regular idea we joked around with and also in some cases employed effectively was to "Put a rug on it" to cover anything in the frame that looked like it was not from that region.

The importance of searching for the absolute right location when you're working on a very tight budget and using production design and cinematography to bring your audience to the "world" of your movie can not be overstated. It is critical to persist.

The budget of one of Amanda Renee Knox's graduate school films, *Rajam*, was $1500. The project was shot in Orange County, California—but it's set in Syria. The film is about a woman living under strict Sharia Law, who is accused of adultery, imprisoned, and sentenced to death by ston- ing. How difficult was it to find Syria in suburban southern California?

Amanda Renee Knox

We (Amanda and her producer, Angelo Ford) went and looked at abandoned buildings and then stumbled upon a paint ball air soft

Photos 19.20 and 19.21 Paint ball field for Syrian desert.

(continued)

(continued)

field that had a Middle Eastern set. It had a full town with blown out cars, vans, and buildings that all we had to do was walk on and shoot (see Photos 19.20, 19.21). We shot the stoning scene at Irvine Lake, which because of the drought was a desert. One of the days we had to end early so we finished shooting the interior of a jail sequence between the two lovers in the back of a grip truck, with matching lights and a wild wall!

Knox's thesis film, *Night Call*, was also shot in and around southern California. The log line for *Night Call*: "When, on a routine patrol, a black female cop living in and patrolling Inglewood gets called to a disturbance she is forced to make an unprecedented life altering decision."

Night Call has not only been an Official Selection at dozens of international film festivals, the recipient of prestigious awards from the Directors Guild of American and the NBC Universal Short Film Festival, it is the 2018 winner of the Jury Prize for Best Student Film at the American Pavilion Emerging Filmmakers Showcase at the Cannes Film Festival.

Amanda Renee Knox

Night Call was shot on a very small budget (for the ambition of the screenplay), which forced us to be resourceful. I think the most challenging aspect of the film, and also the most fun to shoot, was the car chase. It's nearly impossible to shoot a car chase in Los Angeles on a minute budget . . . we found a backlot in Pomona that backed up against a freeway. We used this to stage the car speeding past traffic and also for the chase. As luck would have it, there was a train trestle that passed over the street that we shot on, which made for very cinematic shots. The locations of the film made it what it was. I am so grateful to the local vendors and stages that allowed us to shoot there either for free or deeply discounted. Without their help, the film wouldn't be what it is.

Photos 19.22, 19.23, 19.24 Police chase scene.

(continued)

Photo 19.25 Night shoot on the streets.

Andrew Johnson needed the interior and exterior of a riverside cabin for his school film, *Granpa's River*—so he built them.

Andrew Johnson

The biggest thing was finding and borrowing things for free. I scavenged my garage and basement back home to find anything and everything that might work. This guy (the character) needed to look like his cabin was a mess, but a controlled mess. I also worked with a guy that helped build the exterior and he allowed me to borrow a ton of pieces that really brought the cabin together. That was the most important part, making relationships with people, making sure their stuff was kept safe, and returning it just as I found it. They were happy to help.

The inside works well with the outside of the cabin. We don't see much of the outside, but when you do see it, you don't question whether or not that's what the inside is. That was our biggest concern coming into the project.

Altogether, it took me about 250 hours give or take to complete this over a month. My producer, Abby Johnson, helped on about 100–150 of those hours, and the rest I worked pretty much by myself. With the help of about five crew members, we finished.

A big thing I learned, you can't do it by yourself. It's impossible. You can only get so far and carry so much!

Photo 19.26 Cabin build in progress.

Photo 19.27 Exterior cabin built to match interior on stage.

Chris Read directs and shoots for Studio 10, working mostly on a reality show, *Road Kill*, a car show. He also works on independent narrative projects. While at film school, Chris wrote and directed a project that made unique use of a limited budget and shooting mostly on a (free) stage. His grad thesis film, *The Lost Captain* was about a lonely little boy who builds a cardboard box spaceship. In his fantasies, the ship becomes a true, high-tech, amazing-looking rocket, until the boy's fantasies and reality are shattered.

Chris Read

When I was writing the script, I had a completely different picture of it in my mind. When Brian (his classmate and the production designer of the project) and I were talking about it, we knew we had a very small budget. We wanted the fantasy ship to match the cardboard (reality) version. That was the challenge—making something that matched the practical version that the kids played in. We used similar elements inside and outside that matched in that they had the same feeling.

We talked about how it was going to be lit inside. I wanted lighting panels on the inside so when the alarm (signaling danger, then a crash) goes off, the lights can change to red and flash, and I wanted the elements of the control board to feel as if they were based on toys, since this was the boy's imaginary ship, so there's a joy stick in there, and in the cardboard version there's a joy stick as well but it's more beat up, it's broken there are wires sticking out, whereas in the spaceship (imaginary) version, it's complete, it's working. The cardboard version of the ship, everything had to look as if it came from something. They didn't buy stuff to make a play spaceship, they used duct tape, they used oatmeal containers to make the rockets. There were some of the elements that overlapped. Like their helmets, their spacesuits were better versions of what they had. In the card version, their helmets were bike helmets with cardboard and duct tape. But in the fantasy version they were real helmets but they looked a bit similar to the bike helmets.

The hardest part was staging two kids inside of the spaceship and making it feel bigger than it was. Looking back, there were things we could have done with lenses, using a wide-angle, making it feel like more of an open space, so when he's in there alone (and lonely) it feels drastically bigger than it did when he's in there with his friend. Some of the stuff we used, we didn't buy, we just found. We wanted two doors that opened up and we found these two doors that were elevator doors. We designed it so we put them in and rigged them so they could be pulled open, (like a spaceship's

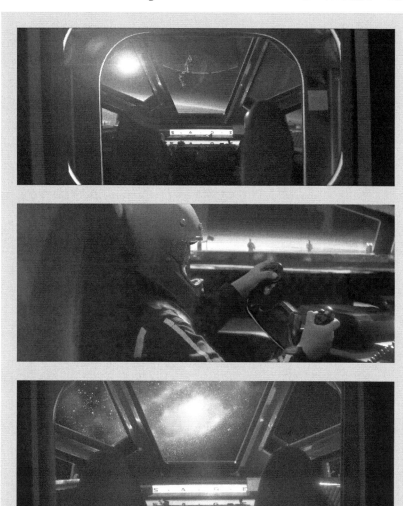

Photos 19.28, 19.29, 19.30 Imaginary space ship.

doors), because he had to walk out of the ship. We rented a few things. We rented a keypad (from a prop house) so it looked like he had to type in something to make the doors open. There were some metal grates—some of the design elements were planned to be something else but we had to figure out how to pay for them all and some of it became, let's look around and see what's available to us without us having to buy it. We were just constantly adding

(continued)

(continued)

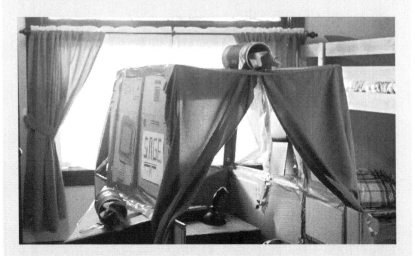

Photo 19.31 Space ship reality.

to it, I don't think it was ever done. Some things would fall down during shooting and you'd have to stop and glue them back on, but on camera it worked. The other thing we had to plan for was, the whole space ship gets destroyed since it was supposed to be a crash landing. We had to shoot it in a certain way—we only had one of each set, the cardboard ship and the "real" space ship. That meant, the way we shot the cardboard stuff was we scheduled it so it was the last thing we shot, because then the kids (the bullies) come in and destroy it. It's really easy to say to a kid, go destroy that now— and they did. Once we were done, it was just a pile of cardboard.

20 Visual Storytelling in Making the Sale

As filmmaking is all about visual storytelling and engaging an audience, it should make sense that the visual advertising possibilities of a project are discussed very early on—by marketers, financiers, and potential distributors. In fact, when producers try to raise funds for projects, they are often armed with a mock-up of a *one-sheet* (a large poster), or a *deck* (a pitch package that relies heavily on visual imagery). For some types of films, these may be more important factors in raising the film's budget than the screenplay itself. The sayings "a picture is worth a thousand words," and "show it, don't say it," hold true. The feeling is, people want to be able to understand elements of the story (tone, characters, genre) in a single glance, because if one image can get an audience excited, there is potential in the marketplace. This is one of the reasons serious, or quirky, character-driven material often has a tougher time at the box office. An audience may love the film or program once they see it, but what kind of quick-hit/initial taste can you give them if there are no guns, no explosions, the setting is contemporary, and the tone is subtle? Other than featuring a big-name cast on the poster, in our current culture in which we have thousands of choices as to how we spend our busy days, how do you get people to commit to sitting down and watching something when they don't have a sense of whether it is going to be worth their time?

Design is a key element at all stages. Visuals are employed in raising the money to make a project, they are employed in the actual production and post-production—and finally, visuals are a key component in finding an audience.

Jim Fredrick is a specialist in creative advertising for motion pictures. He produces and edits film trailers ("previews of coming attractions") and rip-o-matics (conceptual trailers of projects that have not yet been made). He has been an executive at Castle Rock Entertainment, Screen Gems, and Warner Bros. (where he was Senior Vice-President of Creative Advertising) and he oversaw the development of trailers, commercials, and key art (artworks used in ads and posters) for more than 80 campaigns, including the *Harry Potter* franchise.

Jim Fredrick

When a studio greenlights a film for production, the script is passed to the marketing department, where a creative advertising executive is assigned to supervise the production of creative materials for that film.

The assigned executive hires trailer and print vendors that they feel are best suited to the film's genre and story. Have they had success before with a similar film? Have they had success with the cast? Perhaps they have a past relationship with the director or producer?

Poster concepts are the first elements to be created, in preparation for a "special shoot" with the actors you want featured on the poster while they're still on set. If the budget warrants, top photographers are sought to shoot special set ups based on thumbnail sketches created by the vendor. Top photographers can make $100,000 a day on a shoot. Often, big stars insist on choosing who shoots them for the poster.

Hundreds of print "comps" (comparables) are eventually presented to the studio creative executive, who then hones the presentation down to a manageable number for presentation to studio management and the filmmakers. This back-and-forth process continues with research entering the fray. What does the consumer think about the poster(s)? Is it appealing to the target audience? What key art image strikes the most persuasive tone?

Trailers usually begin during production, as vendors often work from dailies of the film, to get a jump on the process. Often a trailer company has an editor cutting their own version of the feature in order for the trailer editor to begin cutting. Trailer scripts are pitched to the studio creative executive, logos and graphics are designed, voiceover narration is considered, though rarely used these days.

The trailer follows a similar route. Big budget Hollywood films require multi- vendors on trailers and print material. Some trailer vendors will cut six or seven different trailers—losing money on editor fees along the way—just to get the coveted "finish" that will find its place in theaters. This valued finish may seem like a money-loser for the vendor, but "winning" this bake-off usually leads to the important and lucrative TV spot assignment, where a vendor can cut as many as 100 TV commercials for the studio (and get paid very well for the huge volume of work). That's right. 100 TV spots from just ONE vendor.

The end goal of this process is rather simple: create an audio-visual and print campaign that monetizes the film on opening weekend. Creating persuasive marketing materials is the most important tool in drawing a paying audience to see the studio "product" on Friday night. In marketing a film, you only have one shot to make an impression. And several millions of dollars go into their creation.

How Do You Take the Essential Story of the Film and Translate That into a Trailer and Poster?

Sometimes—and God help the Movie Marketer—the essential story in a film isn't very commercial. This typifies the epic tussle in the film industry of business vs. art, a fight that has been going on for 100 years and continues. In the world of movie marketing, it's SHOW BUSINESS, not SHOW ART, that guides the process.

The vast majority of films entering the marketplace offer a huge challenge to the marketer: how can we open (get a large audience the minute the project is released) a film with a difficult title (*The Shawshank Redemption*). No major stars (Tim Robbins and Morgan Freeman) in a 2 hour and 40-minute drama that is violent, grim, claustrophobic (prison), has virtually no female characters, and contains several key scenes (secrets) that, if divulged in the marketing materials, would ruin the film-going experience?

In the case of *Shawshank* Castle Rock had a film with tremendous playability and challenging marketability. In our early research screenings, we recognized how much people loved the film, but we struggled to create an inviting, persuasive advertising campaign that could draw in a vast opening weekend audience. We ended up with a Platform release, starting on a small number of screens and expanded theaters as word-of-mouth spread. This was only mildly successful until we garnered seven Academy nominations and went on to be the biggest DVD seller the following year. The film has gone on to become the #1 movie of All-Time on IMDb. But it didn't open.

Every film ever marketed has had the challenge of finding a balance between titillation and information that is presented to the consumer. Even the first Harry Potter film we worked on at Warner Bros—a film that seems today like a guaranteed hit—had many challenges and expectations to overcome. There are no guarantees in this business.

Of course, the common complaint among audiences and film lovers today is, why do trailers "tell me everything?" The answer is research. Once the marketing department signs off on a campaign, it goes to the research department, who measure the interest of the consumer, just like any other product or service. And often, the

(continued)

(continued)

consumer wants more. More story. More laughter. More thrills. More information, before they spend their hard-earned $15 on a movie ticket. Believe me, the studios would LOVE to reveal less moments, less plot, less visual effects, less . . . everything, to gain the interest of audiences. But the customer is always right. So, studios go back and add MORE.

The movie poster is the most difficult job in film marketing: how do you boil the marketing message down to one image, known as the Key Art? Trailers and TV spots have the luxury of using film footage, music, dialogue, graphics, even specially shot material to persuade audiences. They also have time, be it 2:30 for a trailer or 30 seconds for a TV commercial. Not so the poster maker.

Color, and the Placement of Visual Elements in Marketing/ Promo/Sales Materials

There are no design rules when it comes to marketing materials. Every film is different, and every creative group is trying to create a BRAND for that film. One hopes the color palette is consistent throughout the campaign—that the poster design uses similar (or the same) color, photography, logo, etc. as the billboard or bus side or bus shelter or digital or magazine ad. Synergy in message and look are important in the marketing of any product or service.

One of my studio mentors—a brilliant advertising mind—always used white as a background for comedy films. Why? Because it always led to a successful opening. Horror posters often use red type against a black or dark background, to imply fear. But there is no marketing style guide that suggests certain color palettes or other tricks that work every time for a specific film genre.

Visual Elements in a Poster That Help Sell the Movie

If you have two movie stars making $10 million bucks to star in a film—well—there's a good reason they command that kind of salary, in addition to their acting skills, of course. They bring in audiences based on their popularity, which is a major factor why they got hired in the first place. The "Two-Heads-In-The-Sky" movie poster is invariably what studios often resort to. So, for a marketer, two heads on a poster address that problem—though sometimes not to ideal effect.

In the halcyon days of poster illustration—-the 1970s and 1980s—great artists like Bob Peak (*Apocalypse Now*), Drew

Stuzan (*Harry Potter and The Sorcerer's Stone*), and John Alvin (*Blade Runner*) created posters that seamlessly blended a montage of characters with action, environment, and effects with just paint, imagination, and talent. Today, Photoshop accomplishes that task.

Saul Bass created singular posters with geometric design that can't be mistaken for anyone else's work today. (He did the iconic poster for *The Shining*.)

The era of the legendary poster artist has been replaced by teams of art directors and designers, crouched over their Macs using Photoshop and Illustrator. Some campaigns develop over a thousand ideas for their key art.

Does the Visual Design of the Film Itself Often Inspire the Marketing?

I would say often. As mentioned, the concepts for design start with the screenplay before the film even begins production. Sometimes, a visual effect can lead to your central image.

The 100-foot wave from *The Perfect Storm* was described on page 87 of the screenplay. After reading it, I called director Wolfgang Peterson and the visual effects team at ILM and asked when the shot was going to be ready. They fast-tracked it for the teaser trailer I was cutting and it also became the key art for the poster. No two heads! No George Clooney. No Mark Wahlberg. They were probably pissed. But the movie opened [had a good first weekend at the box office], and that's all that counts.

21 Entering the Profession

The end credits of some of the lavish comic book, fantasy, or historical films and/or limited series (multiple episodes but shorter than a normal television series) can number in the hundreds and, in addition to the sheer number of people working together, there is often a complex web of union affiliations. In almost all cases the art and design groups are represented by different locals (think of them as divisions) of the International Alliance of Theatrical and Stage Employees.

Locals and union affiliations can vary according to where the crew is based. New York, Chicago, and Miami are set up slightly differently, but for an example of how the locals are split, in Los Angeles, on a union project you might be a member of:

Local 800—The Art Directors Guild, which covers production designers, art directors, set designers, graphic artists, and scenic artists.

Local 892—The Costume Designers Guild, representing designers, assistant costume designers, and costume illustrators.

Local 44—Property masters, set decorators.

Local 600—The entire camera department.

Directors are represented by the Directors Guild, and the Location Department is represented by Teamster Local 399 on the West Coast and the Directors Guild in the East.

Unions are collective bargaining organizations. In the film and television industry, a union local is usually comprised of people working in similar areas. As listed above, specific departments are represented by specific locals.

For the purpose of understanding how film unions work, think of the union as representing labor (technicians, artists, and craftspeople). They are the workers, the *employees*. Workers are hired by management, the *employers*. In this case, management consists of the people who run the major production companies, the networks, and the studios.

In the business world, individual laborers have very little power. On a film, a single painter or costumer or set dresser doesn't have much leverage when it comes to demanding better wages and working conditions. Management has the money and strength on their side.

They are the bosses and can easily replace anyone who causes problems. BUT, if *all* the laborers band together and instead of thousands of individuals negotiating their individual interests with management, *all* labor (a union of several thousand workers) negotiates the interests they have in common with management then there is a more reasonable balance of power. Each side needs each other. Without labor, you can't make the movie. Without management, you can't make a living.

The issues negotiated are usually wage rates and the increase of the level of benefits (health insurance and pension.) Every year, labor would like raises in both of these areas and every year management, hoping to maximize its profits, doesn't want to increase the amount they've agreed to in the past.

Every few years, a committee for IATSE, the labor union representing most of the creative departments we've discussed in this book meets with management—the big companies making film and television. Point by point, the two opposing groups work together to hammer out revisions to the next two-year contract. Eventually a vote is taken. Each side gets something, each side concedes something. Usually it's settled in a few weeks, but if a consensus can't be reached, there is a labor action—a strike. Pre-production, production, and post shuts down. No one works. No one makes money. That's not good for anyone, so each side goes to great lengths to avoid it if possible. Ultimately a contract is settled and life and work goes on. People make a fair hourly wage, receive benefits, and have enough clout that any unsafe or unsavory working conditions can be fairly dealt with and remedied.

What does this all have to do with you? When starting out on very low-budget projects, usually everyone on the crew is non-union. When you begin your career you can expect low wages, no health insurance or pension, long hours, and very tight resources. If you are straight out of school, you're at the bottom of the totem pole and you're often happy to be making minimum wage. You're working 12–14 hour days. If you're fortunate, you're eligible to remain on your parent's health insurance. If you're not, hopefully you're squeezing enough money out of the small amount you're earning to afford some kind of health insurance on your own. Film and television production is a freelance business, which means you work project to project. If you're employed you're tired all the time. If you're unemployed you're wondering if the phone will ever ring, and you're trying to network and make the contacts that will help you get where you want to go. You want to join the appropriate union so you can work on the bigger projects but without at least 30 days' experience on a union project, you won't be accepted. It feels like a Catch-22 situation, where in order to do this you need that, but in order to get that you need this.

Confusing? First, often you want to get your experience on smaller, non-union films and programs and gradually build up to the bigger projects. That way, by the time the opportunity opens up, you'll be ready. You'll always be learning but the more knowledgeable you are, the more capable you'll be. You'll have a better understanding of handling the stress, the politics, the hierarchy, and the creative and budgetary demands of bigger projects if you build up to them. And you'll have the ability to do things for less, which is appreciated on all sizes and types of projects. Also, you'll meet a lot of people on lower budget projects who are exactly where you are and if you do a good job and they like you, you'll have built a network of people who are rising at the same pace or a little ahead of you. On small projects with tight budgets, there is no place to hide. People notice you for better or for worse. Recommendations and references are your move ahead.

There are times you may feel incredibly discouraged. You just want to tell stories, to express yourself creatively, and there are all these obstacles and barriers. Don't despair. You're trying to break into one of the most competitive industries existing. There is a long line of people who want exactly what you want and it can take a very long time to get established. But something to keep in mind—every person I interviewed for this book LOVES what they do. They get up in the morning and want to go to work. They love transforming empty spaces into vibrant sets, building things that don't even exist except in their mind or the mind of a screenwriter. They love solving problems, helping to tell stories, creating the visual that you the audience remembers long after the movie is over.

Lee Ross, Scenic Painter on What He Likes Best about His Job

The collaboration is what it's all about. It's such an organic thing, everybody is working together. It's like an amoeba. Unless you're watching you don't necessarily see it, but being on a crew is like being part of a dance, or watching an amazing tapestry.

Dave DeGaetano

I started as a construction coordinator in 1978. 1992 I started working on features. I worked with a lot of good people. I retired on December 1st of 2017. A 49-year career and I wouldn't do anything else.

The Final Word: Set Decorator Shirley Starks

It's important to say that this job must make your heart sing. You have to feel like you're bringing your job to the party every day because it's too damn hard if you don't. It's brutal hours. There's a pad by my bed because at 3 o'clock in the morning like clockwork, the solution will come—Oh! I could do that! There is a passion that goes with creating. If you don't love it, if it's not making your heart sing, re-think. There have been some stinker days. 3 o'clock in the morning with Skeet Ulrich and Gerald McRainey up to our knees in mud and hay because we were shooting at 5 to get the sunrise. But we were all laughing and joking . . . that's how it should be! You get to create a brand new world every day. It can be magical.

22 Suggested Viewing

You have hopefully seen or have access to most of the films and television series referred to in this book. Some are very old (*To Kill A Mockingbird*), many are somewhat old (*The Godfather*), and many are quite recent. When you watch the films and episodes that are good and hold your attention, you are probably not looking at the elements of design because they're working on you the way they're supposed to be—subconsciously. After reading this book, possibly you'll want to go back and watch part or all of them again, but this time, turn the sound off for a few scenes and look at the lighting, the camera work, the costumes, and the sets. If you're a filmmaker you probably learn best by doing, so participate in the films by analyzing the look, the color, the tone, the style. What works and feels real? What pulls you out of the action? Why?

The films and series listed here (in order of appearance) are very different, but each is a strong example of an aspect—or many aspects—of successful design for storytelling.

Legally Blonde

Clueless

The Godfather

The Exorcist

Seven

Friday the 13th

Nightmare on Elm Street

Blade Runner

Whiplash

Locke

Twelve Angry Men

Reservoir Dogs

Panic Room

Breakfast Club

Flightplan

To Kill A Mockingbird

The Great Gatsby

Edward Scissorhands

The Aviator

The Truman Show

La La Land

Chinatown

Witness

Mad Men (series)

Lawrence of Arabia

The Verdict

The Shining

Schindler's List

Road to Perdition

Last Emperor

Grand Budapest Hotel

World Trade Center

The Last Samurai

L.A. Confidential

Beast of the Southern Wild

Fight Club

The Hunger Games

Fast and Furious 4

Kong: Skull Island

The King's Speech

Almost Famous

Jericho (series)

Witness

Downton Abbey (series)

Castaway

THX

Casino

Get Out

The Devil Wears Prada

500 Days of Summer

Ladybird

Jane the Virgin (series)

Lovely and Amazing

Apollo 13

Coco

Wall-E

Some of the student films can be accessed on iTunes or online:

Straw Dolls

Rocket

The Bright Side

Heal

Rajam, Night Call

And you can see some of the posters and trailers Jim Fredrick discusses; just go online and check out the marketing campaigns and one-sheets of the *Harry Potter* series, the *Shawshank Redemption*, and *The Perfect Storm*.

Index